THE SOUNDS
OF ENGLISH AND GERMAN

CONTRASTIVE STRUCTURE SERIES

Charles A. Ferguson

General Editor

THE SOUNDS OF

ENGLISH AND GERMAN

William G. Moulton

THE UNIVERSITY OF CHICAGO PRESS

CHICAGO AND LONDON

The research reported herein was performed pursuant to a contract between
the United States Office of Education and the Center for Applied Linguistics
of the Modern Language Association, and is published with permission
of the United States Office of Education.

The University of Chicago Press, Chicago 60637
The University of Chicago Press, Ltd., London

82 81 80 79 78   12 11 10 9 8

Printed in the United States of America

International Standard Book Number: 0-226-54309-9
Library of Congress Catalog Card Number: 62-20024

GENERAL INTRODUCTION TO THE SERIES

This study is part of a series of contrastive structure studies which describe the similarities and differences between English and each of the five foreign languages most commonly taught in the United States: French, German, Italian, Russian, and Spanish. Each of the five languages is represented by two volumes in the series, one on the sound systems and the other on the grammatical systems of English and the language in question. The volumes on sounds make some claim to completeness within the limits appropriate to these studies; the volumes on grammar, however, treat only selected topics, since complete coverage would be beyond the scope of the series. The studies are intended to make available for the language teacher, textbook writer, or other interested reader a body of information which descriptive linguists have derived from their contrastive analyses of English and the other languages.

The Center for Applied Linguistics, in undertaking this series of studies, has acted on the conviction held by many linguists and specialists in language teaching that one of the major problems in the learning of a second language is the interference caused by the structural differences between the native language of the learner and the second language. A natural consequence of this conviction is the belief that a careful contrastive analysis of the two languages offers an excellent basis for the preparation of instructional materials, the planning of courses, and the development of actual classroom techniques.

The project got under way in the summer of 1959. The primary responsibility for the various parts of the project fell to specialists of demonstrated competence in linguistics having a strong interest in the application of linguistics to practical problems of language teaching. Wherever possible, a recognized senior scholar specializing in the foreign language was selected either as a consultant or as an author.

Since it did not seem likely that the users of the series would generally read all five studies, considerable duplication was permitted in the material presented. Also, although a general framework was suggested for the studies and some attempt was made to achieve a uniformity of procedure by consultation among those working on the project, each team was given free rein to follow its own approach. As a result, the parts of the series vary in style, terminology, notation, and in the relative emphasis given to different aspects of the analysis.

Some differences in these studies are also due to the wide range of variation in American English, especially in the pronunciation of vowels. No special consideration was given to English spoken outside America since the studies were primarily intended for language teachers and textbook writers in this country. There are also differences in the studies which depend on the structure of each of the foreign languages under comparison. Thus, if a fact of English agrees well with a feature of German it may merit little mention, if any, in an English-German contrastive study, but if the same fact differs in a complicated and highly significant way from a corresponding feature of Spanish, it may require elaborate treatment in an English-Spanish study.

In the course of the project several by-products were produced, two of which are worth noting as of possible interest to readers of volumes in this series. One, <u>Linguistic Reading Lists for Teachers of Modern Languages</u> (Washington, D.C., 1962) was compiled chiefly by linguists working on the project and contains a carefully selected and annotated list of works which linguists would recommend to the teacher of French, German, Italian, Russian, or Spanish. The other, W. W. Gage's <u>Contrastive Studies in Linguistics</u> (Washington, D.C., 1961) consists of an unannotated listing of all contrastive studies which had come to the attention of the Center by the summer of 1961.

Although the value of contrastive analysis has been recognized for some time, relatively few substantial studies have been published. In a sense then this series represents a pioneering venture in the field of applied linguistics and, as with all such ventures, some of the material may eventually turn out to be of little value and some of the methods used may turn out to be inadequate. The authors and editor are fully convinced of the value of the studies, however, and hope that the series will represent an important step in the application of linguistic procedures to language problems. They are also agreed in their expectation that, while in another ten years this series may seem primitive and unsatisfactory, the principles of contrastive analysis will be more widely recognized and appreciated.

Charles A. Ferguson
Director, Center for Applied Linguistics

PREFACE

This book has been written in the hope that it may be of service to teachers of German, to those preparing to become teachers of German, and to writers of German textbooks. Through a contrastive analysis of the sound systems of English and German it is designed to reveal those points of conflict which underlie the pronunciation difficulties of American students who learn German and to suggest ways in which these difficulties may be overcome. For the first of these two tasks—identifying and explaining our students' pronunciation difficulties—I hope that my training in linguistics has given me some special competence. For the second task—correcting the difficulties once they have been identified —I am no better qualified than any other teacher of German. The various corrective drills which I present should be looked upon only as suggestions. Others with better pedagogical training than I will surely be able to improve on them.

It should be emphasized that this book is not intended for use with students who are learning German but is aimed only at those who already know German. I hope that the organization and content of the book are well adapted to the needs of teachers; I know, on the other hand, that they would be quite unsuitable for use with students. The order of presentation, for example, is based on linguistic principles: first the consonants, then the vowels, then stress, intonation, and juncture. If the book were meant for use with students, it would have a totally different order of presentation, based on pedagogical principles. Similarly, the style of presentation is mildly technical—not too technical for the teacher, I hope, but surely too technical for the student who is learning German. Finally, the book includes some analyses, especially in chapters 10 through 12, which are highly tentative. I believe it is proper to present such material to fellow teachers of German who are fully capable of judging how right or wrong my formulations may be; but it would be quite im-proper to present this material to students with the implication that it represented a tried and true analysis.

Three books were my constant guide as I was writing these pages: Charles Kenneth Thomas, An Introduction to the Phonetics of American English (2d ed.; New York: Ronald Press, 1958); John Samuel Kenyon and Thomas Albert Knott, A Pronouncing Dic-tionary of American English (Springfield, Mass.: G. & C. Merriam Co., 1953); and Siebs: Deutsche Hochsprache, Bühnenaussprache, 16th ed., by Helmut de Boor and Paul Diels (Berlin: Walter de Gruyter, 1957). After I had written most of the work in preliminary form, there appeared a fourth book which enabled me to revise chapters 8 and 9 and to put them on a much sounder footing: Kans Kurath and Raven I. McDavid, Jr., The Pronun-ciation of English in the Atlantic States (Ann Arbor: University of Michigan Press, 1961). Mention of these standard handbooks on the pronunciation of English and German brings me to two fundamental questions which need to be answered right at the start. This book purports to contrast the sound systems of American English and of German. But what do we mean by "American English"? And what do we mean by "German"? Both languages exist in many different varieties. We need a careful explanation of the varieties treated here, especially since the answers to these questions are rather different in the two languages.

In the case of American English we ought, ideally, to include every variety which the teacher is likely to hear from his students. Regardless of how widespread a particular student's pronunciation of English may be, or of how worthy or unworthy of imitation we may consider it, it is his own particular English pronunciation rather than someone else's which will cause interference when he tries to learn the pronunciation of German. Ideally, then, we should have a full description of _every_ type of English spoken by students in the United States. But such an ideal is, of course, unattainable: descriptions of all varieties of American English simply do not exist; and, even if they did, there would not be room for them all within the brief pages of this book. What I have tried to do is to include the major features of pronunciation given by Kurath and McDavid for the Atlantic States, and to supplement these as best I could for the rest of the country. The result is far from a complete presentation of all types of American English pronunciation, and in part it may even be inaccurate; but I hope that it will suffice to alert the teacher to the _kinds_ of pronunciation differences he will hear from his students, even if it cannot possibly cover all the details.

In the case of German the situation is quite different. We do not need to teach our students to pronounce more than one variety of German; we can therefore limit ourselves to that variety which is everywhere regarded as standard, namely the German pronunciation codified in the _Siebs_. This would seem, at least, to be the simple and obvious answer to the question: "What do we mean by 'German'?" Yet even here there are complications. In a few respects the pronunciation prescribed by the _Siebs_, though acceptable on the stage or lecture platform, is much too formal for ordinary conversation. The _Siebs_ insists, for example, on the use of apical or uvular /r/ in postvocalic position after long vowels (e.g. in _Tier_, _lehrt_); yet many millions of standard German speakers would consider this hopelessly formal, even foreign. Here I have not hesitated to describe, even to recommend, the more usual vocalized /r/ transcribed in this book as [ʌ̯] (cf. §5.7). In a number of other cases the _Siebs_ prescribes pronunciations which are acceptable in some parts of the German-speaking area but unacceptable—even slightly ridiculous or offensive—in other parts. In cases of this sort it seems only sensible to recommend that the teacher, provided he is a native speaker of German, continue to use the pronunciation which is considered standard in his area. Thus the teacher from Northern Germany may wish to continue pronouncing long ä as /ẹ:/ rather than /ɛ:/ (e.g. _spät_ as /špẹ:t/ rather than /špɛ:t/), initial _pf_- as /f/ rather than /pf/ (e.g. _Pfund_ as /fu̧nt/ rather than /pfu̧nt/), and perhaps even unvoiced g as /x/ or /ç/ rather than /k/ (e.g. _Tag_ as /tax/ rather than /ta̧:k/, and _Berg_ as /bẹrç/ rather than /bẹrk/). Similarly, the teacher from Southern Germany, Switzerland, or Austria may wish to continue pronouncing initial _s_- as /s/ rather than /z/ (e.g. _See_ as /sẹ:/ rather than /zẹ:/), and unvoiced -_ig_ as /i̧k/ rather than /i̧ç/ (e.g. _König_ as /ˈkọ̈:nik̦/ rather than /ˈkọ̈:nik̦/). There are both theoretical and practical reasons for allowing these deviations from the prescriptions of the <u>Siebs</u>. Theoretically, standard German should not be thought of as having a pronunciation which is rigidly prescribed right down to the last allophone; the <u>Siebs</u> itself makes generous allowance for geographical and stylistic variations. Practically, the native speaker of German should not, as a teacher, try to deviate much from the local standard to which he is accustomed, since he will then tend to become unsure of himself and thus lose the one precious advantage he has over the rest of us non-native speakers: an absolutely genuine pronunciation. Gross deviations from standard German (e.g. pronouncing <u>schön</u> as /šẹ:n/ rather than /šọ̈:n/) should of course be avoided; but no well-educated speaker of German needs to be warned against things like this. (The above remarks apply to teachers who are native speakers of German. Those of us who learned German as a foreign language should be much more wary of not following the <u>Siebs</u>. We have little excuse for deviating from its prescriptions unless we are sure that we have learned a pronunciation which is really genuine despite the fact that it differs from the <u>Siebs</u> in a few details.)

In concluding these prefatory remarks, I am grateful for the chance to acknowledge the help which I received from the author of the other German volume in this series, Herbert L. Kufner, of Cornell University. Each of us read the other's manuscript during various stages of composition. I can only hope that my comments were as helpful to him as his were to me.

W. G. M.

TABLE OF CONTENTS

INTRODUCTION · 1

"Languages are different." Nothing could be better known than this simple and obvious fact. Two languages such as English and German differ in the forms they use. Where the present tense of a typical English verb has only two different forms ("I-you-we-they speak, he-she-it speaks"), the corresponding German verb may have as many as six different forms ("ich spreche, du sprichst, er-sie-es spricht, wir-sie-Sie sprechen, ihr sprecht, sprich!"). They also differ in the way they arrange such forms. Where English typically turns a statement into a question by adding an auxiliary verb in front (statement, "they work here," question, "do they work here?"), German typically turns a statement into a question by putting the verb in first position (statement, "sie arbeiten hier," question, "arbeiten sie hier?"). They differ, further, in the way in which they arrange and symbolize the world of human experience. Where English has a single word know which can be applied to both persons and facts ("I know him; I know who he is"), German divides this area of experience between the words kennen and wissen ("ich kenne ihn; ich weiß, wer er ist"). Finally, they differ in the sounds they use and in the way in which they use them. English has nothing to match the ch of German doch; German has nothing to match the th of English both. It is this last type of difference and the implications it has for the teaching of German to speakers of English which will concern us in the following pages.

When a student sets out to learn a new language, he is willing—intellectually— to accept the fact that it is different and that he must learn some new and unfamiliar sounds to speak it properly. At the same time, he is so imprisoned within the world of his native English that learning these new sounds can be a very formidable task indeed. This matter of being "imprisoned" within the world of his native English manifests itself in two different ways. First of all, it is a matter of habit. Through thousands and thousands of hours of practice the adult or teen-age student has built up a set of muscular habits which make him a positive virtuoso in the pronunciation of English sounds. These muscular habits are so marvelously formed that they almost automatically exclude the possibility of pronouncing anything but English sounds. As a result, the student finds it hard to master new sounds such as the ch of doch or the ü of Tür. He finds it almost equally hard to pronounce familiar sounds when they are used in unfamiliar ways: the cluster [ts] is entirely familiar to him from such English words as sits, sets, cats; but he finds it hard to say this same cluster in German zu, zehn, Zunge, Zimmer because (barring such oddities as tsetse fly) it never occurs at the beginning of a word in English.

Aside from this matter of muscular habits, the student is imprisoned within his native English in another, more subtle way. We stated above that the student may be willing <u>intellectually</u> to accept the fact that the sounds of German are different from those of English. Quite often, however, he is not <u>emotionally</u> able to do this. The sounds of English constitute for him all that is normal in human speech; anything else strikes him as distinctly abnormal. Though reason may tell him otherwise, his emotions tell him that the ü of <u>Tür</u> is a "queer" sound which no normal, sensible human being would seriously use. Likewise, the uvular <u>r</u> of German strikes him as a quite outlandish rendition of what ought properly to be the familiar constricted <u>r</u> of English; and the <u>ch</u> of <u>doch</u> is to many students an almost indecent sound which ought to be kept outside of language entirely and used only for clearing the mouth of phlegm. These are involuntary reactions, of course; but they can be emotionally very strong. Being told to say such sounds as German ü, <u>r</u>, and <u>ch</u> is a little like being told to wear wrong clothing, to behave in a socially improper way. Anyone who has tried to teach German pronunciation will be familiar with the embarrassed giggles and titters and blushing which the new sounds produce during early stages of instruction.

"Languages are different." The point is clear, and the teaching difficulties which it raises are obvious. Oddly enough, however, some of the greatest teaching difficulties come from the fact that two languages such as English and German are in many ways remarkably similar. We have just examined the one extreme: German sounds which are quite unlike anything in English. At the other extreme are a number of sounds which are entirely identical in both languages: the <u>b</u> of <u>bei</u>, the <u>n</u> of <u>nein</u>, and so on. In between these two extremes are a number of sounds which, though not identical with any in English, are remarkably similar to them: the long [e:] and [o:] of German <u>See</u> and <u>so</u>, never as diphthongal as the usual vowels in English <u>say</u> and <u>so</u>; or the <u>l</u> of German <u>will</u>, never as velarized as the usual <u>l</u> of English <u>will</u>. Most exasperating of all are those cases where an English phoneme is composed partly of sounds which are like those of German, and partly of other sounds which are subtly different. For example, in a word like <u>beaten</u> many Americans pronounce a vowel which is phonetically identical with the <u>ie</u> of German <u>bieten</u>; but in a word like <u>see</u> most Americans render this same English phoneme as far more of a diphthong than is used for the <u>ie</u> of German <u>sie</u>. The difficulty with all of these sounds which are so similar in English and German is that, without considerable training, our students do not consciously hear the differences. And, obviously, until they <u>do</u> consciously hear the differences, they cannot learn to pronounce them differently.

Let us summarize, at this point, the pronunciation behavior of the typical teenage or adult student of German so that we can identify the types of errors he makes and consider how we, as teachers, can overcome them. As we have seen, there is a considerable area where the sounds of English and German are identical; here the student can continue to use the pronunciation habits which he has learned so thoroughly in his native English. The speakers of most types of American English can pronounce German <u>mit</u> and <u>Bett</u> as if they were English <u>mitt</u> and <u>bet</u>, and no one will be the wiser. (This is of course not true of <u>all</u> types of American speech.) The real pronunciation difficulties arise with the following types of German sounds:

1. German sounds which are similar to, but not quite identical with, certain sounds of English. Examples: the <u>ie</u> of German <u>sie</u>, the <u>l</u> of German <u>will</u>. The student's error is that of using English sounds in place of the corresponding German ones. The reason

for the error is that he does not consciously hear the difference between the two.

   2. German sounds which are unlike anything in English, such as the ch of Dach or the ü of Tür; or German sounds like the initial [ts] of zu, zehn which, though familiar to the student, are never used in this particular way in English. The student's errors will be of two main types. If he only hears these words and does not see how they are written, he will most likely substitute more or less equivalent English sounds: German Dach will be made to sound like English dock, German Tür like English tear, and German zu, zehn like English sue, sane. If the student sees how these words are written, on the other hand, Dach will probably still be like English dock, but Tür will almost certainly be like English tour, and zu, zehn like English zoo, Zane. The reasons for these errors are threefold. First, new muscular skills are needed for the pronunciation of these new sounds, and at the beginning this requires much effort and concentration. Second, even when the new muscular skills have been developed, they are often not used: an emotional reaction to the "queerness" of these sounds leads to their replacement by familiar English sounds. Third, the student reacts to the spelling as he has long since been taught to react, namely in an English rather than a German way, and the result is again English sounds.

   The one feature common to all these mispronunciations of the typical American student is the fact that he substitutes for German sounds the corresponding sounds of his own type of American English. Sometimes the substitution is inevitable because the student does not hear the difference: he hears the ie of German sie as if it were a good American diphthong (as in see) and hence pronounces it accordingly. At other times the student may hear the difference quite clearly, and the substitution he makes may seem—when viewed objectively—to be quite far-fetched; but he makes it none the less. An example is the use of English k (as in dock) for German ch (as in Dach). At still other times the student makes a substitution which is based not on sound but on spelling: he reads a given letter as if it were symbolizing English rather than German. An example is the pronunciation of German zu, zehn as if they were English zoo, Zane. For whatever the reason, the substitutions are made; and it is these substitutions of English sounds for German ones which lead the student to pronounce German with an "American accent"—which is to say, incorrectly.

   If we as teachers wish to correct these mispronunciations, it is obvious that we must have a full understanding of the sound substitutions which cause them. To gain such an understanding, it is not enough to know all we can about the sounds of German; we must also know as much as possible about the English sounds which our students substitute instead and to know how these substitutions come about. Such a knowledge can be acquired only through a careful, systematic, point-by-point comparison of the sounds of German and of American English. It is such a comparison which we shall try to present in the following chapters. We call it a "contrastive" analysis because it is only the actual points of contrast which need concern us. Where the two languages use one and the same sound (as in the case of [m] and [n], which are identical in English and German), there is obviously no teaching problem. A teaching problem arises only where corresponding sounds in the two languages contrast with one another, because it is only here that the student makes the substitutions which give him an American account.

In analyzing the sounds of both English and German, we shall use two differ-ent approaches: that of phonetics and that of phonemics. The two supplement each other, and each is necessary in its way; but right from the start we need to make clear the dif-ference between the two.

Phonetics seeks to identify and describe every feature involved in the produc-tion of a given sound. In a very real sense this is an impossible task, since the number of minute adjustments which the speech organs can make is practically infinite. As a result, phonetic analysis is usually limited to a rough description of the most obvious features. For example, the p of pin is roughly described as a "voiceless bilabial stop." It is "voice-less" because the vocal cords do not vibrate (as they do for the b of bin); it is "bilabial" because the organs most obviously involved in its production are the two lips; and it is a "stop" because the two lips form a closure which momentarily stops the flow of the breath tream. A more detailed phonetic analysis would mention such further features as: the du-ation of the closure; the degree of muscular energy involved; whether or not the lips are rotruded; whether or not the stop is aspirated (i.e., followed by an audible outflow of the reath stream); the strength and duration of the aspiration; and the vocalic quality of the spiration (influenced by the quality of the following vowel). This is about as far as unaid-d human observation can go; but a great many further details can be added if laboratory 1struments are used to aid in the analysis.

In contrast to phonetics, phonemics seeks to identify and describe, not every eature involved in the production of a speech sound, but only those features which (in a iven language) are DISTINCTIVE—those which serve, for example, to distinguish two dif-erent words. Where phonetics finds an almost limitless number of features in the p of pin, phonemics finds only three distinctive features: (1) it is a STOP, because it is the op-position "stop vs. fricative" which distinguishes pin from fin; (2) it is LABIAL, because it is the opposition "labial vs. dental" which distinguishes pin from tin; and (3) it is VOICE-LESS, because it is the opposition "voiceless vs. voiced" which distinguishes pin from bin. Phonetically, the p of pin requires an almost endless description; phonemically, it is fully described (for English) as a "voiceless labial stop." It is customary to inclose phonemic symbols within slant lines: "the phoneme /p/"; this distinguishes them from phonetic sym-bols, which are written within square brackets: "the sound [p]."

Phonemics is also more helpful than phonetics from another point of view: it allows us to do two things which we feel intuitively to be correct but which we cannot jus-tify on phonetic grounds. First, we feel intuitively that such a word as pin is made up of a certain number of "sounds" strung along in a row, one after the other; yet from a phonetic point of view pin is a continuum of sound, as a spectrogram of this word (or of any other) clearly shows. Only when we analyze pin phonemically can we prove that it consists of three "pieces" or "segments" of sound. We do this by showing that there are three seg-ments which can be replaced and/or deleted: we can replace the initial segment and get such words as fin, tin, bin; we can replace the middle segment and get such words as pan, pun, pine; we can replace the final segment and get such words as pit, pick, pill; and we can delete the initial segment and get in. Accordingly, we conclude that pin consists of three distinctive sound segments representing three different PHONEMES. (Though we are speaking here of sounds and not of spelling, the reader will have noticed that these replacements and deletions of sound segments correspond very closely to replacements and deletions of letters in the regular English spelling. This is because the English spelling system—like all alphabetic systems—is based clearly on the phonemic principle, albeit with a distressing number of irregularities.)

Second, we feel intuitively that the [pʰ] of pin or peer (an aspirated labial stop) and the [p] of spin or spear (an unaspirated labial stop) somehow belong more closely together than either of them does with the [f] of fin or fear (an unaspirated labial fricative). Phonetically, however, we are no more justified in grouping together the two stop sounds [pʰ] and [p] than we are in grouping together the two unaspirated sounds [p] and [f]. Only when we analyze these English sounds phonemically do we find theoretical support for our intuitive judgment. First, the same opposition "stop vs. fricative" which distinguishes the [pʰ] of peer from the [f] of fear also distinguishes the [p] of spear from the [f] of sphere. Second, in words of this type [pʰ] and [p] occur on NON-CONTRASTIVE DISTRIBUTION: [pʰ] occurs only initially, [p] occurs only after [s], and the difference between them never serves to distinguish two different words. Therefore, since these two PHONES (as we may call them technically) (1) share the same distinctive features ("labial" and "stop"), and (2) occur in non-contrastive distribution, we may class them together as ALLOPHONES of a phoneme /p/.

Allophones of a phoneme may occur in two different types of non-contrastive distribution. One is COMPLEMENTARY DISTRIBUTION, as in the example just given: [pʰ] occurs initially but not after [s]; [p] occurs after [s] but not initially. The other type is FREE VARIATION, whereby two or more allophones may occur non-distinctively in the same environment. For example, final /p/ in such a word as nip may be aspirated [pʰ], unaspirated [p], or even unreleased [p̄]: [nɪpʰ], [nɪp], or [nɪp̄]. Since we as English speakers react to all three of these pronunciations as merely different variants of the same thing, they can be analyzed as phonemically the same: /nɪp/. We may say that, in word-final position, the phoneme /p/ can be "realized" as either [pʰ], [p], or [p̄], in free variation.

Phonemics will underlie much of our description of the sounds of English and German; without it we cannot say how sounds are related to each other or even how many of them there are in each language. At the same time, we must not underrate the importance of phonetics; many of the difficulties which our students have with German pronunciation are of a phonetic rather than of a phonemic nature. In addition, we shall often have to consider matters of spelling, since the difference between the English and German spelling systems also contributes its share to our students' difficulties.

PHONETICS: THE CONSONANTS $\boxed{2}$

2.1 VOWEL VS. CONSONANT

When the speech organs interact so as to produce a speech sound, they are said to ARTICULATE the sound. Sounds articulated in such a way that the breath stream flows essentially unhindered along the median line of the vocal tract are classified as VOWELS. Sounds articulated in such a way that the breath stream is hindered in one way or another along the median line are classified as CONSONANTS. This division into vowels and consonants is primarily a matter of convenience; there is no sharp line between the two. For example, the j of German ja is frequently articulated with the tongue humped up so close to the roof of the mouth that friction is produced as the breath stream flows through the narrow opening; the presence of this friction classifies the sound, phonetically, as a consonant. Just as commonly, however, the space between the tongue and the roof of the mouth is wide enough so that no friction results; such a lack of friction then classifies it, phonetically, as a vowel. From a phonemic point of view this means that the German phoneme /j/ is made up of both consonantal and vocalic allophones, in free variation. How, then, should we classify the phoneme: as a consonant or as a vowel? Phonetically, we would have to discuss its consonantal allophones in the present chapter on consonants and its vocalic allophones in a later chapter on vowels. Phonemically, we can classify /j/ as a consonant because it occurs in much the same positions as obvious consonants. We shall therefore discuss it (and other phonemes like it in both English and German) in the present chapter.

The description given in the preceding chapter of the p of pin as a "voiceless bilabial stop" illustrates the rough way in which a preliminary classification of consonants is usually given. It is customary to mention:

1. the simultaneous activity (if any) of the vocal cords
2. the position of articulation
3. the manner of articulation

We now need to discuss each of these features in some detail.

2.2 THE VOCAL CORDS

Stick a finger in each ear and then pronounce alternately the [v] of veal and the [f] of feel: [vvv]—[fff]—[vvv]—[fff]. You will find that the articulation of the vocal or-

gans in the mouth is identical for both sounds but that [v] is accompanied by a loud buzzing whereas [f] is not. This buzzing, called VOICE, is produced by the vibration of the vocal cords: the cords are held together, but held loosely enough so that the breath stream
sets them in vibration as it flows out. Consonants articulated with simultaneous vibration
of the vocal cords are called VOICED, those without it are called VOICELESS. Since [v]
and [f] are articulated identically except that [v] is accompanied by voice and [f] is not,
they are a VOICED-VOICELESS PAIR. Other voiced-voiceless pairs in English are the
[z] of zeal and the [s] of seal, the [ž] of azure and the [š] of Asher, and the [ð] of thy and the
[θ] of thigh. If you will put your thumb and forefinger on your Adam's apple (behind which
the vocal cords are located), you can feel the vibration which accompanies each of the
voiced sounds.

In the articulation of voiced sounds the vocal cords are held loosely together;
in the articulation of voiceless sounds they are held wide apart. Two further types of articulation can be made by the vocal cords. The space between the vocal cords is called
the GLOTTIS. If the glottis is tightly closed so that the breath stream is momentarily
stopped, the result is a GLOTTAL STOP, symbolized [ʔ]. This is the little catch in the
throat that many Americans articulate between the two syllables of uh uh 'no,' or between
the words not at all when they want to avoid saying nota-tall. The glottal stop is extensively used in German (especially in North German pronunciation) before words or parts of
words beginning phonemically with a vowel: Ver[ʔ]ein, ge[ʔ]ändert, [ʔ]eine [ʔ]alte
[ʔ]Eiche.

If the glottis is held open but the vocal cords kept close enough together so
that frication is produced as the breath stream passes through, the result is a GLOTTAL
FRICATIVE. This is often one of the components of the phoneme /h/ in both English and
German. We shall discuss the other components later on.

(Within the larynx, in which the vocal cords are located, still another type of
articulation is possible. If the glottis is closed but the so-called arytenoid cartilages
drawn apart, the breath stream passing through produces a type of friction known as
WHISPER. When we whisper, this type of friction replaces voice, and it is this which en-
ables us to distinguish whispered [v] from [f], whispered [z] from [s], etc.)

2.3 ARTICULATORS AND POINTS OF ARTICULATION

The various articulators and points of articulation are best described with
reference to the accompanying schematic diagram of the vocal organs. Along the bottom
of the mouth are two highly movable organs: the LOWER LIP, which can articulate against
the upper lip and the upper teeth; and the TONGUE, which can articulate against various
parts of the roof of the mouth. Because the tongue in particular is so movable and because
different portions of it can articulate against the same organ, it is convenient to divide it
into several parts. A fundamental division is that between the tip of the tongue or the
APEX, and the top of the tongue or the DORSUM. The dorsum can then be further subdivided into three parts: the BLADE, opposite the alveolar ridge; the FRONT, opposite the
hard palate; and the BACK, opposite the soft palate or velum. (The part of the tongue that

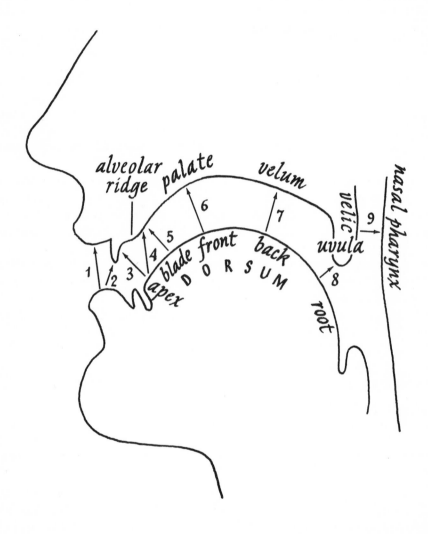

lies opposite the pharyngeal wall is called the ROOT; we can disregard it in any description of the sounds of English and German, though it plays an important role in the sounds of some languages.) This gives the following classification:

	Noun	Adjective	Compounding form
Articulators:	lower lip	labial	labio-
	apex	apical	apico-
	dorsum	dorsal	dorso-

These organs articulate against the following organs in the top of the mouth:

	Noun	Adjective
Points of articulation:	upper lip	labial
	upper teeth	dental
	alveolar ridge	alveolar
	palate	palatal
	velum	velar
	uvula	uvular

Where it is useful, the front, middle, and back of the (hard) palate can be described, respectively, as the "prepalatal," "midpalatal," and "postpalatal" regions. Similarly, one can also use the terms "prevelar," "midvelar," and "postvelar." The term "uvular" usually refers both to the uvula itself and to the extreme back of the velum immediately adjacent to it.

By combining these two sets of terms we arrive at the following POSITIONS OF ARTICULATION. Numbers agree with those on the diagram; each articulation is illustrated by an example.

1. LABIO-LABIAL, though usually called BILABIAL: the [p] of pin.
2. LABIO-DENTAL: the [f] of fin.
3. APICO-DENTAL: the [θ] of thin.
4. APICO-ALVEOLAR: the [t] of tin.
5. DORSO-ALVEOLAR: the [s] of sin (though many speakers articulate this as apico-alveolar).
6. DORSO-PALATAL: the [ç] of German ich.
7. DORSO-VELAR: the [k] of look.
8. DORSO-UVULAR: [ʀ] of German rot (though some speakers articulate this as apico-alveolar [ř]).

The schematic diagram indicates still a ninth position of articulation, in which the VELIC serves as articulator and the NASAL PHARYNX as point of articulation. If the velic articulates against the nasal pharynx, it seals off the nasal cavity and the result is an ORAL sound in which only the mouth functions as a resonance chamber. If the velic does not articulate against the nasal pharynx, the nasal cavity is left open and can also serve (along with the mouth) as a resonance chamber. A sound articulated with the nasal cavity thus open is called NASALIZED if the passage through the mouth is also left open (as is the case with nasalized vowels), but NASAL if there is a closure somewhere in the mouth (as is the case with the nasals [m] and [n]). The use of the velic as an articulator is nicely illustrated by such a word as <u>London</u> when it is pronounced with only one vowel: <u>Lond'n</u>. Throughout the sequence [ndn] an apico-alveolar closure is maintained. The first [n] is articulated with the velic open. (This is therefore a "nasal" sound.) The onset of the [d] is articulated by bringing the velic up against the nasal pharynx, blocking off the nasal passage. (This is therefore an "oral" sound.) The release of the [d] is articulated by pulling the velic away from the nasal pharynx; the result is the second [n].

2.4 MANNER OF ARTICULATION

1. STOPS (also called "occlusives" or "plosives"). The breath stream is stopped momentarily by a closure at some point in the vocal tract. Examples: [p b t d k g] in English <u>pea</u>, <u>be</u>, <u>to</u>, <u>do</u>, <u>cow</u>, <u>go</u>, German <u>Pein</u>, <u>Bein</u>, <u>Tank</u>, <u>Dank</u>, <u>Kunst</u>, <u>Gunst</u>.

2. FRICATIVES (also called "spirants"). The breath stream is forced through a narrow opening in the vocal tract, producing audible friction. Examples: [f v θ ð] in English <u>fee</u>, <u>vow</u>, <u>thigh</u>, <u>thou</u>; [ç x] in German <u>ich</u>, <u>ach</u>.

3. NASALS. The breath stream is stopped by a closure in the mouth (so that, to this extent, these sounds are "stops"), but it flows freely through the nose. Examples: [m n ŋ] in English <u>rum</u>, <u>run</u>, <u>rung</u>, German <u>hemme</u>, <u>Henne</u>, <u>hänge</u>.

4. LATERALS. Though there is a closure along the median line in the mouth, the breath stream flows freely along one or both sides of the tongue. English and German have only one type of lateral, the [l] of English <u>fell</u>, German <u>Fell</u>.

5. TRILLS. The breath stream causes one of the vocal organs to vibrate. Example: the apico-alveolar [ř] or dorso-uvular [ʀ] of German <u>rot</u> is sometimes a trill. In American English, trills are generally used only in imitative words, such as the <u>rrr</u> used in imitation of a telephone bell or a policeman's whistle.

It is often convenient to treat one subvariety of stops, one subvariety of fricatives, and one subvariety of trills as if they were also basic types:

6. AFFRICATES. The release of a stop is made in such a way as to produce the corresponding fricative. For example, if the stop [t] (as in <u>tin</u>) is released in such a way as to produce the fricative [š] (as in <u>shin</u>), the result is the initial segment of <u>chin</u>. This may of course be analyzed simply as stop plus fricative: [tš]. Sometimes, however, it is preferable to analyze it as a separate type of consonant, an affricate. We shall do this for the initial segment of <u>chin</u>, analyzing it as the affricate [č]: [čin]. Its voiced counterpart is the affricate [ǰ] as in <u>gin</u>: [ǰin].

7. SIBILANTS. As the breath stream of a fricative passes through its narrow opening, it may be directed toward the top of the lower front teeth. This adds to the friction characteristic of all fricatives a second type of "sibilant" friction. Examples: the [s] and [z] of <u>seal</u>, <u>zeal</u>; the [š] and [ž] of <u>Asher</u>, <u>azure</u>. (Sibilants also differ from normal fricatives in another way. In normal fricatives the breath stream is forced through a slit-shaped opening; in sibilants it is forced through a groove-shaped opening.)

8. FLAPS. Instead of vibrating two or more times, as in a normal trill, the speech organ vibrates just once. An example is the type of <u>r</u> pronounced in some varieties

of British English in such a word as <u>very</u> (in contrast to the Scotsman's genuine trill in "<u>verrry</u>"). Much the same type of flap is pronounced by most Americans for the /t/ in such a word as <u>city</u>; we can symbolize it as [t̮]. (Here we have considered a flap to be a special subvariety of trill, with only one vibration; it can just as well be considered to be a special subvariety of stop, articulated very quickly.)

It must be emphasized again that this traditional three-way classification of consonant sounds—classifying the [p] of <u>pin</u>, for example, as a "voiceless bilabial stop"— is only the beginning of a full phonetic description. For both English and German we often need to consider at least five further features of articulation: release (of stops), coarticulation, energy, duration, and syllabicity.

2.5 RELEASE

We divide the articulation of any stop into three successive stages: the ONSET, the HOLD, and the RELEASE. The release in particular may occur in a number of ways. English initial /p t k/, as in <u>pin</u>, <u>tin</u>, <u>kin</u>, are released in such a way that the hold is followed momentarily by an audible outrush of breath called ASPIRATION. The result is ASPIRATED [p^h t^h k^h]: [p^hı̣n t^hı̣n k^hı̣n]. But after [s], as in <u>spy</u>, <u>sty</u>, <u>sky</u>, there is no such aspiration; the result is unaspirated [p t k]: [spai stai skai]. (Since aspiration is not phonemically distinctive in English, we have all had years of training in <u>not</u> hearing it as a distinctive sound. To convince yourself of its presence, hold a lighted match in front of your mouth and try blowing it out by saying the word <u>spy</u> [spai] at it. You will find that it is possible to blow it out in this way, but not easy. Now try blowing it out by saying the word <u>pie</u> [p^hai] at it. You will find that the flame goes out almost immediately. It is the aspiration which blows it out.) Before another stop, as in <u>apt</u>, <u>Atkins</u>, <u>act</u>, English /p t k/ are usually not released at all: at the end of the hold the vocal organs simply assume the position needed for the following sound. The result is UNRELEASED [p^- t^- k^-]: [æp^-t æt̄kı̣nz æk^-t]. Before pause, English uses all three varieties, in free variation. The words <u>rap</u>, <u>rat</u>, <u>rack</u> may be [ræp^h ræt^h ræk^h], or [ræp ræt ræk], or [ræp^- ræt^- ræk^-].

Special types of release occur in both English and German before the nasals /m n ŋ/ and the lateral /l/. Before homorganic nasals (i.e., nasals articulated by the same organs as the preceding stop), the stops /p b t d k g/ are released not as usual through the mouth (ORAL RELEASE) but, by opening up the closure between the velic and the nasal pharynx, through the nose (NASAL RELEASE). The result is nasally released [p^N b^N t^N d^N k^N g^N]. This is easiest to hear in such forms as <u>rip 'em</u>, <u>rib 'em</u>, <u>written</u>, <u>ridden</u>, <u>reckon</u>, <u>wagon</u> when they are pronounced with syllabic [m̩ n̩ ŋ̩]: [rı̣p^Nm̩ rı̣b^Nm̩ rı̣t^Nn̩ rı̣d^Nn̩ rε̣k^Nŋ̩ wæg^{N}ŋ̩]. Before the lateral /l/, the stops /t d k g/ show LATERAL RELEASE, that is, the breath stream is released not along the median line of the mouth but along one or both sides of the tongue. The result is laterally released [t^L d^L k^L g^L]. This is easiest to hear before the syllabic [l̩] of such words as <u>metal</u>, <u>meddle</u>, <u>hackle</u>, <u>haggle</u>: [mε̣t^Ll̩ mε̣d^Ll̩ hæk^{L}l̩ hæg^{L}l̩].

2.6 COARTICULATION

When we describe the [k^h] of cool, for example, as an "aspirated voiceless dorso-velar stop," we are describing only the PRIMARY ARTICULATION of this sound—the activity of the vocal organs primarily involved in its production. At the same time, however, it is obvious that all the remaining vocal organs must be doing something. If they are involved in the articulation only in a completely passive way, we can safely leave them unmentioned. But if they are actively involved in any way at all, they are said to COARTICULATE, and their action must be mentioned in a full phonetic description. For the [k^h] of cool the lips are slightly rounded. (Contrast the spread lips for the [k^h] of keel.) If such lip rounding should turn out to be a distinctive feature in English (it is not; but in many languages it is), we would want to use a special symbol for it, perhaps [k^w]. If not, we can content ourselves with adding the verbal description "with lip rounding."

A striking example of coarticulation in English—and one which is of great importance in the teaching of German—concerns the lateral [l]. In terms of primary articulation it is an "apico-alveolar lateral": the apex articulates against the alveolar ridge, and the breath stream flows out along one or both sides of the tongue. At the same time that the apex articulates against the alveolar ridge, the dorsum has to assume one position or another. In most varieties of American English, the back of the dorsum is raised to a greater or lesser degree toward the velum, so that the tongue as a whole is shaped much like the inside of a spoon: high at the front (against the alveolar ridge), low in the middle, but high again at the back (raised toward the velum). This type of coarticulation is called VELARIZATION, because the back of the tongue is raised toward the velum. In most varieties of American English the velarization is slight in initial position: lee, but considerably stronger in final position: eel, especially after a back vowel: pool. If you listen carefully, you may be able to hear a constant increase in the velarization of the /l/'s in such a series as peel, pale, pill, Pell, pal, Poll(y), Paul, pull, pole, pool. This velarized [l] is often called "dark l," in contrast to the "clear l" (without velarization) that is used in German. Where we need to symbolize the difference, we can write the dark l as [ɫ]. Thus English /fɛl/ fell is phonetically [fɛɫ], with dark, velarized [ɫ]; it contrasts in this way with German /fɛl/ Fell, phonetically [fɛl], with clear, non-velarized [l].

2.7 ENERGY

In terms of our rough, preliminary, three-way phonetic description, the [t] of write is a "voiceless apico-alveolar stop" and the [d] of ride is a "voiced apico-alveolar stop." The feature which distinguishes them is therefore the opposition "voiceless vs. voiced." If we examine them more carefully, we will discover that they also differ in the amount of muscular energy expended in their articulation: [t] is FORTIS (articulated with relatively great muscular energy), whereas [d] is LENIS (articulated with relatively little muscular energy). Sometimes, in fact, it is the opposition "fortis vs. lenis" alone which serves to distinguish the two. In a common pronunciation of /raid/ ride, the vibration of the vocal cords ("voice") that is characteristic of the /r/ and the /ai/ ceases before the articulation of the /d/. The result is [raid̥], with VOICELESS LENIS [d̥]. The opposition which distinguishes /rait/ write from this /raid/ = [raid̥] ride is then no longer the double one "voiceless fortis vs. voiced lenis," but simply "fortis vs. lenis."

Our preliminary investigation of English revealed no less than eight "voiceless—voiced" pairs: [p b], [t d], [č ǰ], [k g], [f v], [θ ð], [s z], [š ž]. All of them are at the same time "fortis—lenis" pairs; and very often, when the so-called "voiced" member of the pairs is actually unvoiced, it is only the opposition "fortis—lenis" which serves to distinguish the two. Particularly common in English is the use of voiceless lenis [z̥] in final position. Contrast the voiceless fortis [s] of wince [wɪns] with the voiceless lenis [z̥] of wins [wɪnz] (though this latter can, of course, also be pronounced with voiced lenis [z]: [wɪnz̥]).

The opposition "fortis vs. lenis" is particularly important in German. In Northern Germany the situation is much like that of English: the fortis stops and fricatives are voiceless; the lenis stops and fricatives are typically voiced, but they may also be voiceless. But for many South German speakers the situation is quite different: all stops and fricatives are normally voiceless, and the only feature which groups them into pairs (/p/—/b/, /t/—/d/, /k/—/g/, etc.) is the opposition "fortis vs. lenis." The Siebs condemns this practice and prescribes fully voiced articulation for German /b d g v z ž/ (cf. § 4.2, below). Henceforth we shall therefore describe the stops and fricatives of German as if they were always distinguished by the opposition "voiceless vs. voiced": /p/—/b/, /t/—/d/, /k/—/g/, etc.

2.8 DURATION

A dimension of speech sounds which we have not as yet mentioned is that of time. By their very nature, all fricatives, sibilants, nasals, laterals, and trills can be prolonged indefinitely, until the breath supply is exhausted. Stops are of a different nature, of course. Nevertheless, the "hold" of a voiced stop can continue until the air pressure above the glottis is equal to that below it; and even though the "hold" of a voiceless stop is mere silence, the duration of this silence between surrounding sounds can obviously vary. All such phenomena are matters of DURATION. It is customary to divide the continuum of duration into two dimensions and to speak of SHORT and LONG sounds. If it is useful to do so, we can cut each of these dimensions in half and speak of "over-short," "short," "long," and "over-long" sounds. Sometimes a three-way cut into "short," "half-long," and "long" is more useful.

Depending on the positions in which they occur, English (and German) consonants vary greatly in duration. For example, the final /n/ of English nun is much longer than the initial one; this can be nicely demonstrated by first recording the word on tape or disk and then playing it backward. Similarly, /n/ is considerably longer before lenis consonants than before fortis consonants; contrast the relatively short /n/ of since /sɪns/, cent /sɛnt/ with the relatively long /n/ of sins /sɪnz/, send /sɛnd/. Because such differences in duration are not distinctive in English (or German), we are not conscious of them. The only differences in duration to which we react consciously are those which we interpret as two occurrences of the same phoneme. Phonetically, the difference between my nose and mine knows is (primarily) the difference between short [n] and long [n:]: [mainoz]

my nose vs. [main:oz] mine knows. Phonemically, these phrases are /mai noz/ vs. /main noz/, and this is also the way we react to them intuitively.

2.9 SYLLABICITY

Our analysis thus far has given us no method of distinguishing between the three-syllable word lightening ('lightening the load') and the two-syllable word lightning ('thunder and lightning'). As far as we have gone, both are phonetically [lait^{N}nịŋ]. The difference between them, however, is clear: in lightening the [nʲ forms the nucleus of a separate syllable, whereas in lightning it does not. We can indicate this difference by writing the [n] of lightening as SYLLABIC [n̩]: [lait^{N}n̩ịŋ], but the [n] of lightning as NON-SYLLABIC [n]: [lait^{N}nịŋ]. Syllabic [m̩ n̩ ŋ̩ l̩] are very common in English (and German); we have already met them in such forms as rip 'em, written, reckon, meddle.

Along with these four syllabic consonants we also need to consider at this point three non-syllabic vowels. Two of them are the familiar semivowels [w] and [j], as in [wẹl], [jẹl] well, yell, [wok], [jok] woke, yoke, etc.[1] Phonetically, [w] has the quality of the vowel of to [tu]; it differs from it in being non-syllabic rather than syllabic. The phrase to itch shows this vowel in syllabic function: [tuịč]; the word twitch shows it in non-syllabic function: [twịč]. Similarly, [j] has the quality of the vowel of be [bi]; it differs from it in being non-syllabic rather than syllabic. The phrase be oozing shows this vowel in syllabic function: [biuzịŋ]; the word abusing shows it in non-syllabic function: [əbjuzịŋ].

The third non-syllabic vowel may come as a surprise: it is the [r] of [rẹd] red, [roz] rose, and also (except for those Americans who "drop their r's") in [dir] dear, [dor] door. We are accustomed to thinking of this [r] as a consonant, because phonemically it functions like one. A little thought will reveal, however, that it has none of the phonetic characteristics of a consonant: there is no oral closure with resulting stoppage of the breath stream, as in the case of stops; there is no oral constriction with resulting friction, as in the case of fricatives; there is no oral closure with free passage through the nose, as in the case of nasals; there is no medial closure with lateral opening, as in the case of laterals; and there is (in American English) no vibration of one of the vocal organs, as in the case of trills. In short, [r] fits entirely the phonetic definition of a vowel as a sound "articulated in such a way that the breath stream flows essentially unhindered along the median line of the vocal tract."

Before vowels, probably all varieties of American English have an alveolar [r] "in which the tip of the tongue approaches, but does not touch, the upper gums or the prepalatal region of the roof of the mouth. . . . The middle or the back of the tongue is usually more or less arched toward the roof of the mouth and is laterally constricted," that is, the sides of the tongue are drawn away from the teeth and gums at the sides of

---

1. In American writings on phonetics and phonemics, the second of these semivowels is often written [y]. We choose the symbol [j] for two reasons. First, [j] is the symbol adopted by the International Phonetic Association, and it seems wise to follow this more international practice if we can. Second, [j] is the obvious symbol for the initial sound of German jetzt, ja, jung, etc.; and since English [j] and German [j] are to all intents and purposes phonetically identical, it would be undesirable to symbolize them differently.

the mouth. It is this LATERAL CONSTRICTION which, more than anything else, gives to [r] its special quality.

In so-called "postvocalic position," that is, at the end of a word or before a consonant, as in dear, corn, many speakers along the Atlantic seaboard do not pronounce an [r]. Instead, they use non-syllabic [ə] (the non-syllabic form of the unstressed vowel in [əgo] ago, [sofə] sofa), so that dear is [diə̯]; or else the [r] is lost altogether, so that corn is [kɔ:n], rhyming with lawn. In the rest of the United States, where postvocalic [r] is kept, it usually differs slightly from the prevocalic [r] described in the preceding paragraph. It is "articulated in this position without tongue-tip action." The "body of the tongue is arched toward the roof of the mouth and the sides of the tongue are drawn away from the gums. This lateral constriction of the tongue creates a very complicated resonance chamber, the vibrating breath passing both over the tongue and along its sides." Here also it is this lateral constriction which gives to [r] its special quality. (The above descriptions of [r] are from Kurath and McDavid, The Pronunciation of English in the Atlantic States, p. 115.)

We have seen that non-syllabic [w], as in [twi̯č] twitch, has the phonetic quality of syllabic [u], as in [tui̯č] to itch; and that non-syllabic [j], as in [əbjuzi̯ŋ] abusing, has the phonetic quality of syllabic [i], as in [biuzi̯ŋ] be oozing. In the same way, non-syllabic [r], as in [fret] freight, has the phonetic quality of syllabic [ɝ], as in [fɝet] for eight ("fer eight"). Or, to illustrate with another type of example, non-syllabic [r], as in [stri̯ŋ] string, has the phonetic quality of syllabic [ɝ], as in [stɝi̯ŋ] stirring.

Though the topic belongs properly to a later chapter, it will be helpful to add at this point a few comments on the use of the syllabic vowel [ɝ] in American English. In most of the United States, where postvocalic [r] is pronounced, as in [dir] dear and [kɔrn] corn, syllabic [ɝ] is also used. It occurs not only before vowels, as in [stɝi̯ŋ pɝi̯ŋ fɝi] stirring, purring, furry, but also postvocalically, both in word-final position: [sɝ hɝ fɝ] sir, her, fur, and before consonants: [bɝč pɝt hɝd wɝk bɝn] birch, pert, heard, work, burn. (Note the fantastic variety of spellings for this one sound!) As we have seen, the characteristic articulatory feature of this [ɝ] is the lateral constriction of the body of the tongue. However, in those areas along the Atlantic seaboard where postvocalic [r] is lacking (so that dear is [diə̯], and corn is [kɔ:n], rhyming with lawn), the constriction of [ɝ] is also lacking. The result is unconstricted [ɜ]. In these areas, sir, her, fur are [sɜ hɜ fɜ]; birch, pert, heard, work, burn are [bɜč pɜt hɜd wɜk bɜn]; and stirring, purring, furry are usually [stɜri̯ŋ pɜri̯ŋ fɜri].

In a phonetic notation we will wish to distinguish carefully between the [ɜ] of eastern [hɜ] her etc., without lateral constriction of the tongue, and the [ɝ] of [hɝ] her etc. in the rest of the country, with lateral constriction of the tongue. Phonemically, however, [ɜ] and [ɝ] are merely different geographical pronunciations (different DIAPHONES, to use the technical term) of the same phoneme. We will therefore want to use one and the same phonemic symbol for both of them. For this purpose, following Kurath and McDavid, we shall use the symbol /ɜ/. The phonemic notation /hɜ/ her will therefore mean, phonetically, [hɜ] along most of the Atlantic seaboard, but [hɝ] in the rest of the country.

PHONEMICS: THE CONSONANTS OF ENGLISH

3.1 PHONETICS VS. PHONEMICS

The preceding chapter, short as it is, is long enough to reveal the two aspects of phonetics which we need to keep constantly in mind. From one point of view, phonetics is indispensable: only through phonetics can we give even a rough classification and description of the sounds of any language; without it we could not even make a start. But from another point of view, phonetics seems like a hopeless task: no matter how far we go in trying to describe the sounds even of a single word, we can always go farther; there is simply no end to the number of different features we can find if only we listen hard enough. Much of phonetics seems arbitrary: no two phoneticians will analyze the same utterance in exactly the same way, because one will miss minute features which the other hears, and vice versa; and a third phonetician will hear features which both of them missed. Much of phonetics also seems futile. Why go to the bother of noting that the word nip is sometimes pronounced [nɪpʰ], sometimes [nɪp], and sometimes [nɪp˺], when all three pronunciations are functionally the same in English? Who cares that there are a dozen different kinds of [l] in English, with varying degrees of velarization, when all of them function in exactly the same way? The value of phonetics is that it helps us to hear an immense number of different phonetic features; the dilemma of phonetics is that it cannot tell us which of them are relevant in a given language and which are not.

Phonemics differs from phonetics in a very fundamental way. Instead of treating all languages alike, it treats each language differently. It does this by differentiating between those phonetic features in a language which are distinctive, and those which are non-distinctive. Like phonetics, it notes that English has a dozen or more different kinds of [l]-sounds, with varying degrees of velarization. Unlike phonetics, it also notes that these different sounds are in NON-CONTRASTIVE DISTRIBUTION: they are either in FREE VARIATION (the /l/ of /pɪl/ pill, for example, can be pronounced with varying degrees of velarization) or COMPLEMENTARY DISTRIBUTION (by and large, the degree of velarization is determined automatically by the phonetic nature of the preceding or following vowel). Therefore all of these different PHONES can be grouped together as ALLO-PHONES of a single PHONEME. The choice of a symbol for this phoneme—whether /l/ or

/ɫ/ or something else—is a matter of no importance as far as phonemics is concerned. The usual practice is to choose symbols which are simple and easy to write, type, and print. We shall therefore use the symbol /l/ for both English and German, even though we know that it is usually dark, velarized [ɫ] in English but clear, non-velarized [l] in German.

3.2 PHONEMIC CONTRASTS

The simplest way of determining the phonemes of a language is to look for pairs of words which differ only in a single phone each. Examples: <u>pin</u> vs. <u>bin</u>, <u>pat</u> vs. <u>bat</u>, <u>ripping</u> vs. <u>ribbing</u>, <u>rope</u> vs. <u>robe</u>, <u>cup</u> vs. <u>cub</u>, etc. Such MINIMAL PAIRS make it quite clear that we are dealing with two different phonemes (in these examples /p/ and /b/) rather than with phones which might possibly be allophones of a single phoneme. If we apply this type of analysis to English, we find that it has 24 consonant phonemes. The following list illustrates them, where possible, in three different positions: word-initial, word-medial, and word-final. (The raised tick /'/ at the beginning of each word indicates the point of onset of stress—that is, all of these words are stressed on the first syllable. Contrast with this the form /gə'raǰ/ <u>garage</u> in footnote 1, stressed on the second syllable.)

/p/	/'pel/	pail	/'tæpɪŋ/	tapping	/'rɪp/	rip
/b/	/'bel/	bail	/'tæbɪŋ/	tabbing	/'rɪb/	rib
/t/	/'tel/	tail	/'lætɜ/	latter	/'rɪt/	writ
/d/	/'del/	dale	/'lædɜ/	ladder	/'rɪd/	rid
/č/	/'čen/	chain	/'bæčɪz/	batches	/'rɪč/	rich
/ǰ/	/'ǰen/	Jane	/'bæǰɪz/	badges	/'rɪǰ/	ridge
/k/	/'kel/	kale	/'bækɪŋ/	backing	/'pɪk/	pick
/g/	/'gel/	gale	/'bægɪŋ/	bagging	/'pɪg/	pig
/f/	/'fel/	fail	/'lʌfɪŋ/	luffing	/'lif/	leaf
/v/	/'vel/	veil	/'lʌvɪŋ/	loving	/'liv/	leave
/θ/	/'θai/	thigh	/'iθɜ/	ether	/'loθ/	loath
/ð/	/'ðai/	thy	/'iðɜ/	either	/'loð/	loathe
/s/	/'sil/	seal	/'resɜ/	racer	/'rais/	rice
/z/	/'zil/	zeal	/'rezɜ/	razor	/'raiz/	rise
/š/	/'šel/	shale	/'æšɜ/	Asher	/'ruš/	ruche
/ž/			/'æžɜ/	azure	/'ruž/[1]	rouge
/m/	/'mel/	mail	/'sɪmɜ/	simmer	/'ræm/	ram
/n/	/'nel/	nail	/'sɪnɜ/	sinner	/'ræn/	ran
/ŋ/			/'sɪŋɜ/	singer	/'ræŋ/	rang
/l/	/'len/	lane	/'mɪlɜ/	miller	/'tail/	tile
/r/	/'ren/	rain	/'mɪrɜ/	mirror	/'tair/	tire

---

1. Some speakers do not use /ž/ in word-final position but pronounce <u>rouge</u> as /ruǰ/, <u>garage</u> as /gə'raǰ/, etc.

/j/	/'jel/	Yale
/w/	/'wel/	wail
/h/	/'hel/	hail

3.3 DISTINCTIVE FEATURES

Once we have determined in this way how many consonant phonemes there are in a language, our next task is to see what sort of system they form. We do this by noting the DISTINCTIVE FEATURES which characterize them, i.e., the phonetic features which keep them apart from one another. For example, English /p/ and /b/ are both bilabial stops, but they are kept apart by the fact that /p/ is voiceless, /b/ voiced. We therefore say that these two features form a distinctive OPPOSITION: "voiceless vs. voiced." Similarly, /p b/ and /m/ are all bilabial sounds, but they are kept apart by the fact that /p b/ are stops, /m/ a nasal. These two features thus form the distinctive opposition "stop vs. nasal."

In setting up such phonemic systems, we try to make the distinctive features as inclusive as possible. For example, /p b m/ are all typically bilabial, whereas /f v/ are typically labio-dental. However, the difference between bilabial and labio-dental is not distinctive: we find no minimal pairs in which a labio-dental /p/, /b/, or /m/ contrasts with the usual bilabial one, or a bilabial /f/ or /v/ with the usual labio-dental one. In typical articulations, the stops /p b/ and the nasal /m/ are automatically bilabial, and the fricatives /f v/ are automatically labio-dental. We can therefore group all five of these phonemes under the more inclusive feature "labial."

We are now ready to show the interlocking system of distinctive features which characterize most of the consonant phonemes of English. In the following table, features pertaining to position of articulation are given horizontally at the top, and features pertaining to manner of articulation are given vertically at the left. Where two phonemes appear in the same box (except in the large box at the bottom), the first is voiceless, the second voiced.

	labial	dental	palatal	velar
Stops	p b	t d	č ǰ	k g
Fricatives	f v	θ ð		
Sibilants		s z	š ž	
Nasals	m	n		ŋ
Other		l r j	w h	

The phonemic feature "stop" includes two types of phonetic stops: the plain stops /p b t d k g/ and the affricated stops (affricates) /č ǰ/. This is possible because the opposition "plain vs. affricated" is never distinctive: the palatal stops are always affricated, and the other stops are always plain. (This latter statement needs qualification: though the other stops are typically plain, they are occasionally also affricated. When /k/

is articulated with particular emphasis, it is not infrequently [k^X], with slight affrication. In some areas—New York City, for example—many speakers frequently affricate /t/ as [t^S]. Such deviations from the norm are non-distinctive. They merely give further support to the statement made above that the opposition "plain vs. affricated" is never distinctive in English.)

The phonemic feature "labial" includes two types of phonetic articulation: bi-labial as well as labio-dental. Again, this is possible because the opposition "bilabial vs. labio-dental" is never distinctive: the stops /p b/ and the nasal /m/ are typically bilabial, and the fricatives /f v/ are typically labio-dental. (These statements also need qualification. In the cluster /mf/, as in /'nįmf/ nymph, both phonemes are sometimes bilabial, or both sometimes labio-dental. And in the cluster /pf/, as in /hopfəl/ hopeful, the /p/ is sometimes labio-dental. Both of these exceptions from the norm lend further support to the statement that the opposition "bilabial vs. labio-dental" is not distinctive in English.)

The phonemic feature "dental" is used here as an inclusive term which in effect means something like "usually articulated at or near the teeth, but in any case neither labial, palatal, nor velar." The fricatives /θ ð/ are perhaps always apico-dental. The sibilants /s z/ are apico-alveolar for some speakers (the sibilant groove is made between the apex and the alveolar ridge), dorso-alveolar for others (the sibilant groove is made between the blade and the alveolar ridge). /t d n/ are typically apico-alveolar; but before apico-dental /θ/ they may also be apico-dental: /'etθ 'wįdθ 'tęnθ/ eighth, width, tenth; before dorso-alveolar /s z/ they may also be dorso-alveolar: /'pæts 'pædz 'tęns 'tęnz/ pats, pads, tense, tens; and before or after /r/ they may be apico-prepalatal: /'trai 'drai 'hart 'hard 'barn/ try, dry, heart, hard, barn. As an extreme case, /t/ may even be glottal, as with speakers who use a glottal stop in ['ba?l] = /'batəl/ bottle, where others have laterally released [t^{L}l]: ['bat^{L}l].

The phonemic feature "palatal" might more exactly be called "alveolo-palatal." The onsets of /č/ and /ǰ/ are of course stops, phonetically [t] and [d]; they are articulated against the alveolar ridge, though usually at a point higher than that for /t/ and /d/, i.e., in postalveolar position. The release is by way of the same type of sibilant as for /š/ and /ž/: a wide groove between the tongue and both the alveolar ridge and the front of the palate. The groove for /š/ and /ž/ differs from that for /s/ and /z/ in two ways: it is wider and deeper, and it extends farther back, opposite the front of the palate. Some speakers articulate /č ǰ š ž/ with the apex, others with the blade.

The phonemic feature "velar" refers both to the velum and to the back of the palate. Roughly speaking, /k g ŋ/ are given postpalatal articulation before and after front vowels, prevelar articulation before and after central vowels, and midvelar articulation before and after back vowels. Test this by noting the different qualities of the /k/'s in such a series as keep, cape, kit, kept, cat, cot, caught, could, coat, cool. If all of these vowels are pronounced differently, no two of the allophones of the /k/ before them will sound exactly alike.

The phoneme /l/ is fully defined by the distinctive feature "lateral." The phonemes /r j w/ all share the feature "semivowel"; they are distinguished from one another by the features "central," "front," and "back," respectively. (The terms "central," "front," and "back," as applied to vowels, will be explained in chapter 6.)

The phoneme /h/ is a special case. The sounds which we have called "frica-tives" thus far all involve what is known as LOCAL FRICTION, that is, friction at some specific point in the vocal tract. /h/ involves friction of quite a different type: CAVITY FRICTION, that is, "voiceless resonance of a chamber as a whole caused by air going through it as through an open tube" (Kenneth L. Pike, Phonetics [Ann Arbor, 1943], p. 71). Since the articulation of /h/ does not require the vocal organs to assume any particular position, they take on the position of the next following phoneme. If this next phoneme is a vowel, the result is an /h/ with the quality of this vowel—or, in other words, a voiceless vowel with cavity friction. This means that /h/ has a large number of allophones, depend-ing on the vowel which follows. Test them in such a series as he, hay, hit, heck, hat, hot, hawk, hood, hoe, who. If the phoneme following /h/ is /w/, the /h/ is realized as a voice-less [w̥]: /'hwɪč 'hwɛn 'hwai/ which, when, why (though some Americans say /'wɪč 'wɛn 'wai/, without /h/). If the phoneme following /h/ is /j/, the /h/ is realized as a voiceless [j̥]: /'hju 'hjumɪd 'hjumən/ hue, humid, human (though some Americans say /'ju 'jumɪd 'jumən/, without /h/). This last allophone is of special interest to teachers of German be-cause, if the slit between the dorsum and the palate is narrowed just a bit more until real local friction is produced, the result is the [ç] of German ich, mich, etc.

PHONEMICS: THE CONSONANTS OF GERMAN $\boxed{4}$

4.1 PHONEMIC CONTRASTS

Having analyzed the consonant phonemes of English, we may turn now to those of German. We shall again first determine the number of contrasting phonemes, illustrating each, where possible, in word-initial, word-medial, and word-final position, and then consider the system which they form. We find the following typical contrasts:

/p/	/'pạsə/	passe	/'raupən/	Raupen	/'rị:p/	rieb
/b/	/'bạs/	Baß	/'raubən/	rauben		
/t/	/'tạsə/	Tasse	/'bạ:tən/	baten	/'rị:t/	riet
/d/	/'dạs/	das	/'bạ:dən/	baden		
/k/	/'kạsə/	Kasse	/'hạ:kən/	Haken	/'zị:k/	Sieg
/g/	/'gạsə/	Gasse	/'hạ:gən/	Hagen		
/f/	/'fạsə/	fasse	/'höːfə/	Höfe	/'raif/	reif
/v/	/'vạs/	was	/'löːvə/	Löwe		
/s/	/sa'teⁿ/	Satin	/'raisən/	reißen	/'rais/	Reis
/z/	/'zạts/	Satz	/'raizən/	reisen		
/š/	/'šạts/	Schatz	/'raušən/	rauschen	/'rauš/	Rausch
/ž/	/žẹ:'nị:/	Genie	/'rạ:žə/	Rage		
/ç/	/'çị:na/	China	/'raiçən/	reichen	/'raiç/	reich
/x/			/'rauxən/	rauchen	/'raux/	Rauch
/m/	/'mạsə/	Masse	/'hẹmən/	hemmen	/'rạm/	Ramm
/n/	/'nạsə/	nasse	/'hẹnən/	Hennen	/'rạn/	rann
/ŋ/			/'hẹŋən/	hängen	/'rạŋ/	rang
/l/	/'lạsə/	lasse	/'kọ:lə/	Kohle	/'vịl/	will
/r/	/'rạsə/	Rasse	/'bọ:rə/	bohre	/'vịr/	wirr
/j/	/'jạkə/	Jacke	/'kọ:jə/	Koje		
/h/	/'hạsə/	hasse				

In trying to compile such a list as this, we notice immediately that it is harder to find minimal pairs in German than it is in English. However, even though minimal pairs are a simple and elegant device for proving that two phones stand in contrast with one another, they are by no means necessary. It is sufficient if we can show that the difference between two phones is not automatically determined by the different environments in which they stand. For example, it seems to be impossible to find a minimal pair to demonstrate that German /š/ and /ž/ are contrasting phonemes. This is largely because /ž/ occurs in relatively few words and the chances of finding a minimal contrast with /š/ are therefore reduced. But a minimal contrast is not necessary. A pair such as /'ši:r/ schier vs. /'ži:rọ:/ Giro shows the phones in contrast before /i̥:r/; it would be most unrealistic to assume that the difference between /š/ and /ž/ is conditioned by the absence or presence of the final /ọ:/.

There is only one place where we need to question seriously whether two phones are really in contrast, and that is in the case of /ç/ and /x/. If we examine the full evidence, we find that /ç/ and /x/ are, by and large, in complementary distribution. Compare the following lists:

With /x/		With /ç/		With /ç/	
/'dạx/	Dach	/'dẹçər/	Dächer	/'zi:ç/	siech
/'brạːx/	brach	/'brɛːçə/	bräche	/'zi̥ç/	sich
/'lọx/	Loch	/'löçər/	Löcher	/'blẹç/	Blech
/'hoːx/	hoch	/'höːçst/	höchst	/'raiç/	reich
/'brụx/	Bruch	/'brüçə/	Brüche	/'mạnç/	manch
/'bụːx/	Buch	/'büːçər/	Bücher	/'zọlç/	solch
/'baux/	Bauch	/'bọiçə/	Bäuche	/'dụrç/	durch
				/'çi̥ːna/	China

These lists show that /x/ occurs only after central and back vowels, /ạ ạ: ọ ọ: ụ ụ: au/, whereas /ç/ occurs after front vowels, /i̥: i̥ ɛ: ẹ ü: ü ö: ọ̈ ai ọi/, after the consonants /n l r/, and in word-initial position (China, though in South Germany this is /'ki̥:na/). If this were all the evidence, the occurrence of either /x/ or /ç/ would be automatically regulated, and we could analyze these two phones as allophones of a single phoneme, in complementary distribution. But there is an exception to this complementary distribution. The diminutive suffix spelled -chen shows /ç/ in all positions, even after central and back vowels, and hence it sometimes stands in contrast with /x/. Compare /'kụçən/ Kuhchen vs. /'kụːxən/ Kuchen, or /'tauçən/ Tauchen ('little rope') vs. /'tauxən/ tauchen ('to dive').

How should we account for this discrepancy? One solution would be to say that a minimal pair such as /'tauçən/ Tauchen vs. /'tauxən/ tauchen proves that /ç/ and /x/ are separate, contrasting phonemes, even though they are usually in complementary distribution. Another solution would be to say that the phones [ç] and [x] are allophones of a single phoneme and that the occurrence of [ç] initially in the diminutive suffix -chen is comparable to its occurrence initially in the word China: in both cases the phoneme stands in initial position, and hence the allophone [ç] is used in both cases rather than the allophone [x].

As teachers of German, we do not need to force a choice between these two possible solutions; we need rather to accept them both. On the one hand, we must make our students aware of the fact that the choice of /x/ or /ç/ is largely an automatic matter: except in the diminutive suffix, /x/ is automatic after short /ạ ǫ ụ/, long /a: ǫ: ụ:/, and the diphthong /au/, but /ç/ is automatic in all other positions. It is this automatic complementary distribution which makes it possible for both sounds to be symbolized by the same spelling ch. On the other hand, we also need to make our students aware of the fact that the diminutive suffix -chen is always pronounced /çən/, regardless of the type of sound which precedes it.

4.2 DISTINCTIVE FEATURES

The system formed by the consonant phonemes of German is in many ways very similar to that of English, and we can diagram it in much the same manner. Again, where two phonemes appear in the same box, the first is voiceless, the second voiced.

	labial	dental	palatal	velar
Stops	p b	t d		k g
Fricatives	f v		ç	x
Sibilants		s z	š ž	
Nasals	m	n		ŋ
Other	l	r j	h	

The feature "labial" includes, as in English, both bilabial and labio-dental articulation: /p b m/ are typically bilabial, /f v/ are typically labio-dental. Since bilabial and labio-dental articulation are in complementary distribution, the difference between them is not distinctive. To some extent there is free variation: /p/ before /f/, as in /'pfụnt/ Pfund, /'kǫpf/ Kopf, may be either bilabial or labio-dental; so also may /m/ before /f/, as in /'nümfə/ Nymphe.

The feature "dental" is less of a catchall than in English. German /t d n/ are typically articulated with the apex immediately above the upper teeth or, as in English, against the alveolar ridge; the difference is scarcely audible, and presents no teaching problem. As in English, the sibilants /s/ and /z/ are apico-alveolar for some speakers, dorso-alveolar for others. Before and after dorso-alveolar /s/ the phonemes /t/ and /n/ may also be dorso-alveolar: /'kạtsən/ Katzen, /'kạstən/ Kasten, /'hạns/ Hans; this, too, is like English.

The feature "palatal" also involves some alveolar articulation, since German /š ž/ (like their English counterparts) are alveolopalatal. Some speakers articulate them with the apex, others with the blade. German /ç/, on the other hand, is palatal only.

The feature "velar" refers, as in English, to both the velum and the back of the palate. Again, roughly speaking, /k g ŋ/ are dorso-postpalatal before and after front vowels, dorso-prevelar before and after central vowels, dorso-midvelar before and after back vowels. Note these automatic differences in such a series as Kiel, Kehle, kahl, Kohle, Kuh.

The phoneme /l/ is a lateral consonant. As already noted, it is always "clear" and does not have the varying degrees of velarization which characterize the "dark" /l/ of English.

The phoneme /r/ shows a complicated set of allophones which will be discussed in detail later on. Briefly, we may say the following:

1. Prevocalic /r/. When /r/ is followed by a vowel, as in /'rọ:t 'ịrə 'le̩:rə 'be̩sərə/ rot, irre, leere, bessere, most speakers pronounce it as a uvular trill or fricative, but some use instead an apico-alveolar trill or flap.

2. Postvocalic /r/. When /r/ is not followed by a vowel, its pronunciation varies depending on whether the vowel which precedes it is short or long.

2a. After a short vowel it may again be a uvular trill or fricative (phonetic symbol [ʀ]), or an apico-dental trill or flap (phonetic symbol [r̃]). The word irr /'ịr/ is then phonetically ['ịʀ] or ['ịr̃], and the word irrt /'ịrt/ is phonetically ['ịʀt] or ['ịr̃t]. But after a short vowel /r/ may also be a non-syllabic vowel much like the /ʌ/ of English /'bʌt/ but. The word irr /'ịr/ is then phonetically ['ị̯ʌ], and the word irrt is phonetically ['ị̯ʌt].

2b. After a long vowel, /r/ is always (except in artificial spelling pronunciations) non-syllabic [ʌ̯]. The word leer /'le̩:r/ is then phonetically ['le̩:ʌ̯], and the word leert /'le̩:rt/ is phonetically ['le̩:ʌ̯t].

2c. After unstressed /ə/, the /r/ and the /ə/ combine to give syllabic [ʌ]. The word besser /'be̩sər/ is then phonetically ['be̩sʌ], and the word bessert /'be̩sərt/ is phonetically ['be̩sʌt].

The phoneme /j/ is a front unrounded semivowel. It differs from English /j/ only in the fact that it is more often pronounced with some degree of consonantal friction. This is not a teaching problem, however, since many German speakers use as little consonant friction as do speakers of English for English /j/.

The phoneme /h/, like English /h/, is a cavity friction consonant.

(Before we leave the topic of German consonants, we should raise the question whether the [ts] of German Zahl, Katze, Satz, and the [pf] of Pfahl, Apfel, Napf, should be interpreted as the phonemic clusters /ts/ and /pf/, or as unit phonemes (affricates) which might be written /tˢ/ and /pᶠ/. Though either analysis is possible, we prefer for two reasons to treat them as clusters. First, German has a whole series of clusters of stop plus fricative or sibilant: /ps/ in /'psạlm 'gịps/ Psalm, Gips, /pš/ in /'pšọr 'hụ̈pš/ Pschorr (a name), hübsch, /tš/ in /'tšɛ̩çə 'dọịtš/ Tscheche, deutsch, and /ks/ in /'ksạntən 'zɛ̩ks/ Xanten, sechs. There therefore seems to be no good reason for singling out [ts] and [pf] as phonemically in any way different from the rest. Second, forms such as ['rạ:ts 'rɛ:tst] (des) Rats, (du) rätst are most conveniently analyzed morphologically as stem /'rạ:t/ plus ending /s/, stem /'rɛ:t/ plus ending /st/; and forms such as ['hạts 'tụ:ts] (er) hat's, (er) tut's are most conveniently analyzed syntactically as /'hạt/ plus /s/, /'tụ:t/ plus /s/ (with /s/ as a reduced form of /'ẹs/ es). To analyze ['rạ:ts] as

/ˈrɑːtˢ/, [ˈrɛːtst] as /ˈrɛːtˢt/, [hɑ̣ts] as /ˈhɑ̣tˢ/, and [ˈtṵːts] as /ˈtṵːtˢ/ would put a mor-
pheme and a word boundary right through the middle of a phoneme and hence needlessly
complicate both the morphology and the syntax.)

CONTRASTIVE ANALYSIS: THE CONSONANTS | 5

5.1 TYPES OF TEACHING PROBLEMS

The analyses which we have made of the consonants of English and German now enable us to contrast the two systems, to reveal the conflicts between them, and hence to show the problems which arise in teaching Americans to speak German. We shall classify these teaching problems under four different headings:

1. Phonemic problems. By carrying over English phonemic habits into German, the American student may use the wrong German phoneme. Example: for the unfamiliar /x/ of German he may substitute his familiar English /k/—which, however, happens to equal German /k/. In some cases the substitution will lead merely to gibberish: German /'maxən/ machen will be reproduced as a non-existent /'makən/. In other cases the substitution will produce a word quite different from the one intended: /'naxt/ Nacht will turn into /'nakt/ nackt.

2. Phonetic problems. By carrying over English phonetic habits into German, the American student may use the wrong phone. Example: for the unfamiliar clear [l] of German he may substitute the familiar velarized [ɫ] of American English. This is not a phonemic error, since German has no phoneme ever pronounced [ɫ]. But it sounds very wrong, and it is sometimes incomprehensible.

3. Allophonic problems. By carrying over English allophonic habits into German, the American student may use the wrong phone or even the wrong phoneme. Example: for German /t/ he may use the allophones of his American /t/. In most environments the two correspond very nicely. Non-initially before an unstressed vowel, however, American English frequently shows the flap allophone [t̬], as in /'wɔtɜ/ = ['wɔt̬ɜ] water. If this flapped [t̬] is used for the German /t/ in such a word as /'faːtər/ Vater, the resulting ['faːt̬ʌ] may sound queer but be understood, or it may be incomprehensible, or it may be misunderstood as German /'faːrər/ Fahrer pronounced with apical [ř]: ['faːřʌ].

4. Distributional problems. By carrying over English cluster habits into German, the American student may make a phonemic error. Example: English cluster habits make it easy for an American to say the non-initial /ts/ of German /'zɪts/ Sitz, since English has the same cluster in the same position, e.g., in /'sɪts/ sits. However, English clus-

ter habits do not provide for the initial /ts/ of /'tsu̞:/ zu, since English does not use the cluster in this position. Because the cluster is spelled initially with a z, most students substitute for it their English /z/—which, however, happens to equal German /z/. In some cases this substitution leads merely to gibberish: German /'tsu̞:/ zu will be reproduced as a non-existent /'zu̞:/. In other cases the substitution will produce a word quite different from the one intended: /'tsɔ̞igən/ zeugen will turn into /'zɔ̞igən/ säugen.

5.2 PHONEMIC PROBLEMS

If diagrams of the English and German consonant systems are placed side by side, the phonemic problems stand out very clearly:

English | German

English	German
p b t d [č ǰ] k g	p b t d [ ] k g
f v [θ ð] [ ]	f v [ ] [ç x]
s z š ž	s z š ž
m n ŋ	m n ŋ
l r [w] j h	l r [ ] j h

Dotted lines show areas where an English phoneme is unmatched by anything in German. These areas would present serious problems if we were teaching English to speakers of German, but fortunately they cause little trouble in teaching German to speakers of English. Our students can safely use their English /č/ for the infrequent German cluster /tš/: /'tšɛ̞çə/ Tscheche, /'dɔ̞itš/ deutsch; and they can use their English /ǰ/ for the even more infrequent German cluster /dž/: /'džu̞ŋəl/ Dschungel, /a'da:džo̞:/ Adagio. (In both cases, however, the /š/ and the /ž/ must have lip rounding; see below, § 5.9.) In the case of English /θ ð w/, our students need simply to be told that sounds of these types do not occur in German. The ónly problems which arise are ones of spelling. The student must know that spellings with th (Theater, Goethe) always represent German /t/, and that spellings with w (was, Löwe) nearly always represent German /v/. (The few exceptions are names such as Lützow /lu̞tso̞:/, Treptow /'tre:pto̞:/, and foreign names such as Asow /a'zo̞f/.)

Solid lines show the one area where there is a real conflict to be overcome in teaching German to speakers of English. In discussing it, we shall deal with four different aspects of the teaching problem: (1) the phonetic nature of the German phoneme; (2) ways in which the student can be helped to pronounce the new sound; (3) drills which will help him to control it with ease and accuracy; and (4) the sounds which he will be most likely to substitute for it, together with drills to help him avoid these substitutions.

5.3 GERMAN /x/

1. Phonetic nature. German /x/ is a voiceless dorso-velar fricative. It is articulated by forcing the breath stream through a slit-shaped opening between the back of the tongue and the middle of the velum. The German phoneme most closely related to it is the voiceless stop /k/; but where /k/ is articulated by making a complete closure between the back of the tongue and the velum, /x/ is articulated by bringing the back of the tongue only close enough to the velum so as to produce audible friction as the breath stream passes through.

2. Teaching /x/. Many students are quite able to imitate /x/ successfully without any special instruction. (Some already know it as the sound spelled ch in Scottish Loch Lomond etc.) Those who have trouble with it can often be helped if they are asked to imitate successively a normally aspirated /k/: [ạk^h], then a strongly aspirated /k/ with affricate release: [ạk^x], and finally the /x/ itself: [ạx].

3. Drills for control. These can begin with such forms (largely nonsense syllables) as /ạx ạːx ǫx ǫːx ụx ụːx aux/ (German /x/ occurs only after these seven phonemes), and then go on to such genuine words as:

/'bạx/	Bach	/'bụːx/	Buch	/'tauxt/	taucht
/'naːx/	nach	/'baux/	Bauch	/'vạxən/	wachen
/'dǫx/	doch	/'nạxt/	Nacht	/'vǫxən/	Wochen
/'hǫːx/	hoch	/'kǫxt/	kocht	/'zụːxən/	suchen
/'brụx/	Bruch	/'bụxt/	Bucht	/'hauxən/	hauchen

4. Substitution. The phoneme which American students almost universally substitute for /x/ is /k/. To emphasize the fact that /k/ and /x/ are contrasting phonemes and to give practice in distinguishing them, drills of the following type may be helpful:

/'zạkə/ — /'zạxə/	sacke, Sache	/'taukt/ — /'tauxt/		taugt, taucht
/'dǫk/ — /'dǫx/	Dock, doch	/'štạːkən/ — /'štạːxən/		staken, stachen
/'nạkt/ — /'nạxt/	nackt, Nacht	/'pǫkən/ — /'pǫxən/		Pocken, pochen
/'lǫkt/ — /'lǫxt/	lockt, locht	/'bụːkən/ — /'bụːxən/		buken, Buchen
/'buːk/ — /'buːx/	buk, Buch	/'paukən/ — /'hauxən/		pauken, hauchen

5.4 GERMAN /ç/

1. Phonetic nature. German /ç/ is a voiceless dorso-palatal fricative. It is articulated by forcing the breath stream through a slit-shaped opening between the front of the tongue and the (hard) palate. One phoneme closely related to it in German is the voiceless (alveolo-) palatal sibilant /š/. The difference between the two is primarily the fact that for /ç/ the opening between the front of the tongue and the palate is a shallow slit, whereas for /š/ it is a deep groove. Another phoneme closely related to /ç/ in German is /j/, the palatal semivowel. This is often articulated with the opening between the front of the tongue and the palate so narrow that consonantal friction is produced. This

fricative allophone of /j/ is voiced, however, and it is this which distinguishes it from voiceless /ç/.

    2. Teaching /ç/. Three different approaches can be helpful.

        <u>a</u>. The initial /h-/ of English /'hju/ <u>hue</u>, <u>Hugh</u>, /'hjuʃ/ <u>huge</u>, /'hjumɪd/ <u>humid</u>, /'hjumən/ <u>human</u>, etc. is pronounced by many Americans as a [ç] with rather wide opening. If the student can isolate this sound and then narrow the opening between the front of the tongue and the palate until strong local friction is produced, he will articulate a very acceptable German /ç/. (Many Americans normally pronounce <u>hue</u>, <u>huge</u>, etc. without the initial /h/: /'ju/, /'juʃ/; but even such speakers seem to have little trouble in switching to /'hju/, /'hjuʃ/, etc., so that they can also be taught German /ç/ in the same way.) Since it is often hard for the student to isolate this [ç], he can be helped by being asked to say the vowel [ɪ̯] in front of it, and then imitating such a series as [ɪ̯hju]—[ɪ̯çju]—[ɪ̯ç]. The result, of course, is German /'ɪ̯ç/ <u>ich</u>.

        <u>b</u>. Since German /ç/ and /j/ correspond to one another as voiceless vs. voiced, a good /ç/ can be produced by isolating /j/ and then unvoicing it. Students need first to be made aware of the distinction between voiced and voiceless sounds. This can be done by asking them to pronounce alternately a prolonged [vvv] and a prolonged [fff], while at the same time putting a finger in each ear so as to hear clearly the "buzzing" which is present for [v] but absent for [f]. They can then be told that this buzzing is technically called voice, and that [v] and [f] are identical except for the fact that [v] is accompanied by voice (the "buzzing") whereas [f] is not. To be sure that they can control voice, and turn it on and off at will, it is helpful to ask them to say a prolonged [zzz] and then take the voice away from it. The result, of course, is voiceless [sss]. The next step is to ask them to pronounce a prolonged English /j/ with plenty of friction, as if they were stutterers saying <u>y-y-yes</u>. As a final step, they can be asked to repeat this prolonged [jjj] and then to take the voice away from it. If they have said the [jjj] with plenty of friction, the result will be a prolonged [ççç].

        <u>c</u>. Americans commonly do two types of whistling. For the usual type the lips are rounded and a pure musical tone is produced. But there is also another kind of whistling in which the lips are spread and a fricative sound is produced. For low notes this sounds much like [s], but as the notes get higher and higher the sound becomes more and more like [ç]. (The reason is that for low notes a groove-shaped opening is made between the blade of the tongue and the alveolar ridge, but as the notes become higher the opening moves farther back and is flattened out until it becomes a slit-shaped opening between the front of the tongue and the palate—precisely what is needed to articulate the palatal fricative [ç].) If students are asked to "whistle" in this way the highest note they can reach, the result is a very acceptable German /ç/.

    3. Drills for control. Once a student has isolated the sound [ç] in any one of these ways, he needs practice in controlling it. This is usually best done by having him pronounce such nonsense syllables as the following:

      [ɪ̯:çɪ̯:]   [ɪ̯:ç]   [ɪ̯:çɪ̯:]   [çɪ̯:]
      [ɪ̯çɪ̯]   [ɪ̯ç]   [ɪ̯çɪ̯]   [çɪ̯]

(Examples such as these, with high front vowels, are helpful because the articulation of these vowels automatically places the tongue almost in the proper position for [ç]. The vowel [i:] is that of German /'ri̡:çən/ riechen, /'çi̡:na/ China; [i̡] is the vowel of German /'mi̡ç/ mich, /'i̡ç/ ich.) The /ç/ then needs to be practiced in such environments as the following:

After front vowels		After consonants		Next to /s/ and /š/	
/'ri̡:çən/	riechen	/'manç/	manch	/'ri̡:çst/	riechst
/'mi̡ç/	mich	/'mṳnçən/	München	/'bri̡çst/	brichst
/'pęç/	Pech	/'mi̡lç/	Milch	/'nɛ:çst/	nächst
/'aiçə/	Eiche	/'vęlçər/	welcher	/'hö:çst/	höchst
/'ǫiç/	euch	/'dṳrç/	durch	/'bi̡sçən/	bißchen
/'bü:çər/	Bücher	/'štǫrç/	Storch	/'hǫisçən/	Häuschen
/'brṳçə/	Brüche	/'mɛ:tçən/	Mädchen	/'ti̡šçən/	Tischchen
/'löçər/	Löcher	/'li̡:pçən/	Liebchen	/'flęšçən/	Fläschchen

These examples are arranged in their approximate order of difficulty for American students. Once a student has /ç/ more or less under control, he usually finds it easiest to say after front unrounded vowels: /'ri:çən 'mi̡ç 'pęç 'aiçə 'ǫiç/. He often has difficulty in saying /ç/ after front rounded vowels because the vowels themselves are new and unfamiliar. It may be helpful to lead him to such forms in two steps by having him say first the corresponding front unrounded vowel and then the front rounded vowel: /'bi̡:çər/—/'bü:çər/ Bücher, /'bri̡çə/—/'brṳçə/ Brüche, /'lęçər/—/'löçər/ Löcher. The new /ç/ is somewhat more difficult after consonants. The student can again be led gradually to such forms by having him first say the form with an /i̡/ inserted between the consonant and the /ç/: /'mani̡ç/—/'manç/ manch, /'mi̡li̡ç/—/'mi̡lç/ Milch, etc. The greatest difficulty comes when /ç/ occurs before or after /s/ or /š/, since here the student must shift quickly from a slit fricative (/ç/) to a rather similar groove fricative (/s/ or /š/), or vice versa. This requires some pretty skillful maneuvering of the tongue, switching it quickly from slit-shaped to groove-shaped, or from groove-shaped to slit-shaped. (A similar requirement of skillful maneuvering makes it so enormously difficult for speakers of German to switch from English /θ/ to /s/ and vice versa.) Here again the student can be helped if he is first asked to say a form with inserted /i̡/: /'ri̡:çi̡st/—'ri̡:çst/ riechst, etc. In the case of the diminutive forms, it also helps to have a student begin by exaggerating the syllable boundary between the /s/ or /š/ and the following /ç/: /'bi̡s-çən/—/'bi̡sçən/ bißchen, /'ti̡š-çən/ —/'ti̡šçən/ Tischchen.

  We may recall that, except in the diminutive suffix /'çən/ -chen, /ç/ is in complementary distribution with /x/. The student therefore needs to practice the automatic alternation between /x/ and /ç/ in such forms as the following:

/'dax/—/'dęçər/   Dach, Dächer   /'špra̡:x/—/'šprɛ:çə/   sprach, spräche
/'lǫx/—/'löçer/   Loch, Löcher   /'hǫ:x/—/'hö:çstə/   hoch, höchste
/'šprᶙx/—/'šprṳçə/   Spruch, Sprüche   /'tu̡:x/—/'tü:çər/   Tuch, Tücher
/'braux/—/'brǫiçə/   Brauch, Bräuche

Such an exercise also helps the student realize when the German spelling ch stands for /x/ and when it stands for /ç/.

   4. Substitution. Students commonly substitute any one of three different phonemes for /ç/: /k/, /š/, and /x/. To correct for the substitution of /k/, drills such as the following may be useful:

/'zi̧:k/ — /'zi̧:ç/	Sieg, siech	/'rɛkt/ — /'rɛçt/	reckt, recht
/'ni̧kt/ — /'ni̧çt/	nickt, nicht	/'štraik/ — /'štraiç/	Streik, Streich
	/'ki̧:no̧:/ — /'çi̧:na/	Kino, China	

Particularly troublesome is the cluster /çts/, as in /'ni̧çts/ nichts, /'rɛçts/ rechts. Such words can be drilled by building up to the full form in three steps: /'ni̧ç/ — /'ni̧ç-ts/ — /'ni̧çts/, /'rɛç/ — /'rɛç-ts/ — /'rɛçts/.

   Students who substitute /š/ for /ç/ often complain that they "can't hear the difference," or that "my teacher says /'i̧š/ ich." The reason for this lies in the nature of the English consonant system. If we look at the diagram of this system, we see that the English phoneme /š/ has a great deal of possible latitude: though it is essentially a palatal sibilant, and is therefore articulated with a groove-shaped opening along the tongue, there is no palatal fricative above it (on the diagram) because the slot for [ç] is empty in English. This means that the groove for English /š/ can become quite shallow without resulting in a sound which gets in the way of any other phoneme. American speakers "take advantage" of this possible latitude and commonly articulate allophones of /š/ with a very shallow groove. In addition, they often pronounce their American /š/ with little or no lip rounding. All of this means that some allophones of American /š/ are very close in sound to some allophones of German /ç/. Because of this, when a German speaker articulates a /ç/ with a fairly deep slit-shaped opening, the sound he produces is so similar to a possible allophone of American /š/ that an American listener may actually hear it as the same. It is this which leads the student to say: "My teacher says /'i̧š/ ich." Such a student can be helped by drills which show the clear contrast between German /ç/ and /š/:

/'vi̧ç/ — /'vi̧š/	wich, Wisch	/'fi̧çt/ — /'fi̧št/	ficht, fischt
/'mi̧ç/ — /'mi̧š/	mich, misch!	/'lö̧çər/ — /'lö̧šər/	Löcher, Löscher
/'di̧ç/ — /'ti̧š/	dich, Tisch	/'ko̧içə/ — /'ko̧išə/	keuche, keusche

In examples such as these many German speakers really do pronounce an allophone of German /ç/ which is almost identical with possible allophones of English /š/, but it is always clearly different from any allophones of German /š/. Speakers from some parts of the German speaking area articulate a /ç/ with a relatively deep slit, but it differs from German /š/ in three ways: (1) /š/ is always pronounced with rounded lips, whereas /ç/ is usually pronounced with spread lips; (2) /š/ is always articulated with a groove-shaped opening, whereas /ç/ always has a slit-shaped opening; and (3) the groove for /š/ is always deep, deeper than the usual groove for English /š/, and far deeper than the slit for German /ç/. (The above is true for the standard language, in its various local varieties. Only in some local dialects do /ç/ and /š/ merge in a single phoneme—as in Frankfurt am Main, for example, or in Berlin dialect ['nŭšt] nichts.)

The student who struggles to make a distinction between German /ç/ and /š/ often overcompensates and substitutes /x/ for /ç/. This is especially true of those from a Yiddish background, since Yiddish (in origin a variety of German) has no [ç] but only [x]. Such students can be helped by drills which contrast German /x/ and /ç/ in the same environment:

/ˈtauxən/ — /ˈtauçən/	tauchen, Tauchen
/ˈhauxən/ — /ˈfrauçən/	hauchen, Frauchen
/ˈku̯ːxən/ — /ˈku̯ːçən/	Kuchen, Kuhchen
/bəˈšta̱ːxən/ — /maˈma̱ːçən/	bestachen, Mamachen

5.5 PHONETIC PROBLEMS

Under the heading "phonetic problems" we shall discuss two phonemes, /l/ and /r/, which play entirely equivalent roles in German and English, but which are phonetically quite different in the two languages. In the case of phonemic problems, it is easy to show a student that a faulty substitution (such as /k/ for /x/) can produce a German word very different from the one he intended (such as /ˈnakt/ nackt when he intended /ˈnaxt/ Nacht). In the case of the phonetic problems we are about to discuss, however, it is much less easy to convince a student that he must not carry over English phonetic habits into German. If he says German gelb with a velarized American [ɬ], or German rot with a constricted American [r], he has not substituted one phoneme for another, and hence said a word different from the one he intended. Indeed, he can go through life pronouncing all German /l/'s as velarized [ɬ], and all German /r/'s as constricted [r], and still be understood a good deal of the time. These are not phonemic mistakes, which must inevitably lead to misunderstandings. They are phonetic mistakes, which sometimes lead to incomprehensibility but more often merely sound very foreign and slightly ridiculous. Nevertheless, nothing can ruin an otherwise good pronunciation more than the use of an American /r/ in German. And the use of an American /l/ is not much better.

5.6 GERMAN /l/

1. Phonetic nature. German /l/ is a lateral consonant. It is articulated by placing the apex just above the upper teeth or against the alveolar ridge and allowing the breath stream to flow out unhindered along one or both sides of the dorsum. To this extent it is identical with the commonest type of American /l/. But whereas American /l/ shows varying degrees of velarization, with the back of the tongue humped up toward the velum so as to produce the "dark" quality of the sound, German /l/ is never velarized but is always "clear."

2. Teaching /l/. Before we can attempt to teach the "clear" German /l/ to a student, we need to find out how he pronounces his English /l/. American speakers can be divided into at least four different types:

<u>a</u>. A few speakers do not use an alveolar /l/ at all (or not in all positions), but rather a velar /l/. Instead of placing the apex against the alveolar ridge, they keep the apex and the front and the center of the tongue relatively flat in the mouth and

raise the back of the tongue up close to the back of the velum. The resulting sound is actually not a true lateral, but rather a voiced fricative (with very little friction) articulated with the tongue approximately in the position for the velar semivowel /w/ but with unrounded lips. It is possible to identify speakers who use this velar /l/ by finding out where they place the tip of their tongues when they say /l/. If they do not place it against the alveolar ridge, they must be saying the velar /l/. Before such students can even attempt a clear German /l/, they need to learn how to pronounce an alveolar American /l/. Usually they can do so without much difficulty.

b. Many Americans use a velarized /l/ in all positions. As we have already noted, the velarization is least pronounced initially before a front vowel: leap, somewhat stronger initially before a back vowel: loop, much stronger finally: peal, especially after a back vowel: pool.

c. Many other Americans use a velarized /l/ in most positions, but a non-velarized /l/ before the phoneme /j/. Hence they pronounce a dark [ɫ] in /ˈmɪl/ = [ˈmɪɫ] mill, /ˈbɪl/ = [ˈbɪɫ] bill, but a clear [l] in /ˈmɪljən/ = [ˈmɪljən] million, /ˈbɪljən/ = [ˈbɪljən] billion.

d. Americans in some parts of the South regularly use a clear [l] between vowels: /ˈsɪli/ = [ˈsɪli] silly, and even initially: /ˈli/ = [ˈli] Lee.

The first step in teaching students the clear German /l/ is to make sure that they can hear the difference between [ɫ] (dark, velarized, with the back of the tongue raised toward the velum) and [l] (clear, non-velarized, with the back of the tongue kept flat). Precisely because many of them use both [ɫ] and [l] as non-distinctive allophones of a single phoneme in English, they are likely not to hear the difference. The easiest way of making them aware of it is for the teacher to pronounce comparable English and German words, exaggerating somewhat the velarization of American /l/: English [ˈfiɫ] feel vs. German [ˈfiːl] viel, fiel; English [ˈɫait] light vs. German [ˈlait] Leid. (For further examples, see below.)

3. Drills for control. Once a student has heard and understood the difference between dark [ɫ] and clear [l], he needs practice in consciously pronouncing first the one and then the other. Since most Americans have little trouble in saying a clear [l] before /j/ in such words as million, even if they do not usually do so, words of this type are a good place to begin. An exercise of the following type may prove helpful. Its purpose is simply to give the student practice in controlling velarization—switching it on and off at will.

dark	clear	dark	clear	
[ˈmɪɫjən]	[ˈmɪljən]	[ˈmɪɫjən]	[ˈmɪljən]	million
[ˈbʊɫjən]	[ˈbʊljən]	[ˈbʊɫjən]	[ˈbʊljən]	bullion
[ˈhɛɫjən]	[ˈhɛljən]	[ˈhɛɫjən]	[ˈhɛljən]	hellion
[ˈkaɫjɚ]	[ˈkaljɚ]	[ˈkaɫjɚ]	[ˈkaljɚ]	Collyer

Once velarization is under control in this position, the student can be asked to imitate a clear [l] with and without the following /j/:

['mɪljən] —	['mɪl] —	['mɪljən] —	['mɪl]	million, mill
['buljən] —	['bul] —	['buljən] —	['bul]	bullion, bull
['hɛljən] —	['hɛl] —	['hɛljən] —	['hɛl]	hellion, hell
['kaljɔ] —	['kal] —	['kaljɔ] —	['kal]	Collyer, Col

As a further drill for control, the student can be asked to imitate the clear [l] in such non-sense syllables as the following:

[iːliː] —	[iːl] —	[iːliː] —	[liː]
[uːluː] —	[uːl] —	[uːluː] —	[luː]
[eːleː] —	[eːl] —	[eːleː] —	[leː]
[oːloː] —	[oːl] —	[oːloː] —	[loː]
[aːlaː] —	[aːl] —	[aːlaː] —	[laː]

These syllables are given in the approximate order of difficulty of imitation: Americans usually find it easiest to imitate clear [l] before and after high front [iː], more difficult before and after high back [uː], and progressively more difficult before and after the mid vowels [eː] and [oː] and the low central vowel [aː].

An amusing but effective check on control of the clear [l] can be made by asking the members of a class to take turns pronouncing the German word hell = /'hɛl/, with clear [l]. Pronunciation as ['hɛl] sounds foreign and harmless; but as soon as one of the students says [hɛɬ] the pronunciation becomes improper, since the class, with a bit of a shock, identifies it with the English word hell.

4. Substitution. The sound substituted for clear German [l] is inevitably the velarized American [ɬ]. Students can therefore be helped by drills which contrast American [ɬ] and German [l] in words of similar structure. Such drills can begin with words which have /l/ following a vowel, where the contrast is the most obvious, and then finish with words which have /l/ preceding a vowel, where the contrast is just as real but not as great and hence harder to hear. Examples:

English	German	
/'fil/	/'fiːl/	feel; viel
/'fel/	/'feːl/	fail; fehl
/'pol/	/'poːl/	pole; Pol
/'stul/	/'štuːl/	stool; Stuhl
/'bɪlt/	/'bɪlt/	built; Bild
/'fɛlt/	/'fɛlt/	felt; fällt
/'lif/	/'liːf/	leaf; lief
/'lait	/'lait/	light; Leid
/'plats/	/'plats/	plots; Platz
/'klos/	/'kloːs/	close; Kloß

5.7 GERMAN /r/

1. Phonetic nature. German /r/ consists of several quite distinct allophones, depending in part on the individual speaker and in part on the position of /r/ within a word.

a. Prevocalic /r/. When /r/ is followed by a vowel, it is for most speakers a voiced dorso-uvular fricative or trill, though for some it is a voiced apical flap or trill.

i. Uvular [R] is articulated by raising the back of the tongue toward the uvula and the back of the velum, until a narrow slit-shaped opening is formed, and at the same time forcing the breath stream through this opening. The force of the breath stream may or may not cause the uvula to vibrate against the back of the tongue. The phoneme most closely related to uvular [R] is the dorso-velar fricative /x/, but there is a twofold difference between them: /x/ is articulated against the middle of the velum, whereas [R] is articulated farther back against the back of the velum and the uvula; and /x/ is voiceless, whereas [R] is typically voiced.

ii. Apical [ř] is articulated by bringing the tip of the apex into contact with the alveolar ridge, either once very quickly so as to produce a flap, or two or three times in rapid succession so as to produce a trill, while at the same time the vocal cords vibrate. The phoneme most closely related to apical [ř] is the voiced apico-alveolar stop /d/, but here also there is a twofold difference: the apico-alveolar contact for /d/ includes a wider area of the apex and of the alveolar ridge than does the contact for [ř]; and the hold of /d/ lasts longer than that of [ř]. (When apical [ř] is articulated as a flap, it is similar to the flap allophone [t̬] which many Americans use in such a word as /'si̬ti/ = ['si̬ti] city.)

(Some comments should be added here as to which /r/ should be taught to students, the uvular or the apical variety. The vast majority of German speakers, especially those in cities, use only the uvular /r/. Therefore, if the teacher wishes his students to pronounce German as most German speakers do, he should teach them the uvular /r/. On the other hand, though those German speakers who regularly use apical /r/ are a small minority, their numbers surely run well into the millions [approximate statistics are unknown]; this variety is therefore also acceptable. For strange nationalistic reasons, German orthoëpists have traditionally favored the apical /r/—even the 1957 edition of the Siebs still calls it "das alte deutsche Zungen-r," implying that it must therefore be preferable. However, in 1933 the official advisory committee on pronunciation finally declared the uvular /r/ to be equally acceptable.)

b. Postvocalic /r/. When /r/ is not followed by a vowel, it shows different allophones depending on whether the vowel preceding it is long, short, or /ə/.

i. After long vowels the allophone used is a non-syllabic vowel. In technical terms it is a lower mid unrounded vowel between central and back; in sound it is much like the stressed vowel of English /bʌt/ but. We shall symbolize it as [ʌ], putting a half circle under it to indicate that it is non-syllabic. Examples: /'fi:r/ = ['fi:ʌ̯] vier, /'fü:r/ = ['fü:ʌ̯] für, /'fu̬:r/ = ['fu̬:ʌ̯] fuhr. Note that this postvocalic [ʌ̯] alternates automatically with prevocalic [R] (uvular fricative or trill) or [ř] (apical flap or trill):

	Prevocalic	Postvocalic	
		Before consonant	Finally
Phonetically	['füːʀə]	['füːʌt]	['füːʌ]
Phonemically	/'füːrə/	/'füːrt/	/'füːr/
Spelling	führe	führt	für

ii. After short vowels some speakers use [ʀ] (or [řŗ]), others use [ʌ], and still others alternate between the two. This [ʌ] is therefore partly in complementary distribution with [ʀ] (or [řŗ]), partly in free variation with it, as follows:

	Prevocalic	Postvocalic	
		Before consonant	Finally
Phonetically	['ɨʀə]	['ɨʀt] or ['ɨʌt]	['ɨʀ] or ['ɨʌ]
Phonemically	/'ɨrə/	/'ɨrt/	/'ɨr/
Spelling	irre	irrt	irr

Speakers who use [ʀ] after short vowels often unvoice it more or less completely before a following voiceless /p t k/: ['kʰɒʀˣpʰ] or ['kʰɒx̣pʰ] = /'kɒrp/ Korb, ['haʀˣtʰ] or ['hax̣tʰ] = /'hart/ hart, ['vɛʀˣkʰ] or ['vɛx̣kʰ] = /'vɛrk/ Werk. However, even if the [ʀ] is fully unvoiced (a practice which the Siebs condemns, from which we may deduce that it is quite widespread), it differs from the phoneme /x/: unvoiced [ʀ] is postvelar [x̣], whereas /x/ is midvelar [x], i.e. warte /'vartə/ is ['vax̣tə], whereas wachte /'vaxtə/ is ['vaxtə].

iii. The postvocalic sequence /ər/ is pronounced phonetically as syllabic [ʌ]. We may think of the /r/ as again having the allophone [ʌ], only this time the presence of the /ə/ turns it into syllabic [ʌ]. This postvocalic [ʌ] alternates automatically with prevocalic [əʀ] (or [əřŗ]):

	Prevocalic	Postvocalic	
		Before consonant	Finally
Phonetically	['bɛsəʀə]	['bɛsʌt]	['bɛsʌ]
Phonemically	/'bɛsərə/	/'bɛsərt/	/'bɛsər/
Spelling	bessere	bessert	besser

In careful speech a distinction is made between long vowel plus /r/ and long vowel plus /ər/: sehr is /'zeːr/ = ['zeːʌ] (one syllable), but Seher is /'zeːər/ = ['zeːʌ] (two syllables); or Rohr is /'roːr/ = ['ʀoːʌ] (one syllable), but roher is /'roːər/ = ['ʀoːʌ] (two syllables). In ordinary speech, however, many speakers make no distinction between such pairs: sehr and Seher, Rohr and roher sound alike, and it is impossible to say whether they are pronounced in one syllable or in two. (Compare the similar situation in English, where sear and seer, or hire and higher are usually pronounced alike, and it is impossible to say whether they constitute one syllable or two.)

2. Teaching /r/. The allophones uvular [ʀ], apical [ř], and vocalic [ʌ] are quite separate teaching problems.

a. Uvular [ʀ]. Perhaps the most effective way of teaching uvular [ʀ] is to say to a student: "Tip your head back and enjoy a good dry gargle." This may seem to be a peculiar way of putting things, but it is sound phonetic advice. In gargling, the back of the tongue is raised close to the uvula and the back of the velum; at the same time, the breath stream flows through this narrow opening and the vocal cords vibrate. This is precisely the way in which a uvular [ʀ] is articulated. A second method of teaching the sound, which perhaps seems more scientific but is not any more effective, is based on the fact that uvular [ʀ] as a postvelar fricative is very similar to the midvelar fricative [x]. The student can be asked to say a [x], but to say it as far back in his mouth as possible. The result is voiceless postvelar [x̣]. If he now adds voice to this [x̣], the sound is turned into a voiced postvelar fricative; and this is precisely what the so-called "uvular" [ʀ] is.

b. Apical [ř]. Nearly every American, as a child, has used a trilled apical [ř]—not as a speech sound, but in imitation of such things as a policeman's whistle, a doorbell, etc. Most students therefore have little difficulty in pronouncing the German trilled apical [ř], with two or three vibrations of the apex against the alveolar ridge. Likewise, nearly all Americans pronounce the phoneme /t/ with a flap allophone [t̬] in such English words as city, Betty. They therefore have little trouble in pronouncing the German flapped apical [ř], with a single quick movement of the apex against the alveolar ridge. In both cases the sounds are easy to teach. The real problem is that of persuading students to use these sounds, and not to revert to their usual constricted American [r]. The temptation to revert to [r] is particularly strong because students have heard American /r/ pronounced as a trilled or flapped [ř] in singing and in some varieties of British English, and they have come to react to it as a fancy but abnormal way of pronouncing a sound which ought rightly to be a good old American [r].

c. Postvocalic [ʌ] and [ʌ]. Here again the sound to be learned is hardly new. All Americans use a vowel very close to this in the final syllables of sofa, okra, China, India. For reasons to be discussed in chapter 8, we shall symbolize this vowel in English with the letter /ə/: /'sofə 'okrə 'čainə 'i̜ndiə/. Those Americans along the Atlantic seaboard who "drop their r's" also use this vowel at the end of such words as (with non-syllabic /ə̜/) here, there, pour, poor, or (with syllabic /ə/) father, mother, brother, sister. In the case of these latter speakers, however, one needs to be on guard against the so-called "linking r." Though such speakers drop final /r/ in most environments, they often pronounce it when the next word begins with a vowel. Thus here is /'hiə̜/ and there is /'ðeə̜/, but here and there is /'hiə̜-r-ən 'ðeə̜/; or father is /'faðə/ and mother is /'mʌðə/, but father and mother is /'faðə-r-ən 'mʌðə/. They carry this same habit over to other words which end in /ə/. China is /'čainə/ and India is /'i̜ndiə/, but China and India is /'čainə-r-ən 'i̜ndiə/; or idea is /ai'diə/, but the idea of it is /ði ai'diə-r-əv i̜t/. This habit of pronouncing a "linking r" of any type should not be carried over into German.

3. Drills for control. Probably no special drills beyond simple practice are

needed to help the student gain control over the apical [ř]. For the uvular [R] it is helpful to begin with the nonsense syllables [a̱:ga̱:] (with postvelar [g̱]) and [a̱:x̱a̱:] (with postvelar [x̱]), and then to go from either of these to [a̱:Ra̱:] (with postvelar or uvular [R]):

$$[a̱:ga̱:] \quad — \quad [a̱:Ra̱:]$$
$$[a̱:x̱a̱:] \quad — \quad [a̱:Ra̱:]$$

The purpose of such an exercise is to emphasize the fact that [R] is similar to [g] in being both postvelar and voiced, but differs from [g] in being a fricative rather than a stop; and that [R] is similar to [x] in being both postvelar and a fricative, but differs from [x] in being voiced rather than voiceless. Students usually find it relatively easy to articulate postvelar [g] and [x] if they are told to "pronounce these sounds as far back in your mouth as you can." The transition to postvelar [R] is then relatively simple. The primary difficulty is a psychological one: most American students find it hard to believe that [R] can really function as a perfectly ordinary speech sound.

As a next step the student needs practice in pronouncing [R] before different vowels and in initial position:

$$[a̱:Ra̱:] \quad — \quad [Ra̱:]$$
$$[a̱:Rau] \quad — \quad [Rau]$$
$$[a̱:Ro̱:] \quad — \quad [Ro̱:]$$
$$[a̱:Ru̱:] \quad — \quad [Ru̱:]$$
$$[a̱:Rai] \quad — \quad [Rai]$$
$$[a̱:Re̱:] \quad — \quad [Re̱:]$$
$$[a̱:Ri̱:] \quad — \quad [Ri̱:]$$

There are two reasons for beginning in each case with the low central vowel [a̱:]. First, students seem to find it easiest to pronounce [R] intervocalically after [a̱:], so that such an exercise begins with the least difficult and goes on to the more difficult. Second, use of the vowel [a̱:] means that the student's mouth is wide open, and it is therefore easy for the teacher to see whether the student has his tongue in the proper position. Since uvular [R] is articulated only by the back of the tongue, the apex and the front should be lying flat in the mouth, not taking part in the articulation at all. At the beginning, many students have an almost uncontrollable impulse to raise the apex toward the alveolar ridge, as for an American [r]. If they make this error in trying to say [a̱:Ra̱:], use of the vowel [a̱:] makes it easy for the teacher to see whether the apex flips up or not and, if it does, to identify the error and try to correct it. When the teacher tries to explain the way a uvular [R] is made, it may be helpful to show the student that it is perfectly possible to say a flawless [a̱:Ra̱:] while at the same time holding the front of the tongue down with the little finger. This is clear proof that the front of the tongue does not take part at all in the articulation.

Another helpful drill is to have the student imitate such a series as the following:

(1)		(2)		(3)	
[xau]	—	[fxau]	=	/frau/	Frau
[xai]	—	[fxai]	=	/frai/	frei

(1)		(2)		(3)	
[xaus]	—	[kxaus]	=	/kraus/	kraus
[xais]	—	[kxais]	=	/krais/	Kreis
[xaut]	—	[txaut]	=	/traut/	traut
[xais]	—	[pxais]	=	/prais/	Preis
[xa:t]	—	[txa:t]	=	/tra:t/	trat
[xa:m]	—	[kxa:m]	=	/kra:m/	Kram
[xǫi]	—	[txǫi]	=	/trǫi/	treu
[xo:]	—	[fxo:]	=	/fro:/	froh

In column (1) the student begins the syllable with the phone [x]. In column (2) he repeats the same syllable with a voiceless fricative or stop added on in front. The result is a more or less acceptable pronunciation of the word given in column (3), since most German speakers who use the uvular [ʀ] unvoice it partially after a voiceless fricative or stop. A subsequent exercise can then drill the transition from this more or less voiceless [ʀ] after voiceless phonemes to the fully voiced [ʀ] after voiced phonemes:

[kxau]	—	/grau/	grau
[txai]	—	/drai/	drei
[pxaut]	—	/braut/	Braut
[kxais]	—	/grais/	Greis

A final drill on /r/ needs to emphasize the fact that the uvular [ʀ] (or apical [ɼ]) which occurs before vowels alternates automatically with [ᴀ] or [ʌ] before consonants or in word final position:

[ʀ]	[ᴀ]	[ʀ]	[ᴀ]
zwei Tiere	ein Tier	ich studiere	er studiert
zwei Speere	ein Speer	ich lehre	er lehrt
zwei Jahre	ein Jahr	ich spare	er spart
zwei Tore	ein Tor	ich bohre	er bohrt
zwei Uhren	eine Uhr	wir fuhren	ihr fuhrt
zwei Türen	eine Tür	ich führe	er führt
zwei Öhre	ein Öhr	ich höre	er hört

[ʀ]	[ʌ]	[ʀ]	[ʀ] or [ᴀ]
bittere	bitter	ich irre	er irrt
bessere	besser	ich zerre	er zerrt
die älteren	die Eltern	ich harre	er harrt
ich wandere	er wandert	ich murre	er murrt
ich ändere	er ändert	ich dörre	er dörrt

4. Substitution. The sound which Americans inevitably substitute for German /r/ is the American constricted [r]. There are two reasons for this. The first is the fact that German /r/ is spelled with the letter r. Through years of training in reading, students

automatically react to this visual stimulus by pronouncing the familiar constricted [r] of their native American English. But even when German spelling is never used during the first few weeks of instruction, it does not require much intelligence for a student to figure out that, if ['ʀɪŋ] means 'ring' and ['hi:ʌ] means 'here,' the sounds [ʀ] and [ʌ] must somehow be equivalent to [r]. And once this identification is made, the teaching problem is nearly as great as if German spelling had been used in the first place. Probably the best solution is not to try to hide the equivalence of German [ʀ]—[ʌ] and American English [r], but to recognize it and concentrate on the difference in pronunciation. For this purpose a drill is useful which contrasts German /r/ and American /r/ in words of similar structure or meaning:

[ʀ]		[ʀ]		[ʌ]		[ʌ]	
reef	rief	creak	Krieg	here	hier	bitter	bitter
rest	Rest	fry	frei	air	er	father	Vater
wrote	rot	dry	drei	par	Paar	mother	Mutter
rice	Reis	price	Preis	ore	Ohr	brother	Bruder
Rhine	Rhein	brown	braun	tour	Tour	sister	Schwester

A substitution of quite another sort is made when students hear such a German word as wird /'vɪrt/, do not happen to know how it is spelled, and imitate it as ['vɪɫt], with the American velarized [ɫ]. The reasons for this type of faulty imitation are not hard to find. The German [ʀ] is a velar sound; so also is the American velarized [ɫ]. When an American hears the velar [ʀ] (or [ʌ]) in wird /'vɪrt/, his first reaction is therefore to equate it with the nearest velar sound in his own language—the dark [ɫ]—forgetting, of course, that it cannot be German /l/ because this is always clear [l]. To avoid this type of substitution, he needs practice of two sorts: first, a drill which contrasts German /r/ with American /l/; and second, a drill which contrasts German /r/ with German /l/:

English	German	German			
		/r/	/l/	/r/	/l/
wilt	wird	wird	wild	schwirrt	schwillt
spelt	sperrt	zerrt	Zelt	schmerzen	schmelzen
halt	Hort	ward	Wald	Karte	kalte
fault	fort	Wort	wollt	Warze	Walze
malt	Mord	Kurt	Kult	Schurz	Schulz

5.8 ALLOPHONIC PROBLEMS

Under the heading "allophonic problems" we wish to discuss the teaching problems caused by the presence in English of phonemes which have some allophones identical with those of a corresponding German phoneme, but other allophones which are quite different. The discussion of English and German /l/ might well have been postponed until this section. Since many Americans use both clear [l] (before /j/, as in ['mįljǝn] million, etc.) and dark [ɫ] (in other positions), this would be an example of a phoneme with allophones partly identical with those of a corresponding German phoneme (the German clear [l]). We chose to discuss it as a phonetic problem in part because some Americans seem never to use clear [l], and in part because it presents almost as much of a teaching problem as German /r/.

5.9 GERMAN /š/

A good example of an English phoneme with allophones partly identical to those of a corresponding German phoneme and partly different from them is English /š/ as compared with German /š/. The phonetic facts have already been given in the discussion of German /ç/. First, whereas German /š/ is always articulated with rounded lips, American /š/ may be articulated with or without rounded lips. Second, whereas German /š/ is always articulated with a deep groove in the tongue, American /š/ may be articulated with grooves of varying depth, and some of them may be almost as shallow as the groove for German /ç/. Indeed, if an American /š/ is articulated with a shallow groove and spread lips, it sounds more like German /ç/ than like German /š/. Obviously, then, for at least some students German /š/ will present a real teaching problem. Such students have to learn that, in speaking German, their /š/ can no longer wander freely over such a wide range of allophones as in English, but must be confined to one end of this range. We have already suggested a type of drill which contrasts German /š/ with German /ç/; a drill of the following type may also be helpful in contrasting it with English /š/.

she	—	Schi	session	—	dreschen
sheer	—	schier	nation	—	naschen
shone	—	schon	flashy	—	Flasche
shoe	—	Schuh	ashes	—	Asche
fish	—	Fisch	washing	—	waschen
fresh	—	frisch	mushy	—	Masche
flesh	—	Fleisch	Russian	—	Groschen
bush	—	Busch	rushing	—	rauschen

5.10 GERMAN /p t k/

A second allophonic problem concerns the voiceless stops /p t k/. English and German agree in using strongly aspirated allophones in the following positions (onset of stress marked with a tick):

	Initially at beginning of a stressed syllable		Initially at beginning of unstressed syllable		Medially at beginning of a stressed syllable	
/p/	'pass	'Paß	pa'rade	Pa'rade	a'part	a'part
	'place	'Platz	pla'toon	Pla'net	ap'plause	Ap'plaus
	'print	'Pracht	pro'voke	pri'vat	ap'prove	A'pril
/t/	'take	'Tag	to'day	Ta'blett	at'tain	A'tom
	'try	'Traum	tra'verse	Tra'bant	at'tract	At'trappe
/k/	'come	'Kamm	col'lide	Ka'lender	ac'cord	Ak'kord
	'clean	'klein	cli'matic	kli'matisch	ac'claim	E'klat
	'craft	'Kraft	cre'dentials	Kra'watte	A'cropolis	A'kropolis
	'quite	'Qual	qua'dratic	qua'dratisch	a'quarium	A'quarium

The two languages disagree slightly, however, in the aspiration of /p t k/ in the following positions:

	Medially before unstressed vowel		Finally	
/p/	ripper	Rippe	up	ab
	helper	Tulpe	help	halb
	sharper	Schärpe	harp	Korb
	bumper	Lampe	lump	Lump
/t/	pity	bitte	sat	satt
	salty	sollte	colt	kalt
	party	warte	heart	hart
	county	konnte	want	Hand
/k/	sticky	Stücke	sack	Sack
	bulky	welke	elk	welk
	turkey	wirke	hark	Werk
	inky	sinke	sank	sank

English /p t k/ in both of these positions are usually unaspirated, and in final position they may even be unreleased. For German, the Siebs prescribes strong aspiration in both positions. In actual practice, German speakers often pronounce medial /p t k/ unaspirated, so that (except for the /t/, which is discussed below), there is no serious teaching problem here. Final /p t k/, however, present a minor problem: in English they are very often unreleased; in German they are nearly always released, and they are very often aspirated. If students are told to pronounce German words like the following "more energetically" than their English counterparts, English pronunciation habits will almost automatically produce the aspirated release which is usual in German:

English	German	English	German
reap	rieb	leaped	liebt
lope	Lob	nicked	nickt
mitt	mit	lift	Lift
loot	lud	best	best
seek	Sieg	wished	wischt
lock	Lack	felt	fällt

5.11 MEDIAL /t/

A very serious teaching problem arises in the case of medial /t/. Where medial /t/ occurs before an unstressed vowel, most Americans use the special flap allophone [t̬], and some have no distinction in this position between /t/ and /d/. The first corrective step is to make students aware of this phenomenon, through having them pronounce such pairs of words as the following:

kitty	—	kiddy	filter	—	filled 'er
betting	—	bedding	alter	—	alder
catty	—	caddy	hearty	—	hardy
coated	—	coded	sorted	—	sordid
writing	—	riding	hurting	—	herding

Probably all Americans distinguish these pairs of words in careful speech; and in a pronunciation exercise like this, where the words are said carefully in isolation, many may aspirate the /t/'s in the first and third columns. In ordinary talk, however, most Americans use the special flap allophone [t̬] for /t/; and some make no distinction between /t/ and /d/, so that the two words in each pair sound alike.

In the above examples the /t/ follows a vowel, and /l/, or an /r/. Still another problem arises when it follows an /n/. Here it may be pronounced as the flap [t̬], or it may even drop out altogether, as in the almost universal pronunciation wanna ("I wanna go") for want to. (This pronunciation is often called "sloppy." Perhaps it is. The important point here is that everyone—or nearly everyone—uses it in normal, relaxed speech.) Students therefore need to be made aware of their pronunciation of such pairs of words as the following:

scenting	—	sending	winter	—	winner
mounting	—	mounding	panting	—	panning
canted	—	candid	punting	—	punning
vented	—	vended	runty	—	runny
painter	—	pained 'er	auntie	—	Annie

Once the student has been made aware of the way American /t/ is handled in words of these various types, he needs to be told that this is a peculiarity of English only, and that nothing like this occurs in standard German. He is then ready for a drill like the following, which contrasts the very special /t/ of English with the normal, even aspirated /t/ of German:

[t̬]	[tʰ]	[t̬] or zero	[tʰ]
pity	bitte	"wanta"	wohnte
bitter	bitter	winter	Winter
salty	sollte	painter	lehnte
parted	wartet	county	konnte
partitive	wartete		

5.12 DISTRIBUTIONAL PROBLEMS

These problems are of two sorts. First, German has a number of consonant clusters, such as the /ts/ of /ˈtseːn/ zehn and the /pf/ of /ˈpfʊnt/ Pfund, which cause difficulty. No new sounds are involved here, but merely the use of familiar sounds in unfamiliar ways. Second, German shows an automatic alternation between two sets of consonant phonemes. Stems with voiced /b d g v z/ in some positions (e.g., voiced /b/ in /ˈgraːbən/ Graben) show voiceless /p t k f s/ in other positions (e.g., voiceless /p/ in /ˈgraːp/ Grab). Again, no new sounds are involved, but merely an unfamiliar alternation of familiar sounds.

5.13 CONSONANT CLUSTERS

The consonant clusters which cause teaching problems are almost entirely limited to a few which occur in word-initial position. In order to see why they cause difficulty, we need to compare the initial consonant clusters of English with those of German. The following lists of English initial consonant clusters are by no means complete; they include only those English clusters which correspond more or less closely to comparable German ones, and therefore omit such things as the /θr-/ of /ˈθri/ three, the /kj-/ of /ˈkjut/ cute, etc. The lists of German clusters, on the other hand, are more or less complete. They omit only such abnormal clusters as the /sf-/ of /ˈsfɛːrə/ Sphäre, the /sts-/ of /ˈstseːnə/ Szene, the /pt-/ of /ptoːleːˈmɛːʊs/ Ptolemäus, etc. Abnormal clusters which happen to fit into the systems of the lists are included, but they are placed in parentheses. Rectangles indicate normal German clusters which are not matched by any corresponding clusters in English.

We may begin with the commonest type of initial clusters in both languages, namely those consisting of a stop or fricative followed by a liquid (/l/ or /r/), or a nasal (/n/ or /m/), or German /v/, English /w/. We find the following.

German	/r/	/l/	/n/	/m/	/v/
/p/	Preis	Plan	(Pneu)	. . . .	. . . .
/b/	breit	blau	. . . .	. . . .	. . . .
/t/	treu	. . . .	. . . .	(Tmesis)	(Twist)
/d/	drei	. . . .	. . . .	. . . .	(dwars)
/k/	Kreis	klein	Knie	. . . .	Qual
/g/	grau	Glas	Gnade	(Gmünd)	. . . .
/f/	frei	Flug	. . . .	. . . .	. . . .
/s/	. . . .	(Slawen)	(Snob)	(Smoking)	(Sweater)
/š/	Schrei	schlau	Schnee	schmal	schwer

English	/r/	/l/	/n/	/m/	/w/
/p/	price	plan	. . . .	. . . .	(pueblo)
/b/	broad	blue	. . . .	. . . .	(bwana)
/t/	true	. . . .	. . . .	(tmesis)	twist
/d/	dry	. . . .	. . . .	. . . .	dwarf
/k/	cry	clean		. . . .	queer
/g/	gray	glass		. . . .	(Gwendolyn)
/f/	free	fly	. . . .	. . . .	. . . .
/s/	. . . .	sly	snow	small	sweet
/š/	shrink	(Schlitz)	(Schneider)	(shmoo)	(Schwinn)

As these lists show, the cluster systems of the two languages are remarkably similar. In both of them the stops /p b t d k g/ occur freely before /r/, and all but the dentals occur freely before /l/. When we come to the nasals, however, we find an important difference. English permits only sibilants to occur before nasals (snow, small; Schneider, shmoo), whereas German permits both sibilants (Schnee, schmal) and velar stops (Knie, Gnade). Since clusters of stop plus nasal run counter to the English cluster system, words of this type constitute a real teaching problem. This is all the more true since American students have had years of training in reading the spellings kn- and gn- as symbols for simple /n-/. (Examples: know = /'no/, knot = /'nat/, gnaw = /'nɔ/, gnome = /'nom/. The initial k-, g- of these English words was given up in pronunciation several centuries ago, but the spelling has never been changed.) Special drills on words of this type are probably not needed; but the student certainly needs to be told that the spellings kn-, gn- really do represent the clusters /kn-/, /gn-/ in German, and the teacher needs to see to it that students really do pronounce them as clusters. In trying to handle these new clusters, many students will insert a vowel between the stop and the nasal: Knie will be /kə'niː/, and Gnade will be /gə'naːdə/. (Compare the common pronunciation of the New

York publisher Knopf as /kə'napf/.) Learning to pronounce a proper /kn-/, /gn-/ requires only a little effort and perseverance on the part of the student and a little persuasion on the part of the teacher.

The German clusters with /v/ obviously do not correspond phonetically to English clusters with /w/, but the two types are similar enough so that the German clusters can be learned with little difficulty. Only two of them can really be called normal for German: the /kv-/ of quer, Qual, quellen, and the /šv-/ of schwer, schwarz, schwellen, etc. Again, special drills are probably not needed, but the student needs to be told that the spellings qu- and schw- mean /kv-/ and /šv-/, and the teacher needs to see to it that the corresponding English clusters are not used instead.

The sibilants show an interesting phenomenon. Before /r/, both languages agree in using /š/ rather than /s/, but otherwise they behave in opposite ways:

| Normal for German:
Abnormal for English: | /šl- | šn- | šm- | šv- | (šw-)/ |
| Normal for English:
Abnormal for German: | /sl- | sn- | sm- | sw- | (sv-)/ |

Here also there is no real teaching problem, since the German clusters do not run strongly counter to English pronunciation habits but are merely unusual in English.

A second type of initial consonant cluster common to both languages consists of sibilant plus stop:

German		/r/	/l/	/v/
/sp/	(Spektrum)	(Sprinter)	(Spleen)	. . . .
/st/	(Stop)	(Strategie)	. . . .	. . . .
/sk/	(Skandal)	(Skrupel)	(Sklave)	(Squaw)
/šp/	Spiel	Sprung	Splitter	. . . .
/št/	Stuhl	Strahl	. . . .	. . . .
English		/r/	/l/	/w/
/sp/	spin	spring	split	. . . .
/st/	stop	string	. . . .	. . . .
/sk/	skin	screen	(sclerosis)	squeeze
/šp/	☐	☐	☐	. . . .
/št/	☐	☐	. . . .	. . . .

Again we find that the two languages behave in opposite ways. Clusters of /s/ plus stop are normal in English but abnormal in German; whereas clusters of /š/ plus stop are normal in German but so abnormal in English as to be completely lacking. However, because English makes extensive use of "sibilant + stop" as a general cluster type in initial position, German /šp-/ and /št-/ do not cause any serious difficulty. The real teaching problem arises from the fact that German spelling does not indicate clearly that the sibilant in these clusters is /š/ rather than /s/. Drills in reading aloud such words as Spiel, Spaß, springen, sprechen, Stiel, Staat, stricken, strecken may be of some help. But once the teacher has made the point that initial sp-, st- nearly always stand for /šp-/, /št-/, about all he can do is to persevere in insisting that they be pronounced that way.

A final type of initial consonant cluster consists of stop plus fricative, or stop plus sibilant. We give only a German listing this time, since this general cluster type is totally absent in English.

German		/r/	/l/	/v/
/pf/	Pfund	Pfropfen	Pflaume	. . . .
/ps/	(Psalm)	. . . .	. . . .	. . . .
/ts/	Zahl	. . . .	. . . .	Zweck
/tš/	(Tscheche)	. . . .	. . . .	. . . .
/ks/	(Xanten)	. . . .	. . . .	. . . .

The German initial cluster /tš-/ is phonetically almost identical with the English initial phoneme /č-/, and it therefore presents no difficulty. Otherwise, however, these clusters of stop plus fricative, or stop plus sibilant, constitute a very serious teaching problem, because they run entirely counter to the English cluster system. In the case of /ts-/ this is aggravated by the fact that German spelling symbolizes it with the letter z. American students have had years of training in reading this as a symbol for English /z-/ (as in zoo, zebra, zeal), and this firmly fixed habit is a hard one to break. In the case of both /pf-/ and /ts-/, special drills are probably not particularly helpful. About all the teacher can do is to persevere in insisting on the proper pronunciation.

(A word should be added here on the use of /pf-/ in the German speaking area. The pronunciation /pf-/ is prescribed for standard German, and it is used throughout the South [including Austria and Switzerland] in informal speech and local dialect as well. In Northern Germany, however, there are many millions of speakers who normally pronounce Pfund, Pferd, Pflaume, etc. as /'fụnt/, /'feːrt/, /'flaumə/. The historical reason for this situation is the fact that initial /pf-/ [from earlier /p-/] originally arose in the dialects of the South, spread north, but never reached much of the Rhineland or Northern Germany. As a result, initial /pf-/ is quite lacking in the local speech of the North, and even standard speakers from this area generally substitute simple /f-/ for it. Many such speakers feel no hesitation about teaching /'fụnt/, /'feːrt/, /'flaumə/, etc. as socially acceptable forms, even though they are not strictly standard.)

German has a large number of different consonant clusters in medial and final positions. The teaching problems which they present, however, come not from the clusters as such but from the fact that they contain new sounds such as /ç/, /x/, etc. A single exception is the cluster /nf/ in such words as /'fünf/ fünf, /'hanf/ Hanf. No such cluster occurs in English, and it therefore presents a teaching problem. The commonest error which students make is to nasalize the vowels of the words instead of pronouncing a distinct /n/. A useful corrective drill is to have them first pronounce [fünnn], [hannn], with an exaggerated [nnn], then to add the [f], still exaggerating the [n]: [fünnnf], [hannnf], and finally to shorten the [nnn]: [fünf], [hanf].

5.14 VOICED-VOICELESS ALTERNATIONS

A second type of distributional problem concerns the automatic alternation of phonemes in a given word stem. We may recall that German has six voiced-voiceless pairs of obstruents (stops and fricatives): voiced /b d g v z ž/ and voiceless /p t k f s š/. Though the voiceless obstruents are quite free in their privileges of occurrence, there are two very strict limitations on the positions in which voiced obstruents can occur.

First, though voiced obstruents occur freely in syllable-initial position, they never occur in syllable-final position. For example, the voiced /b/ of the stem /li:b-/ lieb- occurs in syllable-initial position in such forms as /'li:bən/ lieben, /'li:bər/ lieber, /'li:bə/ Liebe; but before a "syllable break" (as we may call it), it is automatically unvoiced to the corresponding voiceless obstruent, /p/. Such syllable breaks occur in three types of positions: (1) at the end of a word, as in /'li:p/ lieb; (2) at the end of part of a compound word, as in /'li:p,ɔigəln/ liebäugeln, /'li:p,raits/ Liebreiz; and (3) before suffixes beginning with a consonant, as in /'li:p+liŋ/ Liebling, /'li:p+liç/ lieblich, /'li:p+lo:s/ lieblos. (Where such a syllable break is not indicated by a space, as at the end of a word, or by a stress mark, as in compounds, we use the symbol /+/ for it.)

Second, though voiced obstruents occur freely in clusters with resonants (/m n l r/), they never occur in clusters with other obstruents. German has clusters of voiceless plus voiceless (such as /pf/, /ts/, /st/), but no clusters of voiced plus voiced (such as /bd/, /dz/, /zd/), or voiced plus voiceless (such as /bt/, /dx/, /zt/), or voiceless plus voiced (such as /pd/, /tz/, /sd/).[1] This again means that the /b/ of /li:b-/ is automatically unvoiced to /p/ in such forms as /'li:pt/ liebt, /'li:ptə/ liebte, /'li:pst/ liebst, /'li:pstə/ liebste.

The following table gives examples of the unvoicing of /b d g v z/ to /p t k f s/; no examples of the unvoicing of /ž/ to /š/ occur in standard German.

---

1. The only exceptions to this statement are clusters of voiceless consonant plus voiced /v/: /kv/ in /'kve:r/ quer etc., /šv/ in /'šve:r/ schwer etc. Many German speakers actually pronounce these clusters with voiceless /f/: /'kfe:r/, /'šfe:r/, though the Siebs condemns this practice—indicating that it must be fairly common. A very rare cluster of two voiced consonants is the /dž/ of a few foreign words such as /'džuŋəl/ Dschungel; most German speakers actually say /'tšuŋəl/, with the normal cluster /tš/. Sequences such as voiceless /s/ plus voiced /g/ in Ausgang etc. are not clusters, since a syllable break occurs between them: /'aus,gaŋ/. So also in such a sequence as the /k/ plus /z/ in /'bi:k,za:m/ biegsam, though many speakers say /'bi:ksam/.

	/b/-/p/	/d/-/t/	/g/-/k/	/v/-/f/	/z/-/s/
Voiced	graben	finden	fragen	Sklave, Motive	lesen
Voiceless finally	Grab	Fund	frag!	Motiv	lies!
Voiceless in compound	Grabmal	Fundort	fragwürdig	motivreich	Lesart
Voiceless before suffix	Begräbnis	Findling	fraglich		lesbar
Voiceless in cluster with /t/	er gräbt	. . . .	er fragt	er versklavt	er liest
Voiceless in cluster with /s/	des Grabs	des Funds	du fragst	du versklavst	. . . .

The unvoicing of /g/ needs some further discussion. In the colloquial speech of the South it is always unvoiced to /k/. In the North, however, it is very commonly unvoiced to /x/ or /ç/. The standard language represents a compromise between these two types of unvoicing: /g/ is in most instances to be unvoiced to /k/, but the suffix ig is to be unvoiced to /iç/. The following table illustrates these different treatments:

Voiced	Voiceless	South	North	Standard
Tage	Tag	/ˈtaːk/	/ˈtax/	/ˈtaːk/
Wege	Weg	/ˈveːk/	/ˈveːç/	/ˈveːk/
Berge	Berg	/ˈbɛrk/	/ˈbɛrç/	/ˈbɛrk/
folgen	folgt	/ˈfɔlkt/	/ˈfɔlçt/	/ˈfɔlkt/
Könige	könig	/ˈköːnɪk/	/ˈköːnɪç/	/ˈköːnɪç/
fertige	fertig	/ˈfɛrtɪk/	/ˈfɛrtɪç/	/ˈfɛrtɪç/
reinigen	reinigt	/ˈrainɪkt/	/ˈrainɪçt/	/ˈrainɪçt/
nötiger	nötigste	/ˈnöːtɪkstə/	/ˈnöːtɪçstə/	/ˈnöːtɪçstə/

(The Siebs adds one rather artificial restriction to this unvoicing of ig: the southern /k/ is to be used if a /ç/ follows closely after it. Hence König = /ˈköːnɪç/ (as above), but königlich = /ˈköːnɪk+lɪç/ and Königreich = /ˈköːnɪk,raiç/.)

It is worth noting that, in all these examples of unvoicing, German spelling keeps the symbol for the voiced sound: lieben, lieb rather than lieben, liep; lesen, lies rather than lesen, ließ; etc. One's first reaction is that this is confusing; and perhaps it is, to foreign beginners. But for native speakers of German (for whom, after all, the spelling is primarily intended) it is rarely confusing and often helpful. First, spellings such as lieb, liebte, liebste are completely unambiguous since the phoneme /b/ cannot occur in these positions, but is automatically replaced by its voiceless counterpart /p/. (The native speaker of German does not, of course, make any such analytical observation. For him the occurrence of /p/ rather than /b/ in these positions is simply a matter of habit, something which seems entirely natural, even inevitable. This habit is so firmly fixed that, when he learns a foreign language, he finds it very difficult to pronounce voiced obstruents in one of these positions. Hence his pronunciation of English cab like cap, bed like bet, bug like buck, leave like leaf, his like hiss, etc.). Second, the use of the letters b, d, g, v, s is is actually more helpful than would be the use of p, t, k, f, ß. The spellings Bund and bunt indicate that, though these words are pronounced alike in their uninflected forms (namely both as /'bʊnt/), they will be pronounced differently before such an ending as -e: Bunde = /'bʊndə/ vs. bunte = /'bʊntə/. Similarly, the spelling blies indicates that the plural is bliesen with /-z-/, whereas the spelling ließ indicates that the plural is ließen with /-s-/. The only ambiguities which can arise concern cases where a syllable break is not indicated in the spelling. Thus only the context can indicate whether the spelling Erblasser is to be interpreted as /'ɛrpˌlasər/ 'testator' or as /ɛr'blasər/ 'one who turns pale.'

Though the unvoicing of /b d g v z/ is an automatic habit for native speakers of German, it is by no means automatic for speakers of English. English has a few forms in which final /f/, /s/ alternate with non-final /v/, /z/: leaf, leaves /'lif 'livz/, house, houses /'haus 'hauzɪz/. These are left over from a much earlier stage of English in which voiced and voiceless fricatives alternated automatically somewhat as they now do in German. Otherwise, however, English has nothing whatever to match the special restrictions which German places on the occurrence of /b d g v z/. All of the voiced obstruents can occur in word-final position: rib, bad, big, give, has, etc. They can also occur in clusters with one another: /bd/ in robbed /'rabd/, /dz/ in lids /'lɪdz/, /gd/ in nagged /'nægd/, /vz/ in lives /'lɪvz/, etc. Furthermore, where English has certain alternations between /s/ and /z/, or between /t/ and /d/, they are in one sense quite the opposite of the German alternations. In German the shape of endings is fixed, and it is the consonant of the stem which alternates: stem /glaub-/ in glauben, but stem /glaup-/ in glaubte; or stem /bʊnd-/ in Bunde, but stem /bʊnt-/ in des Bunds. In English, on the other hand, aside from the few forms like leaf—leaves, wife—wives, the shape of the stem is fixed and it is the consonant of the ending which alternates: ending /-d/ in tabbed, bagged, raised, but ending /-t/ in tapped, backed, raced; or ending /-z/ in tabs, pads, bags, but ending /-s/ in taps, pats, backs.

Fortunately, if the student refuses to let himself be misled by the spelling, the German alternation of voiced and voiceless obstruents is not hard to learn. It can be drilled along with practice in the various forms of nouns and verbs.

Voiceless:	das Grab	das Rad	der Tag	der Preis	der König
Voiceless:	des Grabs	des Rads	des Tags	. . . .	des Königs
Voiced:	die Gräber	die Räder	die Tage	die Preise	die Könige
Voiced:	leben	wenden	zeigen	reisen	reinigen
Voiceless:	lebte	wandte	zeigte	reiste	reinigte
Voiceless:	gelebt	gewandt	gezeigt	gereist	gereinigt

Voiced:	geben	laden	tragen	lesen
Voiceless:	gab	lud	trug	las
Voiced:	gegeben	geladen	getragen	gelesen
Voiceless:	er gibt	er lädt	er trägt	er liest

PHONETICS: THE VOWELS 6

6.1 THE CLASSIFICATION OF VOWELS

We may recall from chapter 2 that vowels are defined phonetically as "sounds articulated in such a way that the breath stream flows essentially unhindered along the median line of the vocal tract." Since this is a rather negative definition, we need now to state the same facts in a more positive way: vowels are sounds produced by using the vocal tract as a resonance chamber. The different ways in which we shape this resonance chamber produce different kinds of resonance; and, if the median line of the vocal tract is left unobstructed, these different kinds of resonance are what we call different vowel sounds.

In order to be able to give an articulatory description of vowel sounds, we need some method of describing the various ways in which the vocal tract can be shaped so as to produce different types of resonance. A full description would be enormously complicated, since it would have to include such details as the height of the larynx, the size of the opening in the pharynx, etc. In practical phonetics a greatly simplified type of description is used. It starts out with the observation that the shape of the vocal tract, as a resonance chamber, can most obviously be influenced by the position assumed by that most mobile of all vocal organs, the tongue. Accordingly, all articulatory descriptions of vowels begin by stating the position of the tongue; other details are then added as they seem necessary.

6.2 HIGH VS. LOW

The position of the tongue is customarily described in terms of two dimensions: high vs. low, and front vs. back. In order to understand the high—low dimension, it is helpful to try the following experiment. Say first the vowel sound of English bee, then the vowel sound of English bah (or German die, then German da). Go back and forth several times, noting as you do the positions assumed by the tongue and the directions in which it moves: ee—ah—ee—ah—ee—ah. For ee the tongue is humped up high in the mouth; for ah it is flattened out and is relatively low in the mouth. We therefore call the vowel sound of bee a HIGH VOWEL, that of bah a LOW VOWEL. The essential difference is the distance between the highest part of the tongue and the roof of the mouth. In a high vowel like that of bee, this distance is very small: the highest part of the tongue is very close to the roof of the mouth. In a low vowel like that of bah, the distance is relatively much greater: not only is the hump in the tongue flattened out, but the distance is often still further increased by a lowering of the whole jaw.

6.3 FRONT VS. BACK

Next, try saying first the vowel sound of English bee, and then that of English boo (or German die, du). Again, go back and forth several times, noting the positions and movements of the tongue: ee—oo—ee—oo—ee—oo. For both of these vowel sounds there is an obvious hump in the tongue, i.e., they are both high vowels. Relatively speaking, the hump for ee is in the front of the mouth, whereas that for oo is in the back of the mouth. We therefore call the vowel sound of bee a FRONT VOWEL, that of boo a BACK VOWEL. Since both of them are high (as opposed to the low vowel of bah), we can further define the vowel sound of bee as a HIGH FRONT VOWEL, that of boo as a HIGH BACK VOWEL. If we now examine the low vowel of bah, we will find that (in the pronunciation of most Americans) it is neither front nor back but CENTRAL. We can therefore describe it as a LOW CENTRAL VOWEL.

The dimensions high—low and front—back now enable us to draw a schematic, two-dimensional diagram, and to place in it the conventional phonetic symbols [i a u] for the vowel sounds of English bee, bah, boo, German die, da, du. These symbols do not, of course, represent exact vowel sounds, but only general vowel types.

	Front	Central	Back
High	i		u
Low		a	

6.4 UNROUNDED VS. ROUNDED

In going back and forth between the vowel sounds of English bee and boo, we notice one other difference between them beside that of front and back. For [i] (as in bee) the lips are more or less spread; for [u] (as in boo) they are more or less rounded. This difference between spread and rounded is even more obvious in German in the contrast between the vowel sounds of die and du. To be more exact, therefore, we should describe the vowel [i] as a high front spread vowel or, as is usually said, HIGH FRONT UNROUNDED VOWEL; and [u] is then a HIGH BACK ROUNDED VOWEL.

Lip rounding has a double effect on the shape of the vocal tract as a resonance chamber. First, it changes the shape of the front opening of the resonance chamber from spread to rounded; second, it increases slightly the length of the resonance chamber, since the lips are not only rounded but also slightly protruded. A matter of particular interest to us here is the fact that lip rounding is quite independent of the position of the tongue inside the mouth: with any given tongue position the lips can be either unrounded or rounded.

6.5 FRONT ROUNDED VOWELS

What would happen if we held the tongue in the position for high front [i], but rounded the lips as for [u]? The result is the HIGH FRONT ROUNDED VOWEL [ü], as in German früh, Mühe, Bücher, etc. To understand the nature of this vowel more fully, try two different types of alternation. First, go back and forth between high front unrounded [i] and high front rounded [ü]: [i—ü—i—ü—i—ü]. Here the tongue stays in the same high front position, but the lips move back and forth between unrounded and rounded. Second, go back and forth between high front rounded [ü] and high back rounded [u]: [ü—u—ü—u—ü—u]. Here the lips stay in the same rounded position, but the hump in the tongue moves back and forth between front and back.

Lip rounding adds a whole new dimension to our description of vowels. By rights, we should now give a three-dimensional diagram: one dimension for high—low, a second for front—back, and a third for unrounded—rounded. In practice, we usually put corresponding unrounded and rounded vowels side by side in the same two-dimensional diagram. Just as [i] is the unrounded high front vowel corresponding to rounded [ü], so there is also an unrounded high back vowel corresponding to rounded [u]. Because it does not occur in either English or German, it is of no real interest to us here, and we need not use any special symbol for it. We can symbolize it in the following diagram simply by an X, but neglect it (and others like it) henceforth:

	Front	Central	Back
High	i,ü		X,u
Low		a	

6.6 THE CONVENTIONAL VOWEL QUADRILATERAL

How many possible vowel sounds are there between front [i] or [ü] and back [u]? Or between high [i], [ü], [u] and low [a]? The answer to both of these questions is of course the same: an infinite number. Asking how many vowel sounds there are in the dimensions front—back and high—low is like asking how many points there are on a line. Theoretically, the answer is always: an infinite number. As a practical matter, however, we divide both of these dimensions into an arbitrary number of segments (just as we divide a line one foot long arbitrarily into 12 inches, or a line one meter long arbitrarily into 100 centimeters). The number of such segments is largely determined by the particular language or languages we are working on. Since our special interest in the present study is a comparison of the vowel sounds of English and German, it will be convenient for us to divide the front—back dimension into three segments, and to divide the high—low dimension also into three segments, each of which can then be further subdivided into three more segments. This procedure gives us the following grid on which we can plot approximately the vowel phones of English and German. In order to distinguish clearly between rounded and unrounded vowels, the symbols for rounded vowels are placed within parentheses.

		Front	Central	Back
High	close	i̩ (ü̩)		(y̩)
	neutral	i (ü)		(u)
	open	i̯ (ü̯)		(y̯)
Mid	close	e̩ (ö̩)		(o̩)
	neutral	e (ö)	ɜ ɝ	(o)
	open	e̯ (ö̯)	ə ʌ	(ɔ̩)
Low	close		a̩	
	neutral	æ	a	(ɔ)
	open		a̱	

The above diagram is highly schematic, and it indicates only in very stylized fashion the relative position of the tongue in the articulation of these various vowel types. In particular, it overlooks the fact that, because the jaw is hinged at the back of the mouth, the dimension high—low covers, physiologically, a greater distance in the front of the mouth (for the front vowels) than it does in the back of the mouth (for the back vowels). That is to say, the absolute distance which the front of the tongue moves in going from high [i] to low [æ] is greater than is the distance which the back of the tongue moves in going from high [u̯] to low [ɔ]. Furthermore, X-ray photographs show clearly that low back vowels are farther back than high back vowels. Finally, in both English and German the open front vowels [i̯] and [e̯] are not as far front as the corresponding close vowels [i̩] and [e̩]; and the open back vowels [y̯] and [ɔ̩] are not as far back as the corresponding close vowels [u̯] and [o̯]. To indicate these differences, another conventional type of vowel diagram assumes the following shape:

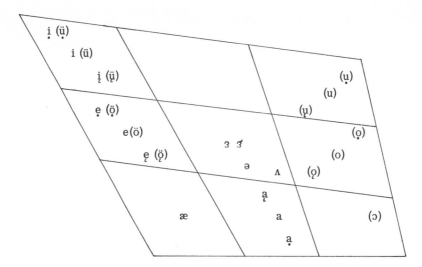

The approximate phonetic values of these symbols can be illustrated by the following examples:

	English	German		English	German
[i̩]		sieht	[u̩]		tut
[i]	seat		[u]	toot	
[i̡]	sits	Sitz	[u̡]	puts	Putz
[e̩]		geht	[o̩]		Boot
[e]	gate		[o]	boat	
[e̡]	bet	Bett	[o̡]		Gott
[æ]	bat		[ɔ]	bought	
[ɝ]	bird		[ü]		fühle
[ə]		(bitt)e	[ü]		
[ʌ]	but		[ÿ]		fülle
[a̩]		Stadt	[ö̩]		Höhle
[a]	far		[ö]		
[a̩]		Staat	[ö̡]		Hölle

6.7 MONOPHTHONGS VS. DIPHTHONGS

From a technical point of view, no vowel ever maintains the same quality throughout its articulation. Acoustic measurements show clearly that every vowel sound in normal speech changes constantly in quality, even though the changes may be very slight. From a practical point of view, however, it is convenient to make a distinction between vowel sounds which very obviously change in quality during their articulation, and vowel sounds which remain relatively constant. Vowels of the former type, which clearly change in quality, are called DIPHTHONGS; vowels which remain relatively constant are called MONOPHTHONGS. For example, the vowel sound which occurs between the /z/ and the /t/ of German seit is obviously a diphthong. It begins in the general area of low central [a] and then glides in the general direction of high front [i]. We may therefore symbolize it phonetically as [ai]—or, in a strict phonetic transcription, as [ai̯], using the symbol [i̯] with a half circle to indicate that this vowel sound is non-syllabic. (In a purely phonetic transcription the notation [ai], without the half circle, would indicate two syllables: [a] + [i].) On the other hand, the vowel sounds of German seht and sieht are, practically speaking, constant in quality. We may therefore symbolize them as [e̜] and [i̜], respectively.

The distinction between monophthongs and diphthongs is a purely practical one; there is no sharp boundary between them but only a gradual transition. Consider, for example, the vowel sounds of English sigh, say, see, and sight, sate, seat. For most Americans the vowels of sigh and sight are obvious diphthongs: [sai] and [sait]. In say and sate we again find diphthongs, something like [sei] and [seit], though their diphthongal quality is less obvious. In see and seat, finally, we face a dilemma. Measurement by instruments will show that these vowel sounds are again diphthongs; but this is a trivial observation, since all vowel sounds, when measured carefully, are found to be diphthongs. The analysis we make will therefore depend on our purposes. If we merely wish to make an approximate phonetic notation of English, we can perfectly well consider them as monophthongs and transcribe these two words as [si] and [sit]. If we want to note the phonetic difference usually made between word-final vowels and vowels checked by voiceless consonants, we can interpret the vowel of see as a diphthong: [si·ⁱ], and that of seat as a monophthong: [sit]. If, finally, our purpose is to contrast the slightly diphthongal quality of these vowels with the essentially monophthongal quality of their German counterparts, we can consider them both to be diphthongs: [si·ⁱ], [si·ⁱt], in contrast to German [zi̜], [zi̜t] sie, sieht.

6.8 SHORT VS. LONG

Vowel sounds, like consonants, can of course also differ in duration. In experimental phonetics, using instruments, it is possible to determine the beginning and end of a vowel sound more or less exactly, and then to measure its duration in hundredths of a second. The resulting measurements are in part quite trivial, since when a given word is spoken slowly it will obviously show a longer vowel than when it is spoken fast. In practical phonetics we therefore try to make rough judgments of vowel length in words spoken at approximately the same speed. For example, if the English words seat, seed, see are all spoken at normal speed, we find that the vowel of seat is shortest, that of seed somewhat longer, and that of see still longer. We can call these durations "short," "half-long," and "long," respectively, and indicate them by writing [sit] seat, [si·d] seed, and [si:] see —or, indicating simultaneously their relative diphthongal qualities, [sit], [si·ⁱd], [si:i]. In much the same way we can classify the vowel of German satt as short: [za̜t], and the vowel of German Saat as long: [za̜:t].

6.9 TENSE VS. LAX

Vowel sounds can also differ in the relative degree of muscular energy involved in their articulation. In comparing English and German we can make the very general observation that, by and large, all German vowels are tenser than their English counterparts—or, vice versa, that all English vowels are laxer than their German counterparts. There are also differences within each language along the tense—lax dimension. The stressed vowels of German bieten, beten are noticeably tenser than the vowels of bitten, Betten. This appears, among other things, in the fact that the [i:] of bieten is higher and farther front than the [i̩] of bitten, just as the [e:] of beten is higher and farther front than the [e̩] of Betten.

The difference between tense and lax vowels in American English is well described by C. K. Thomas: "If you contrast seat with sit, or pool with pull, you will observe another important means of making meaningful distinctions. The primary difference is that for seat and pool the tongue muscles are tense; for sit and pull they are relaxed. You should be able to feel the difference of tension in your muscles. If you touch the skin leading back from your chin to your throat you should be able to feel the muscles bulge for the tense vowel but not for the lax. In addition, you should be able to see in a mirror how the muscles bulge and the point of the larynx rises for the tense vowels. The muscular bulge which you can feel under your chin has its counterpart in a muscular bulge on the upper surface of the tongue" (An Introduction to the Phonetics of American English, 2d ed., p. 37). Thomas goes on to point out that tense vowels are likely to be longer, higher, and more diphthongal than lax vowels.

6.10 CONSTRICTED VS. NON-CONSTRICTED

In the conventional vowel diagrams given earlier, we listed the symbols [ə] and [ɚ] side by side as if they were the same type of mid central vowel. We have already discussed, in chapter 2, the difference between them: [ɚ] has lateral constriction of the body of the tongue (often called simply "r-coloring"), whereas [ə] does not.

6.11 SYLLABIC VS. NON-SYLLABIC

This difference was also discussed in chapter 2. We may recall that syllabic [i] corresponds to non-syllabic [j], syllabic [u] to non-syllabic [w], and syllabic [ɚ] to non-syllabic [r].

6.12 ORAL VS. NASALIZED

In describing the articulation of vowel sounds thus far, we have taken it for granted that the velic was closed and that only the mouth was being used as a resonance chamber. Such vowels are called ORAL. But if the velic is open, and part of the breath stream flows through the nasal cavity, then this latter also serves as an added, supplementary resonance chamber. Such vowels are called NASALIZED. We can symbolize them by writing a superior [n] after the vowel symbol. Thus [a^n] = nasalized [a], [ɔ^n] =

nasalized [ɔ̃], etc. Speakers of American English commonly nasalize vowels which occur before the nasals /m n ŋ/. For example, phonemic /'bɛnt/ bent is often pronounced ['bɛ̃^{n}nt], or even ['bɛ̃^{n}t], with no nasal consonant at all. Speakers in some parts of the country—those who are commonly said to have a "nasal twang"—nasalize vowels in other positions as well, saying things like ['jɛ̃^{n}s] yes, ['no^n] no, etc. Though nasalization is widespread in American English, it is nowhere phonemic. That is to say, there is no meaningful contrast between ['bɛ̃^{n}t] and ['bɛnt], between ['jɛ̃^{n}s] and ['jɛs], or between ['no^n] and ['no].

PHONEMICS: 7
THE VOWELS OF
GERMAN

7.1 PHONETICS VS. PHONEMICS

In making a phonetic analysis of vowels it is more than ever obvious that we are dealing with sound as a continuum of many dimensions, rather than with a specific set of objectively identifiable sounds. In the preceding chapter we mentioned first the three main dimensions along which it is customary to measure vowels: high vs. low, front vs. back, rounded vs. unrounded; and we then added six more dimensions which can be used to give a more exact description: monophthongal vs. diphthongal, short vs. long, tense vs. lax, constricted vs. non-constricted, syllabic vs. non-syllabic, and oral vs. nasalized. Each of these dimensions is a continuum. There is no such thing as a vowel which is high, or rounded, or long in any absolute sense. A vowel can only be more or less high, more or less rounded, more or less long, in relation to one or more other vowels. This means that any phonetic description of vowels is always relative, never absolute.

This dilemma of phonetics, which has to allow for an infinite number of vowels, is removed by the methods of phonemic analysis. Here it is indeed possible to say that a given language has a given number of vowel phonemes, with specific features which distinguish them from one another. The analytical method used is that of relevant contrast: we find out what differences in vowel sound correlate with differences in meaning. In the case of consonants, we began our phonemic analysis with English, on the theory that we should proceed from the more familiar (English) to the less familiar (German). With vowels we shall use the opposite procedure and begin with German. The reason for this is that American English vowels present a number of special problems which do not occur in German, and these problems make their analysis a good deal more complicated. Starting with German vowels will allow us to proceed from the relatively simple to the more complex.

7.2 PHONEMIC CONTRASTS

In stressed position German has seventeen contrasting vowels and diphthongs, plus an eighteenth vowel which is prescribed by the Siebs but is of marginal status for a good many speakers:

1.	/i̯/	bieten	Stiele	ihn	ihre
2.	/i̧̯/	bitten	Stille	in	irre
3.	/e̩/	beten	stehle	wen	zehre
4.	/ȩ/	Betten	Stelle	wenn	zerre
5.	/u̩/	Rute	Buhle	Ruhm	Fuhre
6.	/u̧/	Kutte	Bulle	Rum	murre
7.	/o̩/	rote	Sohle	Sohn	bohre
8.	/o̧/	Rotte	solle	Bonn	Lorre
9.	/ü̩/	Güte	fühle	kühn	führe
10.	/ü̧/	Mütter	fülle	dünn	Dürre
11.	/ö̩/	Goethe	Höhle	tönt	höre
12.	/ö̧/	Götter	Hölle	könnt	dörre
13.	/a̩/	rate	fahle	Bahn	Haare
14.	/a̧/	Ratte	falle	Bann	harre
15.	/ai/	leite	Feile	Bein	. . . .
16.	/o̧i/	Leute	heule	neun	eure
17.	/au/	Laute	faule	Zaun	. . . .
18.	/ɛ/	bäte	stähle	wähne	währe

In addition, German has a nineteenth phoneme which occurs only in unstressed position:

19.	/ə/	ge̲sagt	bitt̲e̲	wart̲e̲t̲e̲	bess̲e̲r̲e̲

7.3 PRELIMINARY CLASSIFICATION

Using the dimensions high—low, front—back, rounded—unrounded, we can plot the first fourteen of these vowels as follows:

		Front	Central	Back
High	close	i̩ (ü̩)		(u̩)
	open	i̧ (ü̧)		(u̧)
Mid	close	e̩ (ö̩)		(o̩)
	open	ȩ (ö̧)		(o̧)
Low	close		a̧	
	open		a̩	

The vowels that are marked with a hook are all relatively near to the center of the diagram; the vowels that are marked with a dot are all relatively far from the center of the diagram. This means that:

/i̧ ü̧ u̧/ are lower and more central than /i̩ ü̩ u̩/
/ȩ ö̧ o̧/ are lower and more central than /e̩ ö̩ o̩/
/a̧/ is higher and more central than /a̩/

These fourteen vowel phonemes therefore fall into two clear phonetic classes, which we may call "centralized" and "decentralized":

centralized: /i̜ ü̜ u̜ e̜ ö̜ o̜ a̜/
decentralized: /i̤ ṳ̈ ṳ e̤ ö̤ o̤ a̤/

(N.B. All phonetic descriptions of German describe /i̜ ü̜ u̜/ as higher than /i̤ ṳ̈ ṳ/, and /e̜ ö̜ o̜/ as higher than /e̤ ö̤ o̤/. Few if any of them, however, describe /a̜/ as higher, and hence more centralized, than /a̤/. It may be that some speakers make only a quantitative distinction between the two: short /a̜/ vs. long /a̤/. All persons whose speech the writer has examined, however, make a clear qualitative difference as well: /a̤/ is pronounced with the jaw lower than for /a̜/. This lower jaw position means that the tongue is also lowered, and hence that /a̤/ is a lower vowel than /a̜/. To test whether a speaker makes this qualitative difference, note whether he lowers his jaw for the second member of such pairs of words with /a̜/—/a̤/ as Bann—Bahn, kann—Kahn, wann—Wahn, Kamm—kam, Lamm—lahm, satt—Saat, Stadt—Staat, schlaff—Schlaf, As—aß, Fall—fahl, Stall—Stahl, all—Aal, Wall—Wahl, Schall—Schal, starr—Star.)

7.4 TENSE VS. LAX

Having used the dimensions high—low, front—back, and rounded—unrounded to make a preliminary classification of the vowel phonemes of German, we may now consider the other phonetic dimensions mentioned in chapter 6 so as to arrive at a more exact description. We have just shown how the vowel phonemes numbered 1 through 14 form seven pairs in each of which one vowel is relatively nearer to the center (is "centralized"), and one vowel is relatively farther from the center (is "decentralized"). If we examine these pairs further, we shall find that each centralized vowel is articulated with relatively less muscular energy, and each decentralized vowel is articulated with relatively more muscular energy. In other words, the centralized vowels /i̜ e̜ a̜ o̜ u̜ ü̜ ö̜/ are LAX, and the decentralized vowels /i̤ e̤ a̤ o̤ ṳ ṳ̈ ö̤/ are TENSE. We can think of this difference in muscular energy as being responsible for the difference in tongue position. The greater muscular energy of the tense vowels causes them to be articulated in more extreme positions; the lesser muscular energy of the lax vowels causes them to be articulated in less extreme positions. The features "lax" and "tense" therefore include the features "centralized" and "decentralized." Since "lax" and "tense" are the more inclusive terms, we shall use them from now on.

7.5 SHORT VS. LONG

When the seven pairs of tense and lax vowels occur in stressed position, the tense ones are noticeably longer in duration than the lax ones. Note such contrasts as the following:

Tense and long		Lax and short	
['liːt]	Lied	['lɪt]	litt
['beːt]	Beet	['bɛt]	Bett
['štaːt]	Staat	['štɐt]	Stadt
['šoːs]	Schoß	['šɔs]	schoß
['muːs]	Mus	['mʊs]	muß
['hüːtə]	Hüte	['hʏtə]	Hütte
['höːlə]	Höhle	['hœlə]	Hölle

These differences in the length of stressed vowels are very striking, and they underlie the customary description of German vowels as "short" and "long" rather than as "lax" and "tense." A more detailed examination shows, however, that lax and tense vowels differ in length only when they are stressed. When they are unstressed, both sets are of equal duration. Consider first the following examples, in which the tense vowel phonemes /i̯ e̯ o̯ u̯/ are long when stressed, but short when unstressed:

Long when stressed	Short when unstressed
/i̯/ = [iː] in ['kri̯ːti̯š] kritisch	/i̯/ = [i̯] in [kri̯'ti̯ːk] Kritik
/e̯/ = [eː] in ['le̯ːbən] leben	/e̯/ = [e̯] in [le̯'bɛndi̯ç] lebendig
/o̯/ = [oː] in ['do̯ːzi̯s] Dosis	/o̯/ = [o̯] in [do̯'zi̯ːrən] dosieren
/u̯/ = [uː] in ['mu̯ːzə] Muse	/u̯/ = [u̯] in [mu̯'ze̯ːu̯m] Museum

Consider next the following examples, in which unstressed tense and lax vowels occur in comparable environments. These examples show that, with one exception, the tense—lax opposition is maintained in unstressed position, even though there are no differences in length:

Tense (and short)	Lax (and short)
/i̯/ in [di̯'ne̯ː] Diner	/ɪ/ in [dɪ'fuːs] diffus
/e̯/ in [de̯'tai̯] Detail	/ɛ/ in [dɛ'seːr] Dessert
(/a/ in [ba'laⁿsə] Balance)	(/a/ in [ba'lɐ̯də] Ballade)
/o̯/ in [ko̯'lʊmbʊs] Kolumbus	/ɔ/ in [kɔ'leːgə] Kollege
/u̯/ in [ku̯'ri̯ːr] Kurier	/ʊ/ in [skʊ'ri̯l] skurril
/ü̯/ in [zü̯na'go̯ːgə] Synagoge	/ʏ/ in [sʏna'löːfə] Synalöphe
/ö̯/ in [ö̯ko̯'no̯ːm] Ökonom	/œ/ in [œstro̯'geːn] Östrogen

These examples, taken from the Siebs (except for the word Östrogen, which does not happen to occur there), illustrate the distribution of unstressed vowel qualities as prescribed for standard German: with few exceptions, a tense vowel is to be pronounced if it is followed in the spelling by a single consonant letter, but a lax vowel if it is followed in the spelling by a double consonant letter or a consonant cluster. Only in the case of un-stressed /a/ is no contrast prescribed between tense and lax: <u>Balance</u> and <u>Ballade</u> both have the same unstressed /a/, despite the difference in spelling (single -l- vs. double -ll-). In linguistic terms we may say that the opposition "tense vs. lax," which we find in stressed position for all seven pairs of vowels, is maintained in unstressed position for the three pairs of high vowels (/i ü u/ vs. /i̬ ü̬ u̬/) and for the three pairs of mid vowels (/e ö o/ vs. /e̬ ö̬ o̬/); but that it is suspended in the case of the low vowels (stressed /a/ vs. /a̬/), giving only a single unstressed low vowel phoneme, /a/.

In the normal relaxed speech of many persons, the suspension of the tense—lax opposition applies not only to the pair /a/ vs. /a̬/, but to all other tense—lax pairs as well. For example, many people who in formal speech distinguish /ko'lumbus/ <u>Kolumbus</u> (with tense /o/) and /ko'legə/ <u>Kollege</u> (with lax /o̬/) often use in informal speech the same vowel in both words: /ko'lumbus/ like /ko'legə/, both with a more or less lax /o/. Simi-larly, formal /filozo'fi/ <u>Philosophie</u> (with tense unstressed /i o o/) may alternate with informal /filozo'fi/ (with more or less lax /i o o/), etc.

To sum up: though the opposition "long—short" is a striking phonetic feature of the German vowel system, it affects vowels only when they are stressed. The one con-stant feature which distinguishes the two sets of vowels in both stressed and unstressed position is the opposition "tense—lax." In formal speech this opposition is suspended in unstressed position only for the pair /a/—/a̬/; in the informal speech of many persons, however, it is suspended for all other pairs as well.

7.6 MONOPHTHONGAL VS. DIPHTHONGAL

The seven tense—lax pairs of vowels which we have discussed thus far are all, practically speaking, monophthongs, with no significant glides in them. If we now look at the three phonemes numbered 15, 16, 17 on the chart given above, we find that they have a very pronounced glide and are clearly diphthongs:

/ai/, as in /'bai/ <u>bei</u>, begins in low central position and then glides to-ward a tongue position which is higher and farther front.

/oi/, as in /'hoi/ <u>Heu</u>, begins in lower mid back rounded position and then glides toward a tongue position which is higher and farther front; the lips may or may not stay rounded.

/au/, as in /'bau/ <u>Bau</u>, begins in low central position and then glides to-ward a tongue position which is higher and farther back, while at the same time the lips are rounded.

A fourth diphthong of very limited occurrence is the /ui/ of the two inter-jections /'hui/ <u>hui</u> and /'pfui/ <u>pfui</u>. It begins in high back rounded position and then glides toward high front position, while at the same time the lips are un-rounded.

(N.B. In two respects we differ from the treatment of these diphthongs given in the <u>Siebs</u>. [1] The <u>Siebs</u> prescribes for the diphthong of <u>Heu</u> etc. a glide during which the lips remain rounded. We indicate an unrounded glide because it is our experience that

most German speakers unround their lips during the glide. In any case, there is no distinctive opposition between a rounded and an unrounded glide, and the presence or absence of
rounding is therefore not phonemically relevant. [2] The Siebs prescribes glides only to
close mid front and back positions, and hence symbolizes the three diphthongs as /ae o̤ö
ao/. This is done in order to warn German readers against using glides to a very high
tongue position, as is the practice in some German dialects. Since there is no danger that
American students will use high glides of this sort (no such high glides occur in American
English), we have retained the phonetically less exact but more traditional symbolization
/ai o̤i au/.)

7.7 SYLLABIC VS. NON-SYLLABIC

In §2.9 we discussed syllabic and non-syllabic vowels, such as the syllabic [i]
of [biuzi̩ŋ] be oozing and the non-syllabic [j] of [əbjuzi̩ŋ] abusing. Such a presentation is
useful in making clear the relationship between a vowel (syllabic) and its corresponding
semivowel (non-syllabic). At the same time, however, it makes the phonetic dimension
"syllabic—non-syllabic" appear to consist only of these two extremes. In actual fact, this
dimension is as much of a continuum as are all the other phonetic dimensions we have discussed, and [i] and [j] merely represent opposite ends of the dimension. In between these
two ends it is quite possible to have phones which are not as fully syllabic as [i], and not
as fully non-syllabic as [j]. German has such phones in words like Indien, Asien, Italien,
etc. Following the Siebs we shall write them as [ĭ]: ['i̩ndĭən], ['a:zĭən], [i̩'ta:lĭən].

To a considerable extent, this [ĭ] is in complementary distribution with [j]:
[ĭ] occurs after long syllables (long vowel + consonant, as in ['a:zĭən], or short vowel +
two consonants, as in ['i̩ndĭən]), whereas [j] occurs after short syllables (short vowel +
one consonant). Examples:

[ĭ]		[j]	
['da̩:lĭə]	Dahlie	['ta̩ljə]	Taille
[la'pa̩:lĭə]	Lappalie	[ka'na̩ljə]	Kanaille
['špa:nĭər]	Spanier	[šam'pa̩njər]	Champagner
[fa'mi̩:lĭə]	Familie	[va'ni̩ljə]	Vanille

However, the Siebs shows the two phones in contrast in such words as the following:

[ĭ]		[j]	
[bi̩'lĭo:n]	Billion	[bi̩l'jɛt	Billet
[mi̩'lĭardə]	Milliarde	[bri̩l'ja̩nt]	brillant

One phonetic difference between the two is the fact that [j] often has spirantal friction,
whereas [i] does not.

Though [ĭ] contrasts with [j], as in the above examples, it does not contrast with [i̯]; [ɪ] and [i̯] may therefore be grouped together as allophones of /i/. The Siebs, to be sure, appears to show a contrast between [ɪ̆] and [i̯], but it does so with such inconsistency as to indicate clearly that they are in free variation in certain environments. Examples, taken from the Siebs:

[ɪ̆]		[i̯]	
[ˈraːdɪ̆u̯s]	Radius	[ˈraːdi̯u̯m]	Radium
[aˈmoːnɪ̆u̯m]	Ammonium	[ˈgeːni̯u̯s]	Genius
[aluˈmiːnɪ̆u̯m]	Aluminium	[akˈtiːni̯u̯m]	Aktinium
[proleˈtaːrɪ̆ər]	Proletarier	[di̯noˈzauri̯ər]	Dinosaurier
[peˈrɪ̆oːdə]	Periode	[peri̯ˈöːkə]	Periöke
[aˈlɪ̆aⁿs]	Alliance	[ali̯ˈants]	Allianz
[ˈkɪ̆anti̯]	Chianti	[fi̯ˈakər]	Fiaker
[ˈpɪ̆aːno]	Piano	[pi̯ˈastər]	Piaster

By and large, [ɪ̆] is commoner in fast speech, [i̯] in slow speech; and [ɪ̆] is commoner in familiar words, [i̯] in unfamiliar words. However, as we have seen, there seems to be no clear contrast between them. The two sets of words above can be pronounced with either [ɪ̆] or [i̯], in free variation.

Following the Siebs, wherever [ɪ̆] is generally used we shall write it (and, to this extent, make our transcription phonetic rather than phonemic). It is especially common before unstressed final /ə/ and /ən/: /ˈlinɪ̆ə/ Linie, /skandiˈnavɪ̆ən/ Skandinavien; and before stressed /on/: /naˈtsɪ̆on/ Nation, /viˈzɪ̆on/ Vision, /mɪ̆ˈsɪ̆on/ Mission, /u̯ˈnɪ̆on/ Union, /mɪ̆ˈlɪ̆on/ Million.

Comparable to [ɪ̆] as a prevocalic allophone of /i/ is [ŭ] as a prevocalic allophone of /u/. The Siebs makes no mention of [ŭ] in its introductory material, but it uses the symbol [ŭ] in its pronouncing dictionary. Again, its use of [ŭ] vs. [u̯] is so inconsistent as to show clearly that the two are in free variation. It writes, for example, the following:

[ŭ]		[u̯]	
[zeˈksŭe̯l]	sexuell	[ˌbiːzɛksu̯ˈel]	bisexuell
[ziˈlŭe̯tə]	Silhouette	[aktu̯ˈel]	aktuell

Though the Siebs does not indicate it, [ŭ] is also commonly used in Statue [ˈʃtaːtŭə], and in fast pronunciations of words like Januar ([ˈjanŭaːr], beside slower [ˈjanu̯aːr]), Situation ([zitŭaˈtsɪ̆oːn], beside slower [zitu̯aˈtsɪ̆oːn]), etc.

German has two other non-syllabic vowels in prevocalic position. One, non-syllabic [ĕ], an allophone of /e/, does not seem to be noted in the Siebs, but it occurs commonly in fast pronunciations of such a word as Petroleum: [peˈtroːlĕu̯m], beside slower [peˈtroːle̯u̯m]. The second, non-syllabic [ŏ], an allophone of /o/, is common in words borrowed from French. The <u>Siebs</u> notes it in such examples as the following:

[bu̯'dŏa̱ːr]	Boudoir	[kŏa'föːr]	Coiffeur
[me̱'mŏa̱ːrən]	Memoiren	[tŏa'lętə]	Toilette
['pŏęⁿtə]	Pointe	[lŏa'ja̱ːl]	loyal

7.8 ORAL VS. NASALIZED

The vowels and diphthongs which we have described thus far are all normally spoken with the velic closed and are therefore oral. Nasalized vowels occur in German only in a few words borrowed from French. Their approximate phonetic qualities, and the phonemic interpretation which we can give to them, are illustrated by the following examples:

[æ^n] = /ę^n/ in /'tę^n/ <u>Teint</u>, /ba'sę^n/ <u>Bassin</u>

[a^n] = /a̱^{n}/ in /'ša̱^{n}sə/ <u>Chance</u>, /ręsto̱'ra̱^{n}/ <u>Restaurant</u>

[o^n] = /o̱^{n}/ in /sa'lo̱^{n}/ <u>Salon</u>, /ba'lo̱^{n}/ <u>Ballon</u>

[ö̧^{n}] = /ö̧^{n}/ in /vęr'dö̧/ <u>Verdun</u>

Two remarks need to be made about the use of these vowels. In the first place, nasalized vowels carry with them an air of elegance and foreignness, and many German speakers feel a bit uncomfortable in using them. It is therefore very common to substitute for any nasalized vowel the corresponding oral vowel plus /ŋ/: /ba'sęŋ/, /ręsto̱'ra̱ŋ/, /ba'lo̱ŋ/, /vęr'dö̧ŋ/. The <u>Siebs</u> condemns this practice; some speakers consider it just a touch vulgar; but many other speakers find it the only natural thing to do. Second, as a given word comes more and more into general use ("bei fortschreitender Eindeutschung," as the <u>Siebs</u> puts it), its nasalized vowel is usually replaced in one of two ways. Sometimes the use of an oral vowel plus /ŋ/ gains acceptance. The <u>Siebs</u>, for example, apparently approves of the pronunciations /bę'to̱ŋ/ <u>Beton</u> and /va'go̱ŋ/ <u>Waggon</u>. Perhaps more often, a German spelling pronunciation is given to the word. Pronunciations such as /bal'ko̱n/ <u>Balkon</u> and /ko̱m'fo̱r/ <u>Komfort</u> are entirely acceptable, beside the more foreign /bal'ko̱^{n}/ and /ko̧^{n}'fo̱r/.

7.9 UNSTRESSED VOWELS

In discussing the dimension short—long, we noted that all of the tense and lax vowels of German can occur both stressed and unstressed—the only irregularity being that the opposition /a/—/a̱/ is suspended in unstressed position. We need now to discuss a vowel phoneme which occurs <u>only</u> in unstressed position, the /ə/. It has two rather different allophones. In forms like the following it is a very lax mid unrounded vowel, central but tending toward front:

[gə'nau]	genau	['reːdətə]	redete	['va̱rtətə]	wartete

Before /m n ŋ l r/, on the other hand, it may show either thı̣   me allophone or an allophone which can best be described as "syllabicity of the follow   :onsonant." Examples:

tippen	/'tɪpən/	= ['tɪpən]	or	/'tɪpəm/	= ['tɪp^{N}m̩]
bitten	/'bɪtən/	= ['bɪtən]	or		['bɪt^{N}n̩]
backen	/'bakən/	= ['bakən]	or	/'bakəŋ/	= ['bak^{N}ŋ̩]
Mittel	/'mɪtəl/	= ['mɪtəl]	or		['mɪt^{L}l̩]
bitter	/'bɪtər/	= ['bɪtəʀ]	or		['bɪtʌ]
		['bɪtəř]	or		['bɪtʌ]

Roughly speaking, the forms with [ə] (['tɪpən], ['bɪtən], etc.) are characteristic of slow and/or formal speech, whereas the forms without [ə] (['tɪp^{N}m̩], ['bɪt^{N}n̩], etc.) are characteristic of fast and/or informal speech. The Siebs specifically warns against the forms without [ə]; but the foreign learner must expect to hear them, and he will need to learn them if he wishes to speak German as the Germans do. In particular, the use of [ʌ] for /ər/ (['bɪtʌ] etc.) is nearly universal.

7.10 THE PHONEME /ɛ/

The vowel phonemes which we have described thus far form a remarkably symmetrical pattern: six high vowels, tense /i ü u/ and lax /ɪ ü̜ u̜/; six mid vowels, tense /e ö o/ and lax /ę ö̜ ǫ/; two low vowels, tense /a/ and lax /a̧/; three diphthongs, /ai ǫi au/; and a single very lax vowel occurring only in unstressed position, /ə/. To this well integrated system of eighteen vowel phonemes we must add a nineteenth, which may occur in the stressed syllables of such words as spät, wählen, Väter, Caesar. Phonetically it has the quality of /ę/, but instead of being short it is long: [ę:]. To avoid confusion with /ę/ we shall write it as /ɛ/.

From a number of points of view this /ɛ/ is not well integrated into the German vowel system. As a stressed vowel it is anomalous because it is long but has no short counterpart. As an unstressed vowel it is doubly anomalous: if long, it is the only phonetically long vowel to occur in unstressed position; and if short, it is phonetically [ę] and hence not /ɛ/ but simply /ę/. Even the Siebs is not quite sure how to handle it. In stressed position it prescribes long /ɛ/ = [ę:] wherever the letter ä is to be pronounced long. This, at least, is consistent. But in unstressed position it sometimes prescribes long /ɛ/ = [ę:], sometimes short /ɛ/ = /ę/. Examples:

/ɛ/ = [ę:]		/ɛ/ = /ę/	
[mɛ:'na̧:də]	Mänade	[dę'mo:nən]	Dämonen
[drɛ:'ni̧:rən]	dränieren	[plę'di̧:rən]	plädieren
[pɛ:'ǫ:nĭə]	Päonie	[prę'a̧mbəl]	Präambel
[fɛ:no̧'tü:p]	Phänotyp	[fɛno̧'mę:n]	Phänomen
[prɛ:'zęnts]	Präsenz	[prę'zęnt]	Präsent

Speakers of German vary widely in their use of /ɛ/. Probably all educated speakers use long /ɛ/ = [ę:] as the name of the letter ä, and as a device for distinguishing such forms as währen /'vɛrən/ = ['vę:rən] vs. wehren /'ve̞rən/ = ['vę:rən], or gäben /'gɛbən/ = ['gę:bən] vs. geben /'ge̞bən/ = ['ge:bən]. Otherwise, though exact details are unknown, it is probably more or less true to say that /ɛ/ is commonly used only in the South, but generally replaced by /e̞/ in the North; and that everywhere /ɛ/ is more frequent in formal (or humorous mock-formal) speech than in informal speech. This general uncertainty in the use of /ɛ/—even on the part of the Siebs—betrays its origin: an artificial phoneme of recent invention, without a phonological history, based only on the spelling system. There are many dialects with long open /ę:/ opposed to long close /e̞:/, but their use of /ę:/ bears little resemblance to the prescribed use of [ę:] = /ɛ/.

7.11 DISTRIBUTIONAL CLASSES

The above paragraphs have given a phonetic classification of the vowel phonemes of German; we now need to add a brief distributional classification. A very obvious distributional difference distinguishes /ə/ from all other vowels: it is the only vowel which never occurs in stressed position. On this basis we may divide all the vowels of German into two classes: an UNSTRESSED class, including only /ə/; and a STRESSED class, including all the others.

The stressed vowels, in turn, fall into two classes which are much more evenly matched. If we disregard a few interjections such as /'nạ/ na, /'hạ/ ha, we find that the lax vowels occur only before consonants (in "checked" position), but that the tense vowels and the diphthongs can also occur before vowels or at the end of a word (in "free" position). This distributional feature divides the stressed vowels of German into a CHECKED class and a FREE class:

Checked		Free			
/'bịn/	bin	/'tsiə/	ziehe	/'zi/	sie
/'de̞n/	denn	/'geə/	gehe	/'ze̞/	See
/'dạn/	dann	/'naə/	nahe	/'zạ/	sah
/'fɔn/	von	/'roə/	rohe	/'zo/	so
/'dụm/	dumm	/'ruə/	Ruhe	/'šụ/	Schuh
/'düṇ/	dünn	/'müə/	Mühe	/'frü/	früh
/'göṇt/	gönnt	/'flöə/	Flöhe	/'bö/	Bö
		/'raiə/	Reihe	/'bai/	bei
		/'rɔiə/	Reue	/'hɔi/	Heu
		/'rauə/	rauhe	/'bau/	Bau
		/'zɛə/	säe	/'jɛ/	jäh

To this we may add the fact that the free vowels can occur in word-final position not only when stressed (as above) but also when unstressed: /'toṇi/ Toni, /'kạfe̞/ Kaffee, /'ɔto̞/ Otto, /'lụlụ/ Lulu, etc.

7.12 TRANSCRIPTIONAL SYSTEMS

The transcriptional system which we have used thus far in the present chapter is only one of many ways in which the vowel phonemes of German can be symbolized. From a theoretical point of view, the choice of phonemic symbols is of no importance whatever. Any system will do, just as long as it is sensibly constructed, adequately described, and consistently used. From a practical point of view the particular system we choose will depend largely on two factors: (1) the medium in which it is to be used, e.g., handwriting, typewriting, or printing; and (2) the purpose for which it is to be used, e.g., as a quick and efficient phonemic transcription, as a "respelling" for pedagogical purposes, as a basis for comparison with the phonemic system of some other language, etc. Before we conclude this chapter, we need to restate the system we have been using, to compare it with the transcription used by the Siebs, to suggest a quick and easy type of transcription for classroom use (if it should be desired there), and to describe the transcription used in the preceding and following chapters.

The transcription which we have used in this chapter is as follows:

Lax			Tense			Diphthongal		Unstressed
i̧	ü̧	u̧	i̠	ü̠	u̠			ə
ẹ	ö̧	ọ	e̠	ö̠	o̠	ọi		
a̧			a̠			ai	au	Special: ɛ

The use of a hook to indicate lax vowels and of a dot to indicate tense vowels is common in German linguistic works. The use of the umlaut sign for front rounded vowels (/ü ü̧ ö ö̧/) is of course taken from the regular German spelling system.

The transcription used in the Siebs is as follows:

Lax			Tense			Diphthongal		Unstressed
I	Y	U	i(:) y(:) u(:)					ə
ɛ	œ	ɔ	e(:) ø(:) o(:)			ɔø		
a			a(:)			ae	ao	Special: ɛ(:)

This system is based on the alphabet of the International Phonetic Association. Though essentially phonemic, it is phonetic to the extent of marking the length of the tense vowels in stressed position: stressed /i:/, /e:/, etc. vs. unstressed /i/, /e/, etc.

Since the Siebs transcription is widely known, we need to explain our reasons for not using it. The fundamental purpose of this book is to compare and contrast the phonemic systems of German and English. For this purpose we need a transcriptional system which will allow us (1) to use the same symbol for phonemes which sound much the same in both languages (e.g., German /i̧/ in Sitz and English /i̧/ in sits); (2) to use similar symbols for phonemes which are similar in sound though usually not quite identical (e.g., German close /i̯/ in <u>sieht</u> vs. English neutral—and often diphthongal—/i/ in <u>seat</u>); and (3) to use different symbols for phonemes which, though comparable, are clearly different in sound (e.g., German /ǫ/ in <u>Kost</u> vs. English /ɔ/ in <u>cost</u>). In particular, we need a system of transcription which will constantly remind us of the fact that German /i̯/ and /u̯/ are higher than English /i/ and /u/ (as in <u>seat</u>, <u>toot</u>), and that German /e/ and /o/ are higher than English /e/ and /o/ (as in <u>gate</u>, <u>boat</u>). To accomplish these various purposes, and at the same time to do as little violence as possible to the traditional symbolizations of German and English phonemes, the system of hooks and dots for lax and tense vowels seems the most useful. At the same time, it allows us to symbolize clearly the important phonetic difference between German /ǫ/ in <u>Kost</u> and English /ɔ/ in <u>cost</u>; and it leaves the symbol /ɛ/ free for the special ä-vowel of German. On the use of /ai ǫi au/ where the <u>Siebs</u> writes /ae ɔø ao/, see above, §7.6.

　　Both the <u>Siebs</u> transcription and our own are needlessly complicated if what we want is a scheme that will allow us to symbolize the vowel phonemes of German in as simple a fashion as possible. For this purpose the following system serves admirably:

Lax			Tense			Diphthongal		Unstressed
i	ü	u	ī	ǖ	ū			ə
e	ö	o	ē	ȫ	ō	oi		
	a			ā		ai	au	Special: ǟ

Here the macron serves simultaneously as an indication of tenseness and as a reminder that, when stressed, the tense vowels are long. For writing on paper or on the blackboard, the macron (/ī ē ā/ etc.) is more legible and easier to write than the colon (/i: e: a:/); but the colon is of course easier to type and cheaper to print.

　　In the chapters preceding this one, and in the chapters to follow, we use the following system:

Lax			Tense			Diphthongal		Unstressed
i̯	ü̯	u̯	i̯:	ü̯:	u̯:			ə
e̯	ö̯	o̯	e̯:	ö̯:	o̯:	ǫi		
	a̯			a̯:		ai	au	Special: ɛ:

Here the opposition tense—lax, so important for German in contrast to English, is purposely overwritten: both by the use of the dot vs. the hook, and by the presence vs. the absence of the colon (or, if we were writing by hand, the macron). At the same time, the colon (or macron) serves as a reminder that these tense vowels are long when stressed.

PHONEMICS: THE VOWELS OF ENGLISH 8

8.1 VARIATIONS IN THE SYSTEM OF VOWELS

In presenting the vowel phonemes of German, we have been able to follow the standardized pronunciation of the <u>Hochsprache</u> as it is described in the <u>Siebs</u> and other similar works. This is everywhere the accepted form of the language; we do not need to mention all the deviations from it which are found in the colloquial speech of many parts of the German-speaking area. The vowel phonemes of "German" are, for us as teachers, the vowel phonemes of this accepted standard.

When we turn now to the vowel phonemes of American English, we face a very different situation. There is no one accepted standard pronunciation which alone is valid for the entire United States. Educated speakers from different parts of the country have different vowel systems, and each of them is entirely "correct" and acceptable in its particular area. The differences which we find are of four sorts:

1. Differences in the number of phonemes. For example, speakers from some areas use in one set of words, e.g. the verb <u>can</u> ('be able'), a vowel which is somewhat lower and shorter than that of another set of words, e.g. the noun <u>can</u> ('tin can'). They therefore have one more phoneme than those who pronounce both sets alike. Similarly, speakers from some areas use in one set of words, e.g. <u>whole</u>, a vowel which is somewhat lower and shorter than that of another set of words, e.g. <u>hole</u>. They, too, have one more phoneme than those who pronounce both sets alike.

2. Differences in the incidence of phonemes. Where two areas have the same number of phonemes, they may differ in the sets of words in which they use them. For example, all areas probably agree in using different vowel phonemes in <u>starry</u> and <u>story</u>. But where some areas use the vowel of <u>starry</u> in both <u>sorry</u> and <u>forest</u>, other areas use in both words the vowel of <u>story</u>, and still others use the vowel of <u>starry</u> in <u>sorry</u>, but the vowel of <u>story</u> in <u>forest</u>. Some areas rhyme <u>fog</u> and <u>dog</u>, others do not; some areas rhyme <u>boot</u> and <u>root</u>, others do not. Many of these differences in the incidence of vowel phonemes are frequent topics of popular discussion: <u>either</u> with the vowel of <u>me</u> or the vowel of <u>my</u>; <u>tomato</u> with the vowel of <u>mate</u> or the vowel of <u>mat</u> or the vowel of <u>far</u>; etc.

3. Differences in the pronunciation of phonemes. Even where two areas have

the same number of phonemes and use them in the same words, they may differ in the way they pronounce them—or, to use the technical term, they may have different DIAPHONES (geographical variants) of the same phoneme. For example, in the North and the North Midland of the Atlantic states, the /ai/ of /'faiv/ five generally shows the diaphone [aˑɪ̈]; but in most parts of the South Midland and the South it shows the diaphones [aˑᵋ] or [aˑᵊ] (sometimes popularly written as "fahv"). Similarly, the /ɔ/ of /'lɔ/ law is a close or open low back vowel in most of the North and the Midland; but in much of the South it is the diphthong [ɔᵊ].

    4. Indeterminacies within the system. In probably all varieties of American English there are parts of the vowel system which are not entirely clear. For example, when the form gonna (as in I'm gonna go) is stressed, does it have the same stressed vowel as the word goner, or as the word gunner, or is it different from both of them? Or: when the word really is stressed, does it have the same stressed vowel as the word mealy, or as the word hilly, or is it different from both of them? For some speakers it is possible to give a clear answer to questions of this sort, but for others it is not.

    Since it is impossible to present a vowel system which is valid for all standard speakers of American English, some sort of compromise system has to be used instead. In the following discussion we shall present a system which, with one exception, includes only those stressed vowel contrasts which seem to be shared by all Americans. That is to say, we shall include such contrasts as those between beat and bit, between bit and bait, etc.; but we shall exclude such contrasts, of limited geographical distribution, as those between (I) can and (tin) can, between whole and hole, between bomb and balm, etc. The one exception concerns the contrast between such words as cot and caught, collar and caller, pa and paw, etc. Though there are large areas in which these pairs of words rhyme and hence all have the same vowel phoneme, the majority of Americans distinguish them from one another and hence use two different phonemes.

8.2 PHONEMIC CONTRASTS

    In stressed position, most Americans have the following fifteen contrasting vowels and diphthongs. The phonemic symbols used for them in this table are intended only to suggest approximate phonetic qualities; allophonic and diaphonic details will be discussed in the following sections. The special problem of vowels before /r/ will be dealt with in §8.7.

						Before /r/	
1.	/i/	beat	leak	dean	nearer	} here	fierce
2.	/i̧/	bit	lick	din	mirror		
3.	/e/	bait	lake	Dane	Mary		
4.	/ȩ/	bet	neck	den	merry	} hair	scarce
5.	/æ/	bat	lack	Dan	marry		
6.	/a/	pot	lock	Don	starry	far	farce
7.	/ɔ/	bought	hawk	dawn	warring	for	horse
8.	/o/	boat	soak	bone	boring	four	hoarse

9.	/ʉ/	put	look		fury	} tour	moors
10.	/u/	boot	Luke	boon	poorer		
11.	/ʌ/	but	luck	bun	hurry		
12.	/ɝ/	Bert	lurk	burn	furry		
13.	/ai/	bite	like	dine	Shirer		
14.	/ɔi/	Hoyt		coin	Moira	coir	coirs
15.	/au/	bout		down	Lowry	hour	sours

In addition, English has a sixteenth vowel phoneme which occurs only in unstressed syllables:

16.	/ə/	a̲bout	gall o̲p	comm a̲

8.3 PRELIMINARY CLASSIFICATION

Using the dimensions high—low and front—back, we can plot the first twelve of these contrasts as follows:

	Front	Central	Back
High	i ɨ		u ʉ
Mid	e ę	ɜ ʌ	o
Low	æ a		ɔ

We may note that lip-rounding is not a distinctive feature in the English vowel system: there are no pairs of vowels which are distinguished solely by the fact that one is unrounded, the other rounded (as is the case with German /iː/—/üː/, /ɨ/—/ü/, etc.). By and large, the front and central vowels of English (including back-central /ʌ/) are unrounded, and the back vowels are rounded. But central /ɜ/, as in /ˈhɜ/ her̲, often has considerable lip-rounding; and the back vowels often have very little lip-rounding.

8.4 TENSE VS. LAX

Unlike German, English does not show any consistent opposition between tense and lax vowels, but makes only partial use of differences in muscular tension:

Tense	Lax
/i/ in feel	/i̧/ in fill
/e/ in fail	/e̦/ in fell
/u/ in fool	/u̧/ in full
/o/ in hole	/o̧/ . . . .[1]

Furthermore, the nature of the tense—lax opposition is somewhat different in English. Instead of being largely an opposition between decentralized and centralized, it is to a considerable extent also an opposition between diphthongal and monophthongal. This aspect of the opposition will be discussed in §8.6

8.5 SHORT VS. LONG

We may recall that, in stressed position, the tense vowels of German are clearly longer than the lax vowels. To a certain extent this is true in English also: the tense /i e u/ of beat, bait, boot tend to be slightly longer than the lax /i̧ e̦ u̧/ of bit, bet, put. Far more striking, however, are the differences in duration which are conditioned by the nature of what follows the vowel. Roughly speaking, stressed vowels are (1) short before voiceless consonants, (2) half-long before voiced consonants, and (3) long in word-final position. Examples:

	Short		Half-long		Long	
1.	['lif]	leaf	['li˙v]	leave	['li:]	lee
2.	['hi̧s]	hiss	['hi̧˙z]	his		
3.	['let]	late	['le˙d]	laid	['le:]	lay
4.	['se̦t]	set	['se̦˙d]	said		
5.	['næp]	nap	['næ˙b]	nab		
6.	['pat]	pot	['pa˙d]	pod	['pa:]	pa
7.	['kɔt]	caught	['kɔ˙d]	cawed	['kɔ:]	caw
8.	['rop]	rope	['ro˙b]	robe	['ro:]	roe
9.	['pu̧t]	put	['gu̧˙d]	good		
10.	['lus]	loose	['lu˙z]	lose	['lu:]	Lou
11.	['mʌt]	mutt	['mʌ˙d]	mud		
12.	['bɜt]	Bert	['bɜ˙d]	bird	['bɜ:]	burr
13.	['rais]	rice	['ra˙iz]	rise	['ra:i]	rye
14.	['bɔis]	Boyce	['bɔ˙iz]	boys	['bɔ:i]	boy
15.	['haus]	(the) house	['ha˙uz]	(to) house	['ha:u]	how

---

1. This lax vowel occurs only in the speech of those New Englanders and New York State speakers who make a contrast between /'hol/ hole and /'ho̧l/ whole, between /'rod/ rode and /'ro̧d/ road, between /'on/ own and /'sto̧n/ stone, etc. /o̧/ is often called the "New England short o."

The above is perhaps the usual distribution of short, half-long, and long vowels. But it is equally important to note that, in effect, any vowel phoneme in English can be long. Probably everywhere in the country vowels can become long through what we may call "expressive lengthening." For example, the vowel of bit occurs before a voiceless conconant and is therefore usually short: ['bɪt]. But a speaker who wishes to give special emphasis to the word bit may do so, among other things, by lengthening its vowel: ['nat ə 'bɪ̥:t] not a BIT. Even aside from such expressive lengthening, long vowels are common in those parts of the country where the speakers are said to "drawl." Here any stressed vowel can be lengthened: ['na:t ə 'bɪ̥:t 'be̥:tɜ] not a bit better, rather than ['nat ə 'bɪt 'be̥tɜ]. Such drawling is particularly common with the low vowels [æ a ɔ]: show me the hat with ['hæ:t]; put it on top with ['ta:p]; look what I bought with ['bɔ:t].

8.6 MONOPHTHONGAL VS. DIPHTHONGAL

The phonetic transcriptions given in the preceding section are deficient in one very important respect: they fail to indicate the amount of diphthongization which occurs especially when vowels are lengthened. This diphthongization is the one feature of American English speech which impresses foreign observers most strongly. The first reaction of a Frenchman, German, or Italian with phonetic training is likely to be that many speakers of American English do not use any monophthongs at all but speak exclusively in diphthongs. This is of course not true; but diphthongization is so widespread a phenomenon that it deserves our careful attention.

We need to examine first the phonemes that we have symbolized as /i e ai/, as in beat, bait, bite, and /u o au/, as in boot, boat, bout. This symbolization, which is traditional in most writings on American English, suggests that the first two phonemes in each set are monophthongs and that only the third is a diphthong. A more accurate statement would be: /i/ and /u/ are diphthongs in some environments; /e/ and /o/ are diphthongs in most environments; and /ai/ and /au/ are diphthongs in all environments. Roughly speaking, diphthongization increases along two dimensions: first, along the dimension "high—mid—low," as we go from /i/ to /e/ to /ai/ (beat, bait, bite), or from /u/ to /o/ to /au/ (boot, boat, bout); and second, along the dimension "short—half-long—long," as we go from [e] to [e˙] to [e:] (mate, made, may), or from [o] to [o˙] to [o:] (rope, robe, roe). The following table is an attempt to show this:

		Short		Half-long		Long	
High	/i/	['lit]	Leet	['li˙ᶦd]	lead	['li:i]	lee
Mid	/e/	['leᶦt]	late	['le˙id]	laid	['le:i]	lay
Low	/ai/	['lait]	light	['la˙id]	lied	['la:i]	lie
High	/u/	['rut]	root	['ru˙ᵘd]	rude	['ru:u]	rue
Mid	/o/	['roᵘt]	wrote	['ro˙ud]	rode	['ro:u]	roe
Low	/au	['raut]	rout	['ra˙ud]	rowed ('fought')	['ra:u]	row ('fight')

In some parts of the country a similar diphthongization also affects lengthened /e̥/, /æ/, and /ɔ/: <u>beg</u> is ['be̞ⁱg], <u>bag</u> is ['bæⁱg], <u>dog</u> is ['dɔᵒg].

The diphthongizations described thus far are all of the type known as "upgliding," that is, the glide is upward toward a higher (front or back) tongue position. But "ingliding" (or "centering") diphthongs also occur, that is, glides inward toward a mid central position. Examples:

$$/i̞/ \quad = \quad [i̞^ə] \text{ as in ['bi̞}^ə\text{d] } \underline{bid}$$
$$/e̞/ \quad = \quad [e̞^ə] \text{ as in ['be̞}^ə\text{d] } \underline{bed}$$
$$/æ/ \quad = \quad [æ^ə] \text{ as in ['bæ}^ə\text{d] } \underline{bad}$$
$$/ɔ/ \quad = \quad [ɔ^ə] \text{ as in ['lɔ}^ə\text{] } \underline{law}$$
$$/u̞/ \quad = \quad [u̞^ə] \text{ as in ['gu̞}^ə\text{d] } \underline{good}$$

This type of diphthong is especially common after front vowels before the typical American velarized [ɫ]:

$$/i/ \quad = \quad [i^ə] \text{ as in ['fi}^ə\text{ɫ] } \underline{feel}$$
$$/i̞/ \quad = \quad [i̞^ə] \text{ as in ['fi̞}^ə\text{ɫ] } \underline{fill}$$
$$/e/ \quad = \quad [ei̞^ə] \text{ as in ['fei̞}^ə\text{ɫ] } \underline{fail}$$
$$/e̞/ \quad = \quad [e̞^ə] \text{ as in ['fe̞}^ə\text{ɫ] } \underline{fell}$$
$$/æ/ \quad = \quad [æ^ə] \text{ as in ['pæ}^ə\text{ɫ] } pal$$

Before we leave the subject of diphthongs, a few words need to be said about common allophones and diaphones of /ai ɔi au/.

1. /ai/. The starting point of the glide in /ai/ may be low front, approaching [æi̞]; or low central: [ai̞]; or low back, approaching [ɔi̞]; or it may be mid central: [əi̞]. The distance of the glide may be relatively great: [ai̞]; or it may be relatively slight and either upgliding: [aᶜ], or ingliding: [aᵊ]. Parts of the South show complementary distribution between [əi̞] before voiceless consonants: ['rəi̞t] <u>right</u>, vs. [a·ᶜ] etc. elsewhere: ['ra·ᶜd] <u>ride</u>.

2. /ɔi/. The starting point of the glide in /ɔi/ may be close low back: [ɔi̞], or mid back: [oi̞]. The distance of the glide may be relatively great: [ɔi̞]; or it may be relatively slight and either upgliding: [ɔᶜ], or ingliding: [ɔᵊ].

3. /au/. The starting point of the glide in /au/ may be low central: [au̞]; or low front: [æu̞]; or mid front: [e̞u]; or it may be mid central: [əu̞]. Again, parts of the South show complementary distribution between [əu̞] before voiceless consonants: ['həu̞s] <u>house</u>, vs. [a·u̞] etc. elsewhere: ['ha·u̞zi̞z] <u>houses</u>.

The above is by no means an exhaustive description of the allophones and diaphones of /ai ɔi au/, but merely a suggestion of the different types which occur. Our purpose is to alert the teacher to the kinds of American diphthongs his students may use and hence to the kinds which they may carry over into German.

8.7 STRESSED VOWELS BEFORE /r/

In the table of phonemic contrasts in §8.2, we listed examples of twelve vowel phonemes (excluding /ai ɔi au/) before intervocalic /r/, and of six vowel phonemes before postvocalic /r/ (i.e., /r/ in word-final position, or /r/ before consonant). Though some Americans actually have this many contrasts, most do not. The matter needs to be considered in some detail—both as regards the vowels which contrast with one another before /r/ and as regards the allophones which they show in this position.

Leaving aside the phonemes /ai ɔi au/, which present no special problems, we find vowel contrasts which can perhaps best be diagrammed as follows, in the shape of the vowel quadrilateral:

Before intervocalic /r/			Before postvocalic /r/	
{ nearer mirror }		{ poorer fury }	fear	poor
{ { Mary merry } marry }	{ furry hurry }	{ boring warring }	fair	{ four for }
	starry		far	

We may consider first the vowel contrasts found before intervocalic /r/.

1. In some areas (much of the Atlantic seaboard, for example) the opposition /i/−/ɪ/ is maintained before intervocalic /r/: /'nirɜ/ nearer vs. /'mɪrɜ/ mirror. Elsewhere the opposition /i/−/ɪ/ is neutralized before intervocalic /r/, and one and the same vowel phoneme is used in both words (and others like them). Such a phoneme, representing the neutralization of an opposition found in other positions, is called by European phonologists an ARCHIPHONEME and customarily symbolized by a capital letter. Hence we may say that, before intervocalic /r/, the opposition /i/−/ɪ/ is represented in most of the country by the archiphoneme /I/: /'nIrɜ/ nearer, like /'mIrɜ/ mirror.

2. In parts of the Atlantic seaboard the double opposition /e/−/ę/−/æ/ is maintained before intervocalic /r/: /'meri/ Mary vs. /'męri/ merry vs. /'mæri/ marry. In some parts of the East (Pennsylvania, for example) the opposition /e/−/ę/ is neutralized: /'mEri/ Mary like /'mEri/ merry, but still opposed to /'mæri/ marry. In the rest of the country both oppositions are neutralized: /'mEri/ = /'mEri/ = /'mEri/ Mary, merry, marry.

3. Everywhere in the country a low vowel /a/ occurs before intervocalic /r/, as in /'stari/ starry, /'barɪŋ/ barring, etc. The variation which we find here is not in the occurrence of this phoneme before /r/, but rather in its incidence. Some areas use /ar/ also in such words as sorry, borrow, or orange, forest; others use it in sorry, borrow but not in orange, forest; and still others use it in none of these words and others like them.

4. In some areas (for example, the Atlantic states except for the Midland area), the opposition /o/−/ɔ/ is maintained before intervocalic /r/: /'borɪŋ/ boring vs. /'worɪŋ/ warring. Elsewhere the opposition is neutralized, and the archiphoneme /O/ is used: /'bOrɪŋ/ boring like /'wOrɪŋ/ warring.

5. Data are not available on areas in which the opposition /u/−/ʉ/ is maintained, as in /'pur3/ poorer vs. /'fjʉri/ fury. It seems probable, however, that the archiphoneme /U/ is used in a large part of the country: /'pUr3/ poorer like /'fjUri/ fury.

6. In parts of the Atlantic seaboard (Metropolitan New York and vicinity, plus scattered points in New England and the South), the opposition /3/−/ʌ/ (with /3/ = non-constricted [ɜ]) is maintained before intervocalic /r/: /'f3ri/ furry vs. /'hʌri/ hurry. Elsewhere the vowel /3/ (with /3/ here = constricted [ɝ]) is used in both words and others like them: /'f3i/ furry like /'h3i/ hurry.

The above analysis shows that, excluding /ai ɔi au/, American English has before intervocalic /r/ a maximum of twelve stressed vowel phonemes and a minimum of five:

Maximum				Minimum	
i			u		
				I	U
ị			ʉ̣		
e	3		o		
				E	O
ẹ		ʌ			
æ			ɔ		
	a				a

The above applies to intervocalic /r/. When we turn now to postvocalic /r/ we find that, by and large, only the minimum system diagrammed above is used, whether before word-final /r/ or before /r/ plus consonant:

/I/	/E/	/a/	/O/	/U/
beer	bare	bar	bore	boor
fierce	scarce	farce	force	moors
weird	dared	hard	board	toured

However, in a considerable part of the country the opposition /o/−/ɔ/ is more or less consistently maintained. It occurs in such pairs as:

/o/	four	wore	more	mourn	hoarse	oar
/ɔ/	for	war	nor	morn	horse	or

Thus far we have spoken only of vowel contrasts before /r/, with no mention of the allophones used in this position. Though it is impossible to treat this complicated topic fully here, we need to mention those allophones which are most troublesome when carried over into German. The one outstanding difficulty is the fact that, in almost all parts of the country, only open [ị ʉ̣ ẹ ọ] are used before /r/, never neutral [i u e o], much less close [i̭ ṷ ḙ o̭]. In areas which preserve the oppositions /i/−/ị/, /u/−/ʉ/, /e/−/ẹ/, /o/−/ɔ/, these phonemes often show the following allophones before intervocalic /r/:

/i/ = [ị˙] or [ị^ə] in <u>nearer</u>　　　/ị/ = [ị] in <u>mirror</u>

/u/ = [ụ˙] or [ụ^ə] in <u>poorer</u>　　　/ụ/ = [ụ] in <u>fury</u>

/e/ = [ẹ˙] or [ẹ^ə] in <u>Mary</u>　　　/ẹ/ = [ẹ] in <u>merry</u>

/o/ = [ọ˙] or [ọ^ə] in <u>boring</u>　　　/ɔ/ = [ɔ˙] in <u>warring</u>

With this we may compare the allophones which these same phonemes typically show before other consonants:

/i/ = [i] or [iⁱ] in <u>leaner</u>　　　/ị/ = [ị] in <u>thinner</u>

/u/ = [u] or [u^u˙] in <u>cooler</u>　　　/ụ/ = [ụ] in <u>fully</u>

/e/ = [eⁱ] or [eị] in <u>rainy</u>　　　/ẹ/ = [ẹ] in <u>penny</u>

/o/ = [o^u] or [oụ] in <u>boning</u>　　　/ɔ/ = [ɔ˙] in <u>dawning</u>

Though the allophones of /ị ụ ẹ ɔ/ are much the same in both cases, the allophones of /i u e o/ are markedly different. Before most consonants they are short neutral vowels or upgliding diphthongs; but before /r/ they are half-long open vowels or open ingliding diphthongs.

Where the oppositions /i/—/ị/, /u/—/ụ/, /e/—/ẹ/, /o/—/ɔ/ are neutralized before intervocalic /r/, the resulting archiphonemes vary in length, but they are always open:

/I/ = [ị˙] or [ị] in <u>nearer</u>, <u>mirror</u>

/U/ = [ụ˙] or [ụ] in <u>poorer</u>, <u>fury</u>

/E/ = [ẹ˙] or [ẹ] in <u>Mary</u>, <u>merry</u>

/O/ = [ọ˙] or [ọ]

　　　or [ɔ˙] or [ɔ] in <u>boring</u>, <u>warring</u>

Both groups of speakers—those who neutralize before /r/ and those who do not—will have serious difficulties in learning to pronounce German, where the tense—lax opposition is consistently maintained before intervocalic /r/ and shows the same phonetic qualities of close-and-long vs. open-and-short as before other consonants: /iː/—/ị/ in /ˈịːrə/ <u>ihre</u> vs. /ˈịrə/ <u>irre</u>, /eː/—/ẹ/ in /ˈleːrə/ <u>lehre</u> vs. /ˈšpẹrə/ <u>sperre</u>, etc. American speakers who neutralize are quite lacking in such an opposition before intervocalic /r/ and will have to learn to make it; and even those speakers who do not neutralize will have to learn to make the opposition in a phonetically different way: close-and-long vs. open-and-short rather than open-and-long (or open-and-ingliding) vs. open-and-short.

Before postvocalic /r/ all Americans neutralize, excepting only those who keep the opposition /o/—/ɔ/ as in <u>hoarse</u> vs. <u>horse</u>. The resulting archiphonemes are phonetically fairly long in some areas, short in others; but almost everywhere they are again open rather than close:

/I/ = [i̯ˑ] or [i̯] in <u>fear</u>
/U/ = [u̯ˑ] or [u̯] in <u>poor</u>
/E/ = [e̯ˑ] or [e̯] in <u>fair</u>
/O/ $\begin{cases} /o/ = [o̯ˑ] \text{ or } [o̯] \text{ in } \underline{four} \\ /ɔ/ = [ɔ̯ˑ] \text{ or } [ɔ̯] \text{ in } \underline{for} \end{cases}$

In this position all speakers of American English will have difficulties in learning German, since it maintains the tense—lax opposition just as consistently before /r/ as before other consonants: /iː/−/i̯/ in /'viːr/ <u>wir</u> vs. /'vi̯r/ <u>wirr</u>, /eː/−/e̯/ in /'heːr/ <u>her</u> vs. /'he̯r/ <u>Herr</u>, etc. The fact that many Americans preserve the opposition /o/−/ɔ/ before postvocalic /r/ (<u>four</u> vs. <u>for</u>, etc.) will be of little help in learning German, since the phonetic nature of the oppositions is quite different in the two languages: American [o̯(ˑ)]−[ɔ̯(ˑ)], but German [oː]−[ɔ̯], as in <u>bohrt</u> vs. <u>Bord</u>.

The above remarks on postvocalic /r/ refer to the pronunciation that is used in most of the United States, by over two-thirds of the total population. But along much of the Atlantic seaboard—in Eastern New England, in Metropolitan New York, and in the greater part of the South—there are millions of speakers who do not use postvocalic /r/. Roughly speaking, instead of [ar] and [ɔr] these speakers have lengthened [aː] and [ɔː]; and instead of the other vowels plus /r/ they have vowel plus non-syllabic [ə̯]. Examples:

		General	Seaboard			General	Seaboard
here	=	['hi̯(ˑ)r]	['hi̯ˑə̯]	beard	=	['bi̯(ˑ)rd]	['bi̯ˑə̯d]
care	=	['ke̯(ˑ)r]	['ke̯ˑə̯]	stairs	=	['ste̯(ˑ)rz]	['ste̯ˑə̯z]
car	=	['ka(ˑ)r]	['kaː]	barn	=	['ba(ˑ)rn]	['baːn]
for	=	['fɔ(ˑ)r]	['fɔː]	horse	=	['hɔ(ˑ)rs]	['hɔːs]
four	=	['fo̯(ˑ)r]	['fo̯ˑə̯]	hoarse	=	['ho̯(ˑ)rs]	['ho̯ˑə̯s]
poor	=	['pu̯(ˑ)r]	['pu̯ˑə̯]	moors	=	['mu̯(ˑ)rz]	['mu̯ˑə̯z]

Furthermore, in parts of the South the high vowels are lowered to [e] and [o] before [ə̯]: <u>here</u> and <u>beard</u> are ['he̯ˑə̯], ['be̯ˑə̯d]; <u>poor</u> and <u>sure</u> are ['po̯ˑə̯], ['šo̯ˑə̯] or, with loss of [ə̯], ['po], ['šo].

In two respects these Atlantic seaboard speakers have an advantage over others in learning German. First, many of them have an /a/−/aː/ opposition, as in /'kat/ <u>cot</u> vs. /'kaːt/ <u>cart</u>, or /'mak/ <u>mock</u> vs. /'maːk/ <u>mark</u>. This makes it considerably easier for them to learn the German /a̯/−/a̯ː/ opposition, as in /'šta̯t/ <u>Stadt</u> vs. /'šta̯ːt/ <u>Staat</u>, or /'ha̯kən/ <u>Hacken</u> vs. /'ha̯ːkən/ <u>Haken</u>. Second, the [ə̯] which they use in ['hi̯ˑə̯] <u>here</u> etc. is very similar to the [ʌ] of German ['hiːʌ] <u>hier</u> etc. However, the problems of vowel quality before German /r/ still remain, since these speakers use neutral (or even open) [i u e o] in ['hi̯ˑə̯ 'pu̯ˑə̯ 'e̯ˑə̯ 'o̯ˑə̯] <u>here</u>, <u>poor</u>, <u>air</u>, <u>oar</u> rather than the close [iː uː eː oː] of German ['hiːʌ 'fuːʌ 'eːʌ 'oːʌ] <u>hier</u>, <u>fuhr</u>, <u>er</u>, <u>Ohr</u>.

8.8 ORAL VS. NASALIZED

Some Americans use nasalized vowels more or less consistently in a few words borrowed from French, for example in [fia^{n}'sei] <u>fiancé(e)</u>. Except for such rather rare forms, however, nasalization is not a distinctive feature of English vowels, that is, it is not used to distinguish a set of nasalized vowel phonemes from a set of oral vowel phonemes. This being the case, Americans are free to nasalize vowels as they wish—and many of them take full advantage of this freedom. In some areas, sporadic nasalization of any and all vowels is common; elsewhere nasalization occurs more or less commonly in the pronunciation of individual speakers.

Very widespread is the nasalization of vowels before a following nasal consonant. Forms such as <u>bent</u>, <u>can't</u>, <u>hunt</u>, phonemically /'bent/, /'kænt/, /'hʌnt/, are often phonetically ['be^{n}nt], ['kæ^{n}nt], ['hʌ^{n}nt], with nasalized vowels before the [n]; or the [n] may drop out entirely, leaving only a nasalized vowel: ['be^{n}t], ['kæ^{n}t], ['hʌ^{n}t]. Americans react to all three pronunciations—['bent], ['be^{n}nt], ['be^{n}t]—as "the same," namely /'bent/.

8.9 UNSTRESSED VOWELS

We saw in chapter 7 some of the ways in which stress affects the German vowel system. In stressed position tense vowels are long and lax vowels are short; but in unstressed position both sets of vowels are short. Further, in stressed position all standard speakers make a consistent distinction between tense and lax vowels; but in unstressed position all speakers give up the distinction between tense /a:/ and lax /a/, and many speakers frequently give up the other tense—lax distinctions as well. Nevertheless, except for /a:/–/a/, all stressed vowels also occur in unstressed position, and the tendency to suspend vowel oppositions in unstressed position affects only the opposition tense—lax and not, for example, such oppositions as high—mid, front—back, etc.

The occurrence of unstressed vowels in American English is a far more complicated matter, and one that cannot be described in a few paragraphs. We shall mention here only a few points which need to be covered in any comparison of English and German.

In word-final unstressed syllables, English shows seven contrasting vowels. One of them occurs only in checked syllables (ending in a consonant); the remaining six occur also in free syllables (ending in the vowel itself). Examples:

	Checked[1]		Free	
/i̧/	/'kændi̧d/	candid	. . . .	
/i/	/'kændid/	candied	/'kændi/	candy
/e/	/'mʌndez/	Mondays	/'mʌnde/	Monday
/o/	/'ekoz/	echoes	/'eko/	echo
/u/	/'i̧šuz/	issues	/'i̧šu/	issue
/ɜ/	/'kʌvɜz/	covers	/'kʌvɜ/	cover
/ə/	/'sofəz/	sofas	/'sofə/	sofa

1. Two additional unstressed checked vowels which occur in very few forms are /u̧/, as in /'ɔfu̧l/ <u>awful</u> (beside /'ɔfəl/) and /ʌ/, as in /'hi̧kʌp/ <u>hiccup</u> (beside /'hi̧kəp/).

The unstressed vowel of <u>candid</u> can be equated with the stressed /ɨ/ of <u>did</u> etc.; and, like stressed /ɨ/, it occurs only in checked syllables. The unstressed vowels of <u>candy</u>, <u>Monday</u>, <u>echo</u>, <u>issue</u>, <u>cover</u> are clearly /i e o u ɜ/; and, like stressed /i e o u ɜ/, they occur in both free and checked syllables. The unstressed vowel of <u>sofa</u> is usually farther front than stressed /ʌ/, but still close enough so that it might be considered as the unstressed allophone of /ʌ/. On the other hand, this unstressed vowel occurs regularly in both checked and free syllables, whereas stressed /ʌ/ occurs only in checked syllables. We shall therefore consider it to be a separate phoneme /ə/.

Unstressed /ɜ/ is limited to the speech of those who have postvocalic /r/, as in /'kar/ <u>car</u>, /'barn/ <u>barn</u>. Those Atlantic seaboard speakers who lack postvocalic /r/ and say /'kaː/ <u>car</u>, /'baːn/ <u>barn</u>, also lack unstressed /ɜ/. <u>Cover</u> is for them /'kʌvə/, <u>covers</u> is /'kʌvəz/, etc. It is not known how many speakers use unstressed /e/ in <u>Monday</u>, <u>Tuesday</u>, etc. Many speakers say /'mʌnˌde/, with /e/ in a syllable bearing secondary stress; others say /'mʌndi/, with unstressed /i/ rather than /e/.

In unstressed syllables other than those at the end of a word, probably all vowels can occur in careful speech. A public speaker, for example, may pronounce <u>affect</u> as /æ'fɛkt/, with /æ-/, and thus distinguish it from <u>effect</u> /ɛ'fɛkt/, with /ɛ-/. In informal speech, however, American English shows a strong tendency toward using in non-final unstressed syllables only the single vowel /ə/. The various vowel oppositions of stressed position are here all neutralized in a single mid central unstressed vowel:

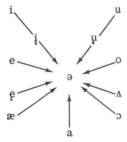

Compare the following forms, in which the various "full" vowels of stressed syllables are all replaced by /ə/ when the stress shifts to the following syllable:

Stressed			Unstressed		
/i/	/'diˌtelz/	details	/i/	/di'telz/	details
			or /ɨ/	/dɨ'telz/	
			or /ə/	/də'telz/	
/e/	/'ebəl/	able	/ə/	/ə'bɨləti/	ability
/ɛ/	/'dɛməˌkræt/	democrat	/ə/	/də'makrəsi/	democracy
/æ/	/'ætəm/	atom	/ə/	/ə'tamɨk/	atomic
/a/	/'prafɨt/	prophet	/ə/	/prə'fɛtɨk/	prophetic
/ɔ/	/'ɔθɜ/	author	/ə/	/ə'θarəti/	authority

Stressed			Unstressed		
/ʌ/	/ˈkʌmiŋ/	coming	/ə/	/kəmˈan/	come on
/o/	/ˈpro͵tɛst/	(the) protest	/ə/	/prəˈtɛst/	(to) protest
/u/	/ˈjunịt/	unit	/u/	/juˈnait/	unite
			or /ụ/	/jụˈnait/	
			or /ə/	/jəˈnait/	

This replacement of stressed vowels by unstressed /ə/ takes place only before consonants. When a vowel follows, the vowel of stressed position is kept in unstressed position as well:

Stressed			Unstressed		
/i/	/ˈriəl/	real	/i/	/riˈæləti/	reality
/e/	/ˈke͵as/	chaos	/e/	/keˈatịk/	chaotic
/o/	/ˈko͵ap/	co-op	/o/	/koˈapə͵ret/	co-operate
/u/	/ˈduəl/	dual	/u/	/duˈæləti/	duality

English also has a class of monosyllabic words, few in number but frequent in occurrence, which have phonemically different stressed and unstressed forms. The stressed forms have "full" vowels, the unstressed forms have /ə/:

Stressed			Unstressed		
/i/	/ˈði/	the	/ə/	/ðə ˈpič/	the peach
/e/	/ˈe/	a	/ə/	/ə ˈpič/	a peach
/æ/	/ˈæn/	an	/ə/	/ən ˈæpəl/	an apple
/æ/	/ˈænd/	and	/ə/	/ˈju ən ˈai/	you and I
/æ/	/ˈkæn/	can	/ə/	/ˈhi kən ˈgo/	he can go
/æ/	/ˈhæv/	have	/ə/	/ˈkụd ə(v) ˈgɔn/	could've gone
/ʌ/	/ˈʌv/	of	/ə/	/ˈkʌp ə(v) ˈkɔfi/	cup of coffee
/ẹ/	/ˈðẹm/	them	/ə/	/ˈlɛt əm ˈgo/	let 'em go
/u/	/ˈdu/	do	/ə/	/ˈhwɛn də ͵ðe ˈliv/	when do they leave?
/u/	/ˈtu/	to	/ə/	/tə ˈdrịŋk/	to drink
/u/	/ˈju/	you	/ə/	/ịf jə ˈdrịŋk/	if you drink

Here again, if a vowel follows, the vowel of stressed position is usually kept in unstressed position:

Stressed			Unstressed		
/i/	/ˈði/	the	/i/	/ði ˈæpəl/	the apple
/u/	/ˈdu/	do	/u/	/ˈhwɛn du ͵ai ˈliv/	when do I leave?

	Stressed			Unstressed	
/u/	/'tu/	to	/u/	/tu 'it/	to eat
/u/	/'ju/	you	/u/	/i̯f ju 'it/	if you eat

The above analysis makes it appear as though /ə/ were the unstressed vowel of English; but to a considerable extent this role is shared by the vowel /i̯/. Probably most speakers of American English use /i̯/ rather than /ə/ in final unstressed syllables before /č/: /'spi̯ni̯č/ spinach; before /ǰ/: /'pæki̯ǰ/ package; before /š/: /'pali̯š/ polish; and before /ŋ/: /'teki̯ŋ/ taking. Before other consonants there is a good deal of variation between /ə/ and /i̯/: olive may be /'aləv/ or /'ali̯v/; Philip may be /'fi̯ləp/ or /'fi̯li̯p/; stomach may be /'stʌmək/ or /'stʌmi̯k/; Dallas may be /'dæləs/ or, in Dallas itself, /'dæli̯s/; etc. This sort of variation also occurs in non-final unstressed syllables: animal may be /'ænəməl/ or /'æni̯məl/; pitiful may be /'pi̯təfəl/ or /'pi̯ti̯fəl/; citizen may be /'si̯təzən/ or /'si̯ti̯zən/; etc. Some speakers have clear minimal contrasts between /ə/ and /i̯/: /'rʌšəz/ Russia's vs. /'rʌši̯z/ rushes; /'rozəz/ Rosa's vs. /'rozi̯z/ Rose's. But other speakers have no such minimal contrasts and hence no clear opposition between /ə/ and /i̯/. The treatment of unstressed vowels is another of the indeterminacies which we find in the English vowel system.

The phonetic differences between English /ə/ and German /ə/ will be discussed in the next chapter. We need to note here a similarity between the two. English /ə/ shows before /m n ŋ l/ the same two allophones as does German /ə/: either the vowel [ə], or an allophone which can best be described as "syllabicity of the following consonant." Examples:

happen	/hæpən/	=	[hæpən]	or	/'hæpəm/	=	['hæp^{N}m̩]
bitten	/'bi̯tən/	=	['bi̯tən]	or			['bi̯t^{N}n̩]
sicken	/'si̯kən/	=	['si̯kən]	or	/'si̯kəŋ/	=	['si̯k^{N}ŋ̍]
middle	/'mi̯dəl/	=	['mi̯dəɫ]	or			['mi̯d^{L}ɫ]

8.10 DISTRIBUTIONAL CLASSES

In the case of German it was possible to classify the vowel phonemes on the basis of their distribution within words. The vowel /ə/ was the only one limited to unstressed position. The remaining vowels fell symmetrically into a checked class, which occurred only before consonants, and a matching free class, which also occurred before vowels and in word-final position.

Like German, English has a vowel /ə/ which occurs only in unstressed position. It also has, in stressed position, a class of checked vowels and a class of free vowels; but these two classes are neither as evenly matched nor as clearly differentiated as in German:

Checked		Free			
/ˈpi̧t/	pit	/ˈsii̧ŋ/	seeing	/ˈsi/	see
/ˈpȩt/	pet	/ˈsei̧ŋ/	saying	/ˈse/	say
/ˈpæt/	pat				
/ˈpat/	pot			(/ˈpa/	pa)
		/ˈsɔi̧ŋ/	sawing	/ˈsɔ/	saw
/ˈpʌt/	putt	/ˈsoi̧ŋ/	sewing	/ˈso/	sew
/ˈpu̧t/	put	/ˈdui̧ŋ/	doing	/ˈdu/	do
		/ˈpɜi̧ŋ/	purring	/ˈpɜ/	purr
		/ˈbaii̧ŋ/	buying	/ˈbai/	buy
		/ˈbɔii̧š/	boyish	/ˈbɔi/	boy
		/ˈbaui̧ŋ/	bowing	/ˈbau/	bow

This list shows, in word-final position, nine (or ten) different stressed free vowels. When they are unstressed, however, only five of them occur in word-final position: /i/ in /ˈkændi/ candy, /e/ in /ˈmʌnde/ (beside /ˈmʌndi/) Monday, /o/ in /ˈȩko/ echo, /u/ in /ˈi̧šu/ issue, /ɜ/ in /ˈkʌvɜ/ cover (but where postvocalic /r/ is lost, cover is /ˈkʌvə/, and there is no final unstressed /ɜ/).

In this list we have classified /æ/ and /ʌ/ as checked vowels; the forms /ˈbæ/ baa (of sheep) and /ˈðʌ/ (beside /ˈði/) the are not sufficient evidence to justify us in classifying them as free. The status of /a/, on the other hand, is not fully clear. English certainly has words with final stressed /a/: spa, ra, shah, pa, ma, ah, hah, bah, fa, la, hurrah. But there are very few such words, and nearly all of them are of types (loanwords, nicknames, interjections) which commonly show atypical phonemic structure. Furthermore, examples of /a/ before a following vowel (such as /həˈrai̧ŋ/ hurrahing) are practically non-existent. All in all the evidence suggests that, though /a/ is not clearly a checked vowel, it is by no means as clearly free as are /i e ɔ o u ɜ ai ɔi au/.

8.11 TRANSCRIPTIONAL SYSTEMS

At the end of the previous chapter we discussed several different ways in which the vowel phonemes of German can be symbolized. No linguistic problems were involved in this discussion. We were concerned only with such practical matters as the medium in which the symbolization is to be presented (handwriting, typewriting, or printing), and the purpose for which the symbolization is to be used. The vowel system was in each case the same.

When we turn now to the various transcriptional systems which are in use for the vowel phonemes of American English, some very serious linguistic problems arise. First and foremost, there simply is no one standard variety of American English, comparable to the standard German of the Siebs, whose vowel system can be described. There are, instead, many different geographical standards, and each is quite acceptable in its own way. Second, many Americans—most of all, perhaps, the better educated—use not just one variety of English, but a mixture of two or more. A description of their vowel system is therefore especially difficult, since it must try to systematize something which is not wholly systematic. Finally, even those vowel systems which are relatively unmixed can be analyzed from two rather different phonemic points of view.

Since the reader may wish to consult works which use different analyses and transcriptions of American vowels, we need to describe those in widest use and to compare them with our own analysis and transcription. In order to do so, we shall first give a list of words which illustrate widespread phonemic contrasts, and then show the various analyses and transcriptions which have been used for them. The list is as follows:

Stressed						Unstressed
bee			too			
bit			put			
bay	her		tow			(calm)er
bet		but				(comm)a
bat			law		boy	
	pot			buy	bough	

The most widely used transcriptional system for the vowels of American English is probably that of the Kenyon and Knott Pronouncing Dictionary of American English and the essentially identical system in C. K. Thomas, An Introduction to the Phonetics of American English. It uses the following symbols:

Stressed						Unstressed
i			u			
ɪ			ʊ			
e	ɝ ɜ		o			ɚ
ε		ʌ				ə
æ			ɔ		ɔɪ	
	a			aɪ	aʊ	

Additional symbols are: low front [a] as in some pronunciations of ask [ask] (lower than [æsk], fronter than [ɑsk]); low back rounded [ɒ] as in some pronunciations of watch [wɒč] (lower than [wɔč], not unrounded like [wač]); and the diphthong [ɪu] as in fuse [fɪuz], where others say [fjuz]. This system is in some respects phonetic rather than phonemic: [ɝ] with tongue constriction and [ɜ] without it are diaphones of a single phoneme; and [ɝ] and [ɚ] are, respectively, the stressed and unstressed allophones of a single phoneme.

A phonemic adaptation of this system to the speech of the Atlantic seaboard is given in Kurath and McDavid, The Pronunciation of English in the Atlantic States, based on the materials of the Linguistic Atlas of the Eastern United States. These show the following phonemic system in a considerable part of this area:

	Stressed			Unstressed
i		u		
ɪ		ʊ		
e	ɜ	o		
ɛ	ʌ			ə
æ	ɔ		ɔi	
a		ai	au	

This is the system which we have used in our presentation of the vowels of American English. We differ only in the choice of four symbols: /ɨ ʉ ẹ/ in place of /ɪ ʊ ɛ/, and /a/ in place of /α/.

The different phonemic systems used in other parts of the Atlantic seaboard require the use of a few additional phonemic symbols:

1. In parts of the Atlantic seaboard—roughly speaking, in Metropolitan New York, in the Upper South, and in the Lower South—the loss of postvocalic /r/ has led to the contrast /'pat/ pot vs. /'pɒt/ part, giving a sixteenth stressed vowel phoneme, low back unrounded /ɒ/. We have written this contrast as /a/—/a:/: /'pat/ pot vs. /'pa:t/ part.)

2. In Eastern New England the loss of postvocalic /r/ gives low front unrounded /a/ in /'pat/ part; but here pot has the same phoneme as law, open low back rounded /ɒ/: /'pɒt/ like /'lɒ/. A sixteenth stressed vowel phoneme occurs, however, in the speech of those Eastern New Englanders who contrast /'rod/ rode and /'rɵd/ road, with open (and slightly centralized) mid back rounded /ɵ/. (This is the "New England short o," which we have symbolized as /ǫ/.)

3. In Western Pennsylvania the vowels of pot and law have merged in open low rounded /ɒ/: /'pɒt/ like /'lɒ/. This area therefore has fifteen rather than sixteen stressed vowel phonemes. (We have indicated the merger of these two phonemes by writing /å̦/. Cf. §9.2[5].)

If we arrange the stressed vowels of the main Atlantic seaboard system into checked and free classes, we get the following:

	Checked			Free		
ɪ		ʊ	i		u	
ɛ	ʌ		e	ɜ	o	
æ					ɔ	ɔi
	a				ai	au

We may note, first, that the free vowels /ai ɔi au/, as in buy, boy, bough, could very well be interpreted as vowel plus semivowel: /ay ɔy aw/ (following the American custom of writing /y/ rather than /j/). Buy, boy, bough are then /'bay 'bɔy 'baw/. Second, free /i e o u/, as in bee, bay, tow, too, are commonly upgliding diphthongs, and hence they

also could be interpreted as vowel plus semivowel: /iy ey ow uw/. Bee, bay, tow, too
are then /'biy 'bey 'tow 'tuw/. This has led a number of scholars to suggest that all
free vowels consist of vowel plus semivowel, and that the only true "vowels" in English
are the checked ones. To the six checked vowels listed above they have added three more
which occur in one variety or another of American English: the Eastern New England
"short o" or road etc., which they write simply /o/; the checked open low back rounded
vowel of watch, mentioned above, which they write /ɔ/; and the open high central /ɨ/
which many Americans use, for example, in the adverb /'ǰɨst/ just (as opposed to the ad-
jective /'ǰʌst/ just). Then, writing /ʌ/ as /ə/, and simplifying the other checked vowel
symbols, they propose the following nine-vowel system:

i	ɨ	u
e	ə	o
æ	a	ɔ

Each of these vowels can occur before either of the semivowels /y/ and /w/. In addition,
to take care of such free vowels as those of pa and law, which usually show neither a /y/-
glide nor a /w/-glide, a third semivowel /h/ is assumed. The total system then consists
of the nine vowels listed above, each of which (in one variety or another of American English) can occur before each of the semivowels /y/, /w/, and /h/.

Using this "nine-vowel" system, our original list of seventeen words can be
transcribed as follows:

Stressed						Unstressed
'biy		'tuw				
'bit		'put				
'bey	'hər	'tow				'kahmər
'bet	'bət					'kamə
'bæt		'lɔh		'bɔy		
	'pat		'bay		'baw	

This analysis of English vowels was first presented in full detail by George L.
Trager and Henry Lee Smith, Jr., An Outline of English Structure ("Studies in Linguistics,
Occasional Papers," No. 3 [Norman, Okla., 1951]). In one respect it is very useful in contrasting the vowels of English with those of German. The most striking difference between
the vowels of English see, say, so, shoe and German sie, See, so, Schuh is the fact that the
English vowels are usually diphthongized: ['siⁱ 'sei 'sou 'šuᵘ], whereas the German vowels are monophthongal: ['ziː 'zẹː 'zọː 'šụː]. Full emphasis is placed on this difference if
we symbolize the two sets of forms as /'siy 'sey 'sow 'šuw/ vs. /'ziː 'zẹː 'zọː 'šụː/.

For a number of reasons, both practical and theoretical, we have chosen not
to use this nine-vowel analysis. Though for our purposes it is useful insofar as it empha-
sizes the diphthongal nature of the vowels of see, say, so, shoe by writing them /iy ey ow
uw/, it does this at the price of obscuring the fact that these same vowels are essentially

monophthongal in many other positions. This is only a minor objection to the system. It amounts to little more than saying that the analysis is not phonetic—which it was never intended to be.

A more serious objection to the nine-vowel system is the fact that it is not phonemic. First, it forces us to give different symbolizations to what, by the accepted techniques of phonemic analysis, are clearly allophones (positional variants) of the same phoneme. Many speakers use short /æ/ before voiceless consonants as in ['bæt] bat, but long /æ/ before voiced consonants as in ['bæ·d] bad. The nine-vowel system forces us to write this allophonic difference as if it were phonemic: /'bæt/ vs. /'bæhd/. Many speakers use an upgliding diphthong for the word-final vowel of ['siⁱ] see, but an ingliding diphthong for the same phoneme before intervocalic /r/, as in ['nⁱᵊrɜ] nearer. The nine-vowel system forces us to write this allophonic difference as if it were phonemic: /'siy/ vs. /'nihrər/. In parts of the South the phoneme /ai/ is [əi̯] before voiceless consonants: ['rəi̯t] right, but [a·ɛ̯] before voiced consonants: ['ra·ɛ̯d] ride. The nine-vowel system forces us to write this allophonic difference as if it were phonemic: /'rəyt/ vs. /'rayd/.

Second, the nine-vowel system forces us to give different symbolizations to what are clearly diaphones (geographical variants) of the same phoneme. We have seen that the diphthong /au/, as in /'aut/ out, shows an infinite series of diaphones ranging from [ęu̯] through [æu̯] to [au̯], and from [au̯] up to [əu̯]. The nine-vowel system forces us to single out four areas of this infinite series and to phonemicize them as /ew/ vs. /æw/ vs. /aw/ vs. /əw/.

The nine-vowel system has been called a "transcriptional arsenal" from which symbols can be drawn for describing different varieties of American English; but for this purpose a full phonetic alphabet is preferable. It has also been called an "overall pattern" analysis giving the total English vowel system, different parts of which are used in different areas; but it has been shown that even nine vowels and three semivowels do not suffice for a description of all varieties of American English. The great value of the system is that it has stimulated much useful thinking about vowel systems in general, and about English vowel systems in particular. In the present contrastive analysis of English and German, however, it has seemed preferable to give the vowel systems of the two languages according to more generally accepted methods of phonemic analysis. We have included this discussion of the nine-vowel system as an aid to those who may run across it in their readings and will wish to know how it differs from the more conventional analysis which we have presented.

CONTRASTIVE ANALYSIS: THE VOWELS

9

9.1 THE TWO SYSTEMS

In contrasting the vowels of English and German, it is not enough to make simple phonemic diagrams of the two systems and place them side by side, as we did for the consonants. Particularly in the case of English we must also try to show allophones. Though we cannot show them all, we can at least indicate some of those involving lowering before /r/, lengthening, and diphthongization. The following diagram attempts to do this for all of the stressed vowel phonemes except English /ai ɔi au/ and German /ai ọi au/.

English		German		
[i⋅ⁱ i i̧⋅ i̧ᵊ] [u⋅ᵘ u ṳ⋅ ṳᵊ]		i:	ü:	u:
i̧(⋅) ṳ(⋅)		i̧	ü̧	ṳ
[ei e ȩ⋅ ȩᵊ] ɜ(⋅) [ou o ǫ⋅ ǫᵊ]		e:	ö:	o:
ȩ(⋅) ʌ(⋅)		ȩ	ö̧	ǫ
æ(⋅) ɔ(⋅)			a̧	
a(⋅)			a̧:	

On the English side, the parenthesized dots indicate the allophonic length that is common before voiced consonants and is always possible under expressive lengthening or drawl; the spellings [i⋅ⁱ u⋅ᵘ ei ou] indicate the diphthongal allophones which in many environments are typical of the phonemes /i u e o/; and the notations [i̧⋅ ṳ⋅ ȩ⋅ ǫ⋅] and [i̧ᵊ ṳᵊ ȩᵊ ǫᵊ] indicate the lowering and lengthening or diphthongization that are so widespread before /r/.

9.2 POINTS OF CONFLICT

Inspection of the above table reveals a host of conflicts between the English and German vowel systems.

1. German /ü: ü̯ ö: ö̯/. These constitute a major phonemic problem because they represent a combination of distinctive features unmatched in English: that of "front" plus "rounded." In English, the only front vowels are unrounded, and the only rounded vowels are back. A further conflict arises from the fact that German /ö:/ and /ö̯/ are vaguely similar to American English /ɜ/, which may allophonically show considerable lip rounding. As a result, American students frequently imitate both /ö:/ and /ö̯/ as /ɜ/—pronouncing, for example, German /šö:n/ schön as ['šɝ'n] (with [ɝ] as in /'bɜn/ burn), or German /'könən/ können as ['kɟnən] (with [ɟ] as in /'kɜnəl/ kernel). Despite their vaguely similar sounds, the articulatory difference between /ö: ö̯/ and /ɜ/ is sharp: German /ö: ö̯/ are front, rounded, and quite without lateral tongue constriction; whereas American /ɜ/ is central, only moderately rounded (if at all), and in most parts of the country constricted.

2. German /i̯: u̯: e̯: o̯:/. These constitute a number of phonetic problems. Before a voiceless consonant an American will substitute his monophthongal allophones [i u] and (perhaps) [e o]; but these will be too open and probably also too short, so that sieht, tut, geht, Boot will be ['zit 'tut 'get 'bot] (like English seat, toot, gate, boat) rather than ['zi̯:t 'tu̯:t 'ge̯:t 'bo̯:t]. For German /e̯: o̯:/ the American is more likely to use his diphthongal allophones [eⁱ oᵘ]: ['geⁱt 'boᵘt] (like English gate, boat). Before voiced consonants and in word-final position an American will substitute his diphthongal allophones, so that sie, Schuh, See, so will be ['ziⁱ 'šuᵘ 'zei 'zou] (like English see, shoe, say, so) rather than ['zi̯: 'šu̯: ze̯: zo̯:]. And before /r/ an American will substitute whatever allophones he uses for the archiphonemes /I U E O/, so that ihr, Uhr, er, Ohr will be ['i̯'r 'u̯'r 'e̯'r 'o̯'r], or ['i̯r 'u̯r 'e̯r 'o̯r], or (where postvocalic /r/ is not used) ['i'ə 'u'ə 'e'ə 'o'ə] (corresponding in each case to the local pronunciation of ear, poor, air, oar), rather than ['i̯:ʌ 'u̯:ʌ 'e̯:ʌ 'o̯:ʌ].

3. German /a̯/ and /a̯:/. This harmless looking pair constitutes a very difficult phonemic problem because American English does not use the opposition lax—tense (realized phonetically as short-and-close vs. long-and-open) to distinguish two different low central vowel phonemes. For both /'šta̯t/ Stadt and /'šta̯:t/ Staat most Americans will substitute their single, drawlable /a/ as in /'pat/ pot, and pronounce both words with perhaps a half-long [a']: ['šta't]. But this ['šta't] is too low and too long for ['šta̯t] Stadt, and it is too high and too short for ['šta̯:t] Staat. The only Americans who are at all prepared for the German /a̯/—/a̯:/ opposition are those who use short vs. long vowels in such forms as /'pat/ pot vs. /'pa:t/ part (with loss of postvocalic /r/). However, many speakers who distinguish such pairs do so in quite another way: pot has low back [ɔ] (rhyming with bought), and part has low central or low front [a:]. Such persons are then no better off than the vast majority who use the drawlable /a/ in pot.

4. German /o̯/. This presents a serious phonetic problem for nearly all speakers of American English. The only exceptions are those few who happen to have the opposition tense—lax in the mid back vowels, and distinguish tense /o/ in /'hol/ hole from lax /o̯/ in /'ho̯l/ whole etc. (this latter being the "New England short o"). These speakers can successfully use this rare /o̯/ for German /o̯/. The overwhelming majority of Americans, however, have no such lax mid back /o̯/, but only a low back /ɔ/, as in ['kɔ'st] cost, ['fɔ'ł] fall, ['dɔ'n] dawn. The use of this American phoneme in German Kost, voll, Bonn

will give ['kɔ·st 'fɔ·l 'bɔ·n], with a vowel that is markedly lower and longer than the /ǫ/ of German /'kǫst 'fǫl 'bǫn/.

     5. German /a̱: a̱ ǫ/. The above remarks on German /ǫ/, and the statement that Americans will substitute their /ɔ/ for it, refer only to those Americans who actually have in their English an /ɔ/ (as in caught, caller, paw) opposed to an /a/ (as in cot, collar, pa). As we have already noted in chapter 8, however, there are many Americans—in western Pennsylvania, in the Great Lakes area, and throughout the Northwest—who have no /a/—/ɔ/ opposition in their English at all, but only a single phoneme which we can note as /å̧/. They use this /å̧/ not only in caught, caller, paw but also in cot, collar, pa, so that these pairs are identical: /'kå̧t 'kå̧lɜ 'på̧/. Such speakers—and there are millions of them —will then have a double problem in German. Like everyone else they will fail to distinguish German /a̱/ and /a:/, because their English lacks such a distinction. In addition, they will also fail to distinguish German /a̱ a̱:/ from German /ǫ/, since they also have no distinction resembling this in their English. As a result, German Kamm, kam, komm /'ka̱m 'ka:m 'kǫm/ will all be ['kå̧m]; German hacken, Haken, hocken /'ha̱kən 'ha:kən 'hǫkən/ will all be ['hå̧kən]; and so on.

     6. German /i̱ e̱ u̱/. Except where they occur before /r/ (see the following section), these three vowels present only minor allophonic difficulties. American /i̱ e̱ u̱/ are subject to allophonic lengthening (in some areas accompanied by diphthongization), whereas German /i̱ e̱ u̱/ are not.

     7. Stressed vowels before /r/. We may recall the extraordinary limitations which American English places on the occurrence of vowel phonemes before /r/. Some Americans, to be sure, maintain nearly their full set of stressed vowel contrasts before intervocalic /r/; but most Americans drastically reduce these contrasts before intervocalic /r/, and all Americans drastically reduce them before postvocalic /r/. If we disregard /ai ɔi au/, it is typical for most Americans to use before /r/ only /a/ and the four archiphonemes which we noted as /I E O U/. This produces a very sharp conflict with German, where the student must learn to distinguish no less than fourteen stressed vowel phonemes before /r/: both tense /i: e: a̱: o: u: ü: ö:/ and lax /i̱ e̱ a̱ ǫ u̱ ü̱ ö̱/. It is precisely these tense—lax oppositions which students tend to merge, on the analogy of their American archiphonemes. Before intervocalic /r/ they tend to merge

/'i̱:rə/	ihre	and	/'i̱rə/	irre	as	['i̱(·)rə]
/'tse̱:rə/	zehre	and	/'tse̱rə/	zerre	as	['tse̱(·)rə]
/'ha̱:rə/	Haare	and	/'ha̱rə/	harre	as	['ha(·)rə]
			etc.			

Before postvocalic /r/ they tend to merge

/'vi̱:r/	wir	and	/'vi̱r/	wirr	as	['vi̱(·)r]
/'he̱:r/	Heer	and	/'he̱r/	Herr	as	['he̱(·)r]
			etc.			

     The above is a phonemic problem: in each tense—lax pair of German, two phonemes correspond to only a single phoneme in English. For those Americans who maintain the tense—lax oppositions before intervocalic /r/ (i.e., for those who distinguish the vowels of <u>nearer</u> and <u>mirror</u>, <u>Mary</u> and <u>merry</u>, etc.), the conflict shifts from the phonemic to the allophonic level. Their distinction between (relatively) tense /i u e o/ in <u>nearer</u>, <u>poorer</u>, <u>Mary</u>, <u>boring</u> vs. lax /i̜ u̜ e̜/ plus /ɔ/ in <u>mirror</u>, <u>fury</u>, <u>merry</u>, <u>warring</u> is phonemically more or less comparable to the German distinction between (strongly) tense /i̤: ṳ: e̤: o̤:/ in <u>ihre</u>, <u>Uhren</u>, <u>Ehre</u>, <u>Ohren</u> vs. lax /i̜ u̜ e̜ o̜/ in <u>irre</u>, <u>murre</u>, <u>Sperre</u>, <u>Lorre</u>. Allophonically, however, the tense vowels of the two languages are quite different. For where German keeps its usual close [i: u: e: o:] before /r/, these American speakers use open [i̜ˑ u̜ˑ e̜ˑ o̜ˑ] or open and ingliding [i̜ᵊ u̜ᵊ e̜ᵊ o̜ᵊ]. The resulting "American accent" can be illustrated as follows:

German		"American accent"		
[ˈi̤:ʀə]	<u>ihre</u>	[ˈi̜ˑrə]	or	[ˈi̜ᵊrə]
[ˈṳ:ʀən]	<u>Uhren</u>	[ˈu̜ˑrən]	or	[ˈu̜ᵊrən]
[ˈe̤:ʀə]	<u>Ehre</u>	[ˈe̜ˑrə]	or	[ˈe̜ᵊrə]
[ˈo̤:ʀən]	<u>Ohren</u>	[ˈo̜ˑrən]	or	[ˈo̜ᵊrən]

8. German /ai ɔi au/. These three diphthongs present so many minor allophonic problems that it was not possible to present them within the space of the above table contrasting English and German vowels. Perhaps the most widespread problem is the allophonic lengthening to which English /ai ɔi au/ are subject, especially before voiced consonants and in word-final position. Because of this automatic lengthening, American students will tend to reproduce German <u>nein</u>, <u>neun</u>, <u>Baum</u> as [ˈnaˑin ˈnɔˑin ˈbaˑum], and German <u>bei</u>, <u>Heu</u>, <u>Bau</u> as [ˈbaːi ˈhɔːi ˈbaːu]. But, as the <u>Siebs</u> says (pp. 33-34): "Diphthonge mit langem Vokal (Langdiphthonge) gibt es im Deutschen nicht." These diphthongs must be short: [ˈnain ˈnɔin ˈbaum] and [ˈbai ˈhɔi ˈbau]. In addition, American students will tend to transfer to German the particular pronunciation of American /ai ɔi au/ which is used in their local speech. Hence German /ai/ may be rendered as [æi], [ɔi], [əi], [aˑɛ̯], [aˑᵊ]; German /ɔi/ as [ɔi], [oi], [ɔᵊ]; and German /au/ as [æu], [ɛ̜u], [əu].

9. Unstressed /ə/ and [ʌ]. In our transcription we have followed tradition in using the symbol /ə/ both for the unstressed vowel of German <u>bitte</u> and for the unstressed vowel of English <u>sofa</u>. In addition, we have used the symbol [ʌ] both for the stressed vowel of English <u>but</u> and for the unstressed vowel (phonemically /ər/) of German <u>bitter</u>. We need now to consider the conflict caused by the partial overlap of English unstressed [ə] with German [ə] in one direction and with German [ʌ] in another direction. The matter is perhaps most clearly presented in the form of a diagram of the vowel quadrilateral:

	Front	Central	Back
High	ị		ụ
	į	X Y Z	ų
Mid	ẹ	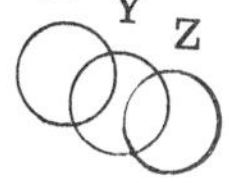	ọ
	ę		ǫ
Low	æ	ą	ɔ
		ạ	

Circle X represents schematically the allophonic range of German /ə/ in /'bįtə/ bitte etc. It is a mid central vowel tending toward high and front; we may call it "[e]-colored." Circle Y represents the allophonic range of English /ə/ in /'sofə/ sofa. It is a mid central vowel tending, if anything, a bit toward low and back; we may call it slightly "[ʌ]-colored." Circle Z represents the allophonic range of German [ʌ] in ['bįtʌ] bitter. It is a mid central vowel tending clearly toward low and back; it is strongly "[ʌ]-colored."

This is a classic example of a phonemic conflict caused by the fact that the allophonic range of a single phoneme in one language (English) overlaps with parts of the allophonic ranges of two different phonemes in another language (German). The result, as one might predict, is a very serious teaching problem. Students simply do not hear the difference between bitte (with [ə]) and bitter (with [ʌ]) because both sounds fall most of the time within a phonetic range which years of experience with English have taught the student to react to as linguistically "the same."

10. Other unstressed vowels. We may recall that all the vowels of German may occur in unstressed position (except that the /ą/—/ạ:/ opposition is then neutralized), whereas the only common unstressed vowels of English are /ə/ and /į/. This difference between the two languages creates serious distributional problems. Most Americans who have learned to control the vowels of German in stressed position still find it hard to use them in unstressed position. Following American distributional patterns, they imitate German philosophisch /fị:lọ:'zọ:fįš/ as [ˌfįlə'zọ:fįš], German diplomatisch /dị:plọ:'mạ:tįš/ as as [ˌdįplə'mạ:tįš], etc. Most difficult of all is German unstressed /a/. German Aroma /a'rọ:ma/ is usually imitated as [ə'rọ:mə], German Afrika /'ạ:frị:ka/ as ['ạ:frįkə], etc.

Though we have described /ə/ and /į/ as the unstressed vowels of English, we have also pointed out that the opposition between them is often suspended. One position where the two seldom contrast is that before final /n/: one and the same unstressed vowel phoneme is generally used in such forms as basin, beaten, button, etc. This is in sharp contrast to German, where /ə/ and /į/ are clearly opposed in such pairs as Wirten (dative plural) vs. Wirtin, or Königen (dative plural) vs. Königin.

11. Expressive lengthening. We have described the expressive lengthening which can affect any stressed vowel in English. The free vowel of /'no/ no can be lengthened from ['nou] to ['no:u]; the checked vowel of /'jęs/ yes can be lengthened from ['jęs] to ['ję:s]; etc. Expressive lengthening is also common in German; but in sharp contrast

to English it affects only the free vowels and, among these, only the monophthongs. Thus the free vowel of /'ja:/ ja, already long, can be lengthened still further; so also can the free vowels of /'zo:/ so, of /'ni:/ nie, etc. On the other hand, the diphthong of /'nain/ nein and the checked vowel of /'jetst/ jetzt are not subject to lengthening. If anything at all is lengthened in such words, it is the consonant which follows the diphthong or checked vowel. The word /'imər/ immer, for example, often becomes ['im:ʌ] (with long [m:]) under expressing lengthening. By and large, however, expressive lengthening is simply not used in German words with a stressed diphthong or checked vowel. A good many different expressive features—overloud stress, overhigh pitch, overtense articulation—can be given to such words as /'raus/ 'raus!, /fer'damt/ verdammt!, but lengthening is not one of them.

12. Nasalization. We have described the different ways in which English and German handle nasalized vowels. In ordinary English they are never separate phonemes but merely allophones of normally oral vowels. In German they constitute separate phonemes, though only in a limited number of words borrowed from French. The American who customarily pronounces /'hʌnt/ hunt as ['hʌ^{n}nt] or even ['hʌ^{n}t] will carry this habit over into German and imitate /'hant/ Hand as ['ha^{n}nt] or even ['ha^{n}t]. This is unlikely to cause any misunderstanding on the part of a German listener, but it will sound strange and constitute another part of an "American accent."

9.3 CORRECTIVE DRILLS

In the following sections we shall examine most of these twelve points of conflict in further detail and suggest corrective drills which may help overcome them. The order in which we shall consider the different points is partly pedagogical. For example, front rounded /ü: ü ö: ö/ are best taught as having the tongue position of /i: i e: e/ and the lip-rounding of /u: u o: o/; there is therefore little point in trying to teach them until these latter eight vowels are reasonably well under control.

The corrective drills which we shall suggest will be of two different types. First we shall present English-German contrasts, that is, contrasts between the German sound we wish to teach and the American English sound which our students are most likely to substitute for it. Only after a student has heard the difference between the two can he be expected to imitate the German sound correctly. Following this we shall present German-German contrasts, that is, contrasts between German phonemes which the student may tend to confuse with one another. Even if the student cannot imitate the German phonemes perfectly, he must at least learn to keep them apart. Only control of allophones will make his German perfect; but control of phonemes will at least make his German intelligible.

9.4 GERMAN /i:/ AND /u:/

We begin with these two vowels because, among the conflicts we must resolve, these two probably present the least difficulty. The sounds which the student will tend to substitute for them are of course the allophones of his English /i/ and /u/. These are near-always lower than German /i̩:/ and /u̩:/; usually, especially in word-final position, they are too diphthongal; and, in the speech of many Americans, /u/ is too far front (its allophonic range may extend from back to central or almost front), and it has too little lip-rounding. To a person used to articulating English /i/ and /u/, the features which go to make up German /i̩:/ and /u̩:/ all seem to be exaggerated: /i̩:/ is pronounced with the tongue very high and very front and with the lips very spread; /u̩:/ is pronounced with the tongue very high and very back and with the lips very rounded; and both vowels are exaggeratedly tense and monophthongal.

Drills like the following may help the student to hear and imitate the difference between the corresponding English and German sounds:

[iⁱ̩]	[i̩:]	[u⁰̩]	[u̩:]
fee	Vieh	too	tu'
she	Schi	do	du
knee	nie	coo	Kuh
sheen	schien	moose	Mus
deep	Dieb	hoot	Hut

The phonemes which the student must be sure to keep distinct from tense /i̩:/, /u̩:/ are lax /i̩/, /u̩/:

/i̩:/	/i̩/	/u̩:/	/u̩/
mied	mit	Mus	muß
Lied	litt	Fuß	Fluß
liest	List	bucht	Bucht
hießen	hissen	Buße	Busse
bieten	bitten	Huhne	Hunne

9.5 GERMAN /e̩:/ AND /o̩:/

The sounds which the student will tend to substitute for German /e̩:/ and /o̩:/ are the allophones of his English /e/ and /o/. As we have seen, these are nearly always far too diphthongal ([ei], [ou]); and even when students manage to suppress the diphthongal glide, the vowel sounds they produce are usually too low: [e: o:] rather than [e̩: o̩:]. As in the case of /i̩:/ and /u̩:/, a person used to articulating American /e/ and /o/ finds the articulation of German /e̩:/ and /o̩:/ highly exaggerated: for /e̩:/ the tongue is very high and very front and the lips are very spread; for /o̩:/ the tongue is very high and very back and the lips are very rounded; and both vowels are exaggeratedly tense and monophthongal.

An English-German contrastive drill might take the following form:

[ei]	[e̞:]	[ou]	[o̞:]
pay	P (letter name)	owe	O (letter name)
bay	B (letter name)	so	so
gay	geh	tone	Ton
vain	wen	shone	schon
bait	Beet	boat	Boot

Because German /e̞:/ and /o̞:/ are so much closer and more monophthongal than English /e/ and /o/, many beginning students confuse them with the relatively open /i/ and /u/ of English. On hearing German /'ge̞:t/ geht, for example, students often say with considerable annoyance: "I can't tell whether you're saying ['ge^it] or ['gi^it]" (using English allophones). Drills showing the contrast of German /e̞:/ vs. /i̞:/ and of German /o̞:/ vs. /u̞:/ may therefore be needed:

/e̞:/	/i̞:/	/o̞:/	/u̞:/
See	sie	schob	Schub
weh	wie	Ton	tun
wen	Wien	tot	tut
denen	dienen	Moos	Mus
beten	bieten	logen	lugen

Additional drills are needed to emphasize the contrast between tense /e̞:/, /o̞:/ and lax /e̞/, /o̞/:

/e:/	/e̞/	/o̞:/	/o̞/
den	denn	bog	Bock
wen	wenn	Schoß	schoß
Beet	Bett	Ofen	offen
stehlen	stellen	Sohle	solle
fehlen	fällen	wohne	Wonne

Finally, for the teacher who uses /ɛ:/, drills are needed to contrast it with both long /e̞:/ and short /e̞/:

/e:/	/ɛ:/	/e̞/	/ɛ:/
je	jäh	rette	Räte
lege	läge	Betten	bäten
lese	läse	esse	äße
gebe	gäbe	spreche	spräche
sehen	sähen	Vetter	Väter

9.6 GERMAN /a̧/ AND /a̧ː/

Most speakers of American English have only a single low central vowel phoneme, /a/, with allophones of various lengths, depending on phonemic environment, drawl, and expressive lengthening. It is this drawable /a/ which students tend to substitute, indiscriminately, for both German /a̧/ and /a̧ː/. The only students who are at all prepared for this German contrast are those who distinguish short /a/ as in /'kat/ cot from long /aː/ as in /'kaːt/ cart (with loss of /r/). But even here the allophonics are not quite right. German /a̧/ is not only shorter than /a̧ː/, but also higher and laxer. The usual German /a̧/, in fact, is phonetically a good deal closer to American English /ʌ/ (as in /'kʌt/ cut) than to American English /a/ (as in /'kat/ cot). Two types of drill are therefore needed: one to show the difference between English /a/ and German /a̧ː/ and another to show the similarity between English /ʌ/ and German /a̧/:

/a/	/a̧ː/	/ʌ/	/a̧/
par	Paar	up	ab
calm	kam	hut	hat
not	Naht	luck	Lack
tot	Tat	bus	Baß
lock	lag	come	Kamm

Extensive drills are also needed to make clear the contrast between German /a̧/ and /a̧ː/:

/a̧/	/a̧ː/	/a̧/	/a̧ː/
Kamm	kam	Masse	Maße
kann	Kahn	Ratte	rate
satt	Saat	schaffe	Schafe
Stadt	Staat	Hacken	Haken
schlaff	Schlaf	harre	Haare

9.7 GERMAN /ǫ/

In the preceding section we listed a number of English words with /a/: par, calm, and not, tot, lock. In some parts of the country all five of these words do indeed have the phoneme /a/. But in other parts—eastern New England, for example—par and calm have /a/, but the remaining three have /ɔ/, so that not and tot sound just like naught and taught. In still other parts of the country—western Pennsylvania, the Great Lakes region, and the Northwest, where pa and paw sound the same—all five have /å/. This brings us to the difficult problem of German /ǫ/, which is not matched by any phoneme in most varieties of American English. The sound which nearly all Americans substitute for the German /ǫ/ of /'bǫn/ Bonn, for example, is either their vowel in dawn or (partly on the

basis of the spelling) their vowel in <u>Don</u> and/or in the name <u>Kahn</u>. In the Northwest, etc.,
all three have the phoneme /ȧ/; in eastern New England <u>dawn</u> and <u>Don</u> have /ɔ/ but <u>Kahn</u>
has /a/; elsewhere <u>dawn</u> has /ɔ/ but <u>Don</u> and <u>Kahn</u> have /a/. Schematically we may put it
this way:

Northwest etc.	Eastern New England		Elsewhere	
/ȧ/	/a/	/ɔ/	/a/	/ɔ/
Kahn	Kahn	Don	Kahn	
Don		dawn	Don	dawn
dawn				

(This is surely not a full description of these phenomena, and in part it is probably not
even a correct one. Exact details are not as yet known for the entire country. The purpose
in mentioning the whole matter here is simply to alert the teacher to the pronunciations
he may expect to hear from the students in his particular area.)

Faced with this complicated situation in American English, we may expect that
German /ọ/ will need a good deal of corrective drilling. The first task is to make the student aware of the difference between German /ọ/ and whatever similar vowels he may have
in his English:

X	/ọ/	X	/ọ/	X	/ọ/
top	topp	Ross	Roß	caught	Gott
stop	stop	tossed	Post	sought	sott
cot	Gott	cost	Kost	hawk	hocke
dock	Dock	fall	voll	balk	Bock
lock	Locke	tall	toll	calk	Koch
sock	Socke	Saul	soll	naught	Motte

Once the student has been made aware, in this way, of the difference between German /ọ/
and whatever vowel phoneme is most similar to it in his English, he needs to drill the contrasts between German /ọ/ and /ạ/, and between German /ọ/ and /ạ:/. (The contrast between German /ọ/ and /o:/ has already been dealt with in §9.5.)

/ạ/	/ọ/	/ạ:/	/ọ/
Kamm	komm	kam	komm
Bann	Bonn	Bahn	Bonn
Fall	voll	fahl	voll
Dach	doch	nach	noch
sacke	Socke	Laken	Locken
Hacken	hocken	Haken	hocken
Gassen	gossen	Gas	goß

9.8 GERMAN /ü̲: ṳ̈ ö̲: ö̤/

These front rounded vowels represent a combination of distinctive features which is never used in English. They can best be understood if they are compared with their front unrounded and back rounded counterparts:

(1)	(2)	(3)	(4)
i̲:	ü̲:	u̲:	ü̲:
i̤	ṳ̈	ṳ	ṳ̈
e̲:	ö̲:	o̲:	ö̲:
e̤	ö̤	o̤	ö̤

In articulating these sounds, as one goes from any front unrounded vowel in column (1) to the corresponding front rounded vowel in column (2), the tongue stays in exactly the same position but the lips change from spread to rounded. And as one goes from any back rounded vowel in column (3) to the corresponding front rounded vowel in column (4), the lips stay in exactly the same rounded position but the tongue shifts from back to front. To give students practice in this kind of shifting back and forth from spread to rounded lips and from back to front tongue position, drills of the following type may be helpful:

/i̲:/	/ü̲:/	/u̲:/	/ü̲:/
Kien	kühn	Fuß	Füsse
Biene	Bühne	Hut	Hüte
Stile	Stühle	Schub	Schübe
Ziege	Züge	Zug	Züge
liegen	lügen	gut	Güte

/i̤/	/ṳ̈/	/ṳ/	/ṳ̈/
mißt	müßt	Schuß	Schüsse
Kiste	Küste	Busch	Büsche
sticke	Stücke	Bund	Bünde
Lifte	Lüfte	Kunst	Künste
Kissen	küssen	Mutter	Mütter

/e̲:/	/ö̲:/	/o̲:/	/ö̲:/
Sehne	Söhne	Sohn	Söhne
Lehne	Löhne	Ton	Töne
Hefe	Höfe	Hof	Höfe
lese	löse	Stoß	Stöße
bete	böte	Ofen	Öfen

/ę/	/ǫ̈/	/ǫ/	/ǫ̈/
Gent	gönnt	Stock	Stöcke
helle	Hölle	Bock	Böcke
stecke	Stöcke	Kopf	Köpfe
fällig	völlig	Topf	Töpfe
kennen	können	konnte	könnte

The substitutions which students make for /ü: ü ö: ö̤/ are largely matters of spelling: they simply overlook the umlaut on the written symbols ü and ö. The only cure for this is persistence on the part of the teacher. The one phonetic substitution commonly made is the use of English /ɜ/ for German /ö̤:/ and /ö̤/. Here an English-German contrastive drill may be of help in getting rid of tongue constriction in the pronunciation of German /ö̤:/ and /ö̤/.

/ɜ/	/ö̤:/	/ɜ/	/ö̤/
burn	schön	Burke	Böcke
earl	Öl	hurler	Hölle
Bergen	Bögen	shirker	Stöcke
learner	Löhne	girder	Götter
sterner	stöhne	kernel	können

9.9 STRESSED VOWELS BEFORE GERMAN /r/

Two types of conflict are involved here. (1) Many millions of Americans use only a drastically reduced set of vowel phonemes before intervocalic /r/, and all Americans use only a drastically reduced set of vowel phonemes before postvocalic /r/ (or, in the case of those who do not use postvocalic /r/, before the /ə/ which replaces it in their speech). German, on the other hand, uses all fourteen of its stressed monophthongs (fifteen, if we include /ɛ:/) before intervocalic and postvocalic /r/. (2) The high and mid vowels which Americans do use before their /r/ are nearly always very lax and open. German, on the other hand, uses its full set of tense and close vowels before /r/. As a result, (1) Americans find it hard to pronounce (and even to hear) the fifteen stressed vowel contrasts which occur before /r/ in German; and (2), in particular, they find it hard to pronounce tense, close vowels before German /r/.

An English-German contrastive drill of the following type may be helpful in making the student aware of the difference between his lax, open American vowels before /r/ and the tense, close vowels of German:

[i̩(˙)]	/i:/	[u̩(˙)]	/u:/
beery	Biere	surer	fuhren
deary	Tiere	poorer	Spuren

[i̯(ˑ)]	/i̦ː/	[y̯(ˑ)]	/u̦ː/
nearer	Niere	touring	Touren
fear	vier	poor	pur
mere	mir	cure	Kur
pier	Pier	moor	nur

[e̦(ˑ)]	/e̦ː/	[ɔ(ˑ)]	/o̦ː/
Mary	Meere	tory	Tore
vary	wehre	dory	bohre
hairy	Heere	story	schmore
air	er	ore	Ohr
dare	der	more	Moor
lair	leer	four	vor

Since most varieties of English do not contrast tense and lax vowels before /r/, this feature of German must be drilled:

/i̦ː/	/i̦/	/u̦ː/	/u̦/
ihre	irre	Uhren	murren
zieren	klirren	fuhren	surren
schmieren	schwirren	Fluren	knurren
wir	wirr	Geburt	geknurrt
ziert	wird	fuhrt	Kurt
studiert	geirrt	fuhrst	kurz

/e̦ː/	/e̦/	/a̦ː/	/a̦/	/o̦ː/	/o̦/
Speere	sperre	Haare	harre	Lore	Lorre
zehre	zerre	Schare	scharre	bohrt	Bord
lehre	plärre	sparen	Sparren	Tor	dort
Heer	Herr	Star	starr	vor	fort
begehrt	gesperrt	wahrt	ward	schmort	Sport
gezehrt	gezerrt	Bart	hart	Moor	Mord

Finally, since both /r/ and the front rounded vowels cause difficulty, the student may need to practice them both in the same word and to contrast the front rounded vowels with their front unrounded and back rounded counterparts:

/i̦ː/	/ü̦ː/	/u̦ː/	/i̦/	/ü̦/	/u̦/
Tieren	Türen	Touren	irre	Dürre	murre
schmiere	schnüre	Flure	Wirbel	mürbe	Kurbel

/i̥:/	/ü̥:/	/u̥:/	/i̥/	/ü̥/	/u̥/
gebiert	gebührt	Geburt	irden	würden	wurden
schmiert	schnürt	Schnur	Wirte	Kürze	kurze
vier	für	fuhr	Viertel	Gürtel	Wurzel

/e̥:/	/ö̥:/	/o̥:/	/e̥/	/ö̥/	/o̥/
Meere	Möhre	Moore	zerre	dörre	Lorre
wehre	Föhre	Tore	Kerne	Körner	vorne
ehren	hören	Ohren	Wärter	Wörter	Worte
er	Öhr	Ohr	Wärme	Hörner	worden
lehrt	stört	bohrt	herrsche	Mörtel	Porsche

9.10 GERMAN /ai ɔ̯i au/

A conflict between English /ai ɔi au/ and German /ai ɔ̯i au/ which probably applies to all varieties of American English is the fact that the American diphthongs are subject to allophonic lengthening whereas the German ones are not. Beyond this, the problems which German /ai ɔ̯i au/ present will depend entirely on the particular allophones used for English /ai ɔi au/ in the area where the student learned his English. The teacher can use the following words to compare a student's English pronunciation with standard German pronunciation and then see where the difficulties lie:

/ai/	/ai/	/ɔi/	/ɔ̯i/	/au/	/au/
by	bei	Troy	treu	bough	Bau
fry	frei	ahoy	Heu	row	rauh
mine	mein	annoy	neu	brown	braun
dine	dein	boiler	Beule	house	Haus
bright	breit	loiter	Leute	mouse	Maus
lighten	leiten	royal	Greuel	Cowan	kauen

9.11 GERMAN /ə/ AND [ʌ]

As we have seen, the difficulty with these phones is the fact that most of the time they fall within the allophonic range of the single phoneme /ə/ in English. Without considerable training our students cannot even hear the difference between German /ə/ and [ʌ], much less imitate it. It is as if they had spent all their lives speaking a language in which a single phoneme sounded now pretty much like [p], now pretty much like [b], and were then asked to learn a language in which /p/ and /b/ were contrasting phonemes.

Faced with such a problem as this, there is little point in beginning with drills contrasting English /ə/ and German /ə/, and then English /ə/ and German [ʌ]. Our students would simply not hear any difference. More useful will be German-German drills, contrasting /ə/ and [ʌ] in comparable environments. Such drills can first be used for listening practice. Once a student has learned to hear the difference between /ə/ and [ʌ], he can then use the same drills for active imitation.

We shall begin with a drill contrasting /ən/ = [n̩] vs. /ərn/ = [ʌn], since it is relatively easy for an American to hear and imitate the difference between these two. We shall then give drills contrasting /ət/ vs. [ʌt], and /əs/ vs. [ʌs], since these are only a bit harder to hear and imitate. Finally, we shall give drills contrasting /ə/ vs. [ʌ], which by this time should be somewhat easier to learn.

/ən/ = [n̩]	/ərn/ = [ʌn]	/ət/ = [ət]	/ərt/ = [ʌt]
Minden	mindern	wettet	wettert
Wunden	wundern	endet	ändert
reiten	Reitern	leistet	meistert
öffnen	Öffnern	bindet	hindert
enden	ändern	schneidet	schneidert

/əs/ = [əs]	/ərs/ = [ʌs]	/ə/ = [ə]	/ər/ = [ʌ]
Rittes	Ritters	bitte	bitter
Bannes	Banners	leide	leider
Sieges	Siegers	zeige	Zeiger
Ringes	Ringers	lese	Leser
Bundes	Wunders	Wunde	Wunder

Easy for students to hear but difficult for them to imitate at first is the contrast between word-final German /ən/ vs. /ɪn/, since English unstressed /ɪn/ is rare in word-final position. The problem is largely one of calling the student's attention to this German contrast, through such a German-German contrastive drill as the following:

/ən/	/ɪn/
Wirten	Wirtin
Fürsten	Fürstin
Baronen	Baronin
Köchen	Köchin
Königen	Königin

We may recall that English stressed /i/ (as in /'ði/ the) is often replaced by unstressed /ə/ before a consonant (/ðə 'pič/ the peach) but not before a vowel (/ði 'æpəl/ the apple). This English habit of using /ə/ before consonant but /i/ before vowel is often carried over into German. Students who correctly use German /ə/ before consonants: /bə'gɪnən/ beginnen, /bə'dɔitən/ bedeuten, /gə're:gnət/ geregnet, then incorrectly use [i] before vowel: [bi'ɛndən] beenden, [bi'amtʌ] Beamter, [gi'aignət] geeignet. Extensive drills on this point are probably not needed, but the teacher needs to recognize and correct it when it occurs.

One final conflict between English /ə/ and German /ə/ concerns the frequency with which they function, allophonically, as mere syllabicity of a following nasal. In English, it is common for /ə/ to show this allophone after a preceding stop or fricative, e.g.:

<u>beaten</u> = ['bitən] or ['bit^{N}n̩]

If the preceding stop is a labial or a velar, the syllabic nasal is assimilated to it:

<u>happen</u> = ['hæpən] or ['hæp^{N}m̩]

<u>reckon</u> = ['rɛkən] or ['rɛk^{N}ŋ]

After a preceding nasal, however, this allophone is not very commonly used:

<u>Mennen</u> is usually ['mɛnən], less often ['mɛnn̩]
<u>common</u> is usually ['kamən], less often ['kamm̩]

German also uses syllabic nasals in words of similar structure, and it shows the same assimilation after labials and velars:

<u>bieten</u>　 = ['bi̱:tən] or ['bi̱:t^{N}n]

<u>Lappen</u>　 = ['la̱pən] or ['lap^{N}m]

<u>recken</u>　 = ['ʀɛkən] or ['ʀɛk^{N}ŋ]

Furthermore, many speakers frequently use these syllabic nasals not only after stops (as in the above examples) and fricatives but also after nasals:

<u>nennen</u>　 = ['nɛnən]　or　['nɛnn̩]
<u>kommen</u> = ['kɔmən] or　['kɔmm̩]
<u>singen</u>　 = ['zi̱ŋən]　or　['zi̱ŋŋ̩]

The <u>Siebs</u> calls this type of pronunciation "verwahrlost" and "häßlich"; but the very vehemence of these adjectives is good evidence that millions of Germans normally talk this way.

Because they are not used to hearing syllabic [m̩ n̩ ŋ] after nasals, American students often misinterpret ['nɛnn̩] <u>nennen</u> as ['nɛn] <u>nenn</u>, ['kɔmm̩] <u>kommen</u> as ['kɔm] <u>komm</u>, ['zi̱ŋŋ̩] <u>singen</u> as ['zi̱ŋ] <u>sing</u>, etc. Though it is not necessary to teach them to pronounce such forms with syllabic [m̩ n̩ ŋ] after nasal, they may perhaps need a listening drill of the following type so that they can distinguish them when they hear them:

[n]	[nn̩]	[m]	[mm̩]	[ŋ]	[ŋŋ̩]
ihn	ihnen	kam	kamen	Ring	ringen
den	denen	nehm'	nehmen	fing	fingen
Bahn	bahnen	schwamm	schwammen	eng	engen
Lohn	lohnen	klomm	klommen	sang	sangen
Wein	weinen	Reim	reimen	lang	langen

9.12 OTHER UNSTRESSED VOWELS

We may recall that English places very strict limitations on the number of unstressed vowels it uses and on the positions in which they occur within words. With some exaggeration we said that /i̯/ and /ə/ were the unstressed vowels of English: they are by far the most frequent, and they can occur freely in almost all positions. Much the same thing can be said of German as long as we stay within the realm of ordinary, everyday words. There are countless examples of unstressed /i̯/, as in fertig, Bildnis, sächsisch, Wirtin, Frühling; and there are even more examples of /ə/, as in bitte, wartete, bessere, genug, beginne, etc. To be sure, unstressed /u̯/ occurs frequently in the suffix -ung (Wohnung etc.), unstressed /e̜/ occurs in the prefixes emp-, ent-, er-, ver-, zer-, and German has a few everyday words with other unstressed vowels, such as the /a/ in Monat, the /o̜/ in Bischof, and the /ai/ in Arbeit. Nevertheless, as in English, /i̯/ and /ə/ are by far the most frequent unstressed vowels—as long as we consider only the common words of everyday speech.

As soon as we leave these everyday words, however, and examine the great masses of loanwords that have been borrowed during the past several centuries, especially from Greek, Latin, and French, the picture changes drastically. No longer are the unstressed vowels more or less limited to /i̯/ and /ə/; beside them we find all the other vowels as well. Indeed, the occurrence of these other vowels in unstressed syllables is one of the features which mark these words as Fremdwörter. The only restriction on the occurrence of unstressed vowels in Fremdwörter is still the fact that the seven checked vowels /i̜ e̜ a̜ o̜ u̜ ü̜ ö̜/ may not occur in word-final position.

The occurrence of "full vowels" in the unstressed syllables of Fremdwörter creates some very sharp conflicts with the English distribution of unstressed vowels and hence some very serious teaching problems. We shall need to examine these conflicts one by one, ordering them according to their position within words. Wherever we can, we shall try to place similar English and German words side by side so as to highlight the vowel substitutions which students tend to make.

To help us in our discussion, we shall need some sort of formulaic symbolization of the unstressed vowels and of their relation to syllables bearing primary and secondary stress. We shall let /'V/ = any vowel with primary stress, /,v/ = any vowel with secondary stress, /v/ = any full unstressed vowel, /ə/ = either of the common unstressed vowels /ə/ and /i̯/. Examples:

Formula	German example		English example	
'V-ə	/'ko̜mə/	komme	/'kamə/	comma
'V-v	/'auto:/	auto	/'ɔto/	auto
'V-ə-ə	/'re̜:dətə/	redete	/'æljəbrə/	algebra
'V-v-v	/'ne̜:gati̜:f/	negativ	/'redio/	radio
ə-'V	/bə'zu̜:x/	Besuch	/ə'go/	ago
v-'V	/be̜:'to̜ⁿ/	Beton	/ri'ækt/	react

Formula	German example	English example
v-v-'V-ə ˌv-ə-'V-ə	/deː moˑ'kraːti̦š/ demokratisch	/ˌdɛmə'kræti̦k/ democratic

We may consider first the type /'V-v/. In free final syllables German places no structural limitations on the occurrence of free vowels (though the writer knows of no examples of final /üː/ or /öː/), and all but one of those which occur are matched by the corresponding vowels of English:

German			English		
'V-i̦ː	/'beːbi̦ː/	Baby	'V-i	/'bebi/	baby
'V-eː	/'kafeː/	Kaffee	'V-e	/'mʌnde/	Monday
'V-aː[1]	/'kɔmaː/	Komma	('V-ə	/'kamə/	comma)
'V-oː	/'autoː/	Auto	'V-o	/'ɔto/	auto
'V-uː	/'tsuːluː/	Zulu	'V-u	/'zulu/	Zulu

In imitating the full final vowels of these forms, American students will have only their usual difficulties with German /iː eː oː uː/: they will tend to make them too low, too lax, and too diphthongal. The one new problem here is German final unstressed /aː/, which is quite unmatched by anything in English. A contrastive drill of the following type may be of help:

English /ə/	German /aː/	English /ə/	German /aː/
comma	Komma	Ida	Ida
sofa	Sofa	Eva	Eva
alpha	Alpha	Anna	Anna
beta	Beta	Allah	Allah
gamma	Gamma	Cuba	Kuba

In checked final syllables, of the type /'V-vc/ (letting /c/ = any consonant or consonants), the conflict between German and English is far more striking. German places no restrictions on the occurrence of checked vowels in this position (though the writer knows of no example of /ö̦/); English, on the other hand, shows only its usual unstressed vowels /i̦/ and /ə/:

---

1. Though German [aː] and [a̦] do not contrast in unstressed position, we shall write them in the remainder of this chapter as /aː/ and /a̦/ wherever they are parallel to the other unstressed tense and lax vowels.

German				English		
'V-ǜc	/'o:nüks/	Onyx			/'anịks/	onyx
'V-ịc	/'ọptịk/	Optik	'V-ịc	{	/'aptịks/	optics
'V-ęc	/'de:bęt/	Debet			/'karpịt/	carpet
'V-ạc	/'ạtlạs/	Atlas			/'ætləs/	atlas
'V-ǫc	/'bịšǫf/	Bischof	'V-əc	{	/'bịšəp/	bishop
'V-ǚc	/'mi:nụs/	minus			/'mainəs/	minus

English shows full vowels in words of this type only when the final syllable bears second-ary rather than weak stress: /'pe,θas/ pathos, /'nai,lan/ nylon; contrast German /'pạ:tǫs/ Pathos, /'nailǫn/ Nylon.

Where the stressed syllable is followed by two or more unstressed syllables, English commonly shows full /i/ in the final syllable: type /'V-ə-i/ in /'ligəli/ legally, type /'V-ə-ə-i/ in /'ęfəkəsi/ efficacy, etc. But in non-final syllables English shows full vowels only before a following vowel: /i/ before /ə/ in /'rediəm/ radium, /'siriəs/ seri-ous; /u/ before /ə/ in /'vækjuəs/ vacuous, /'vɜčuəl/ virtual. German, on the other hand, can show full vowels in any syllable following primary stress. Contrast the unstressed vowels in the following German and English words:

German /'V-v-v/		English /'V-ə-ə/	
/'mi:ni:mụm/	Minimum	/'mịnəməm/	minimum
/'nụ:me:rụs/	Numerus	/'numərəs/	numerous
/'ne:ga:tịf/	negativ	/'nęgətịv/	negative
/'pę:ga:zụs/	Pegasus	/'pęgəsəs/	Pegasus
/'pęrgo:la:/	Pergola	/'pɔgələ/	pergola

German /'V-v-v-v/		English /'V-ə-ə-ə/	
/'no:mi:na:tịf/	Nominativ	/'namənətịv/	nominative
/'kọmpa:ra:tịf/	Komparativ	/'kampərəbəl/	comparable
/'zụ:perla:tịf/	Superlativ	(/sə'pəlatịv/	superlative)

English shows full vowels in words of this type only when the final (or pre-final) syllable bears secondary rather than weak stress: /'pazə,tran/ positron, /'ælkə,hɔl/ alcohol; con-trast German /'pọ:zịtrǫn/ Positron, /'ạlkǫ:hǫ:l/ Alkohol.

In the type /v-'V/, German shows both tense and lax vowels if the unstressed syllable is free, but usually only lax vowels if the syllable is checked:

		In free syllables			
/i:/	/mị:'li:ts/	Miliz	/ị/	/mị'lęni:ụm/	Millenium
/e:/	/ẹ:'ro:tịš/	erotisch	/ę/	/ę'ra:tịš/	erratisch
/o:/	/kọ:'lɔnə/	Kolonne	/ǫ/	/kǫ'le:gə/	Kollege

	In free syllables				
/u:/	/ku:'rant/	kurant	/u̯/	/ku̯'rɛnt/	kurrent
/ü:/	/dü:'na:mɪš/	dynamisch	/ü̯/	/zü̯'me:trɪš/	symmetrisch
	In checked syllables				
/ɪ/	/ɪn'takt/	intakt	/ɔ/	/brɔn'çi:tɪs/	Bronchitis
/ɛ/	/bɛn'tsi:n/	Benzin	/u̯/	/bu̯l'ga:rɪən/	Bulgarien
/a/	/bak'te:rɪən/	Bakterien	/ü̯/	/zü̯m'bo:lɪš/	symbolisch

Words of this second type, with full vowels in checked syllables, cause relatively little difficulty to students, because English has many words of similar structure (though often with secondary rather than weak stress on the first syllable). Compare English intact, benzene, bacteria, bronchitis, Bulgaria, symbolic. Of course, the English and German vowels do not always correspond; but the principle of using full vowels in checked unstressed syllables is familiar from English. A real conflict arises only in words which have /ə/ in a checked syllable in English: /kəm'plit/ complete, /kən'træst/ (to) contrast; cf. German /kɔm'plɛt/ komplett, /kɔn'trast/ Kontrast.

Far more of a conflict is caused by German words of the first type: those with full vowels in free syllables. The corresponding words in English usually show /ə/ or /ɪ/:

	German /v-'V .../		English /ə-'V .../	
/i:/	/tsi:'garə/	Zigarre	/sɪ'gar/	cigar
/ɪ/	/dɪ'fu:s/	diffus	/dɪ'fjus/	diffuse
/e:/	/e:'lɛktrɪš/	elektrisch	/ə'lɛktrɪk/	electric
/ɛ/	/ɛ'fɛkt/	Effekt	/ə'fɛkt/	effect
/a/	/a'fɛkt/	Affekt	/ə'fɛkt/	affect
/a:/	/ba:'na:nə/	Banane	/bə'nænə/	banana
/ɔ/	/kɔ'laps/	Kollaps	/kə'læps/	collapse
/o:/	/ko:'lumbus/	Kolumbus	/kə'lʌmbəs/	Columbus
/u̯/	/ru̯'pi:n/	Ruppin		
/u:/	/hu:'ma:n/	human	(/hju'men/	humane)
/ü̯/	/zü̯'me:trɪš/	symmetrisch	/sɪ'mɛtrɪk/	symmetric
/ü:/	/psü:'ço:zə/	Psychose	(/sai'kosɪs/	psychosis)

If two or more syllables precede the primary stress, one or more of them almost always bears secondary stress in English, and the others usually show the typical unstressed vowels /ə/ and /ɪ/. Compare:

/,v-ə-'V .../ in /,kampə'tɪšən/ competition

/ə-,v-'V .../ in /ə,lɛk'trɪšən/ electrician

/ˌv-ə-ə-'V .../ in /ˌrætəfə'kešən/ <u>ratification</u>
/ə-ˌv-ə-'V .../ in /ə,palə'ǰɛtɪk/ <u>apologetic</u>
/ˌv-ə-ˌv-ə-'V .../ in /ˌɛkskə,mjunə'kešən/ <u>excommunication</u>

German shows a totally different pattern. As many as five unstressed syllables may precede the primary stress, and any or all of them may show full vowels. Compare:

/v-v-'V/ in /eːleː'fạnt/ <u>Elefant</u>
/v-v-v-'V/ in /fiːloːzoː'fiː/ <u>Philosophie</u>
/v-v-v-v-'V/ in /ạntroːpoːloː'giː/ <u>Anthropologie</u>
/v-v-v-v-v-'V/ in /deːmoːraːliːzạ'tsĭoːn/ <u>Demoralisation</u>

American students unconsciously carry over into German the English habits
of using secondary stresses and of pronouncing all unstressed vowels as /ə/ or /ɪ/. The
secondary stresses are a minor nuisance; but the use of /ə/ and /ɪ/ in place of full vowels produces a very strong American accent. To learn the full unstressed vowels of German, students need to have the typical American use of /ə/ and /ɪ/ pointed out to them
and to practice German words with full unstressed vowels. If an English-German contrastive drill is needed, forms such as the following might be included. (Vowels which need
particular attention are underlined.)

English /ˌv-ə-'V .../		German /v-v-'V .../	
philosophic	/ˌfɪlə'safɪk/	phil<u>o</u>sophisch	/fiːloː'zoːfɪš/
automatic	/ˌɔtə'mætɪk/	aut<u>o</u>matisch	/autoː'maːtɪš/
academic	/ˌækə'dɛmɪk/	ak<u>a</u>demisch	/aːkaː'deːmɪš/
alcoholic	/ˌælkə'holɪk/	alk<u>o</u>holisch	/ạlkoː'hoːlɪš/
democratic	/ˌdɛmə'krætɪk/	dem<u>o</u>kratisch	/deːmoː'kraːtɪš/
aromatic	/ˌærə'mætɪk/	ar<u>o</u>matisch	/aːroː'maːtɪš/
algebraic	/ˌælǰə'breɪk/	algebraisch	/ạlge'braːɪš/
atmospheric	/ˌætməs'fɛrɪk/	atmosphärisch	/ạtmo'sfɛːrɪš/
affidavit	/ˌæfə'devɪt/	Affidavit	/ạfiː'daːvɪt/
apparatus	/ˌæpə'rætəs/	App<u>a</u>rat	/ạpaː'raːt/
macaroni	/ˌmækə'roni/	Makk<u>a</u>roni	/mạkaː'roːnɪ/
Alabama	/ˌælə'bæmə/	Alab<u>a</u>ma	/aːlaː'baːmaː/
Colorado	/ˌkalə'rædo/	C<u>o</u>lorado	/koːloː'raːdoː/
California	/ˌkælə'fɔrnjə/	Kalif<u>o</u>rnien	/kạːliː'fɔrnĭən/

English /ˌv-ə-ə-'V .../		German /v-v-v-'V .../	
aquamarine	/ˌækwəmə'rin/	aqu<u>a</u>mar<u>i</u>n	/aːkvaːmaː'riːn/
anthropological	/ˌænθrəpə'laǰɪkəl/	anthr<u>o</u>pologisch	/ạntroːpoː'loːgɪš/
entomological	/ˌɛntəmə'laǰɪkəl/	ent<u>o</u>m<u>o</u>logisch	/ɛntoːmoː'loːgɪš/
sentimentality	/ˌsɛntəmɛn'tæləti/	sent<u>i</u>mental	/zɛntiːmɛn'taːl/

English /ˌv-ə-ˌv-ə-'V .../		German /v-v-v-v-'V .../	
immatriculation	/ˌi̯məˌtri̯kjə'lešən/	immatrikulieren	/i̯maːtri̯ːku̯ː'li̯ːrən/
excommunication	/ˌe̯kskəˌmjunə'kešən/	exkommunizieren	/e̯ksko̯muːni̯ːˈtsi̯ːrən/
English /ə-ˌv-ə-ə-ə-'V .../		German /v-v-v-v-v-'V .../	
Americanization	/əˌme̯rəkənə'zešən/	Amerikanisierung	/a̯ːme̯ːri̯ːka̯ːni̯ːˈzi̯ːru̯ŋ/

STRESS 10

10.1 INTRODUCTORY

The term "stress" is used to refer to the relative prominence that is given, in both English and German, to particular words in phrases and to particular syllables in words. For example, we can vary the meaning of the sentence That's my hat depending on whether we stress it THAT'S my hat, or That's MY hat, or That's my HAT. Similarly, we can vary the meaning of the phoneme sequence spelled insert depending on whether we stress it INsert (a noun) or inSERT (a verb). German also uses stress in these same two ways. Compare DAS ist mein Hut; Das ist MEIN Hut; Das ist mein HUT. Or: AUgust (the name of a man) and AuGUST (the name of a month).

In the following paragraphs we shall make some tentative remarks about stress in English and German. We must call them "tentative" because stress is less well understood than the so-called segmental phonemes (consonants and vowels) which we have discussed in the preceding chapters. Fortunately for us, the English-German conflicts involving stress are relatively minor. In terms of the classification which we have used, we can say that teaching problems involving stress are neither phonemic, phonetic, nor allophonic, but only distributional. Both English and German seem to have the same stress systems; they differ only in the ways in which they use them. (The situation would be vastly different if we were teaching French.)

10.2 SYNTACTICAL STRESS

Consider a sentence like John lives here, German Hans wohnt hier. Both English and German allow us to place the strongest stress on any one of these three words, depending on the meaning we wish to convey. If we mark the stressed word by putting the symbol /°/ in front of it, we can write the three possibilities as follows:

(Who lives here?)	°John lives here.
(What does John do here?)	John °lives here.
(Where does John live?)	John lives °here.
(Wer wohnt hier?)	°Hans wohnt hier.
(Was macht Hans hier?)	Hans °wohnt hier.
(Wo wohnt Hans?)	Hans wohnt °hier.

This type of stress is one of the fundamental devices used in syntax—in structuring words into phrases, clauses, and sentences. We shall therefore call it SYNTACTICAL STRESS.

The above sentence is a short one and, as we have marked it, it contains only one syntactical stress. If we expand it into a longer sentence of the same general structure, we will find that it is likely to be broken into two (or more) STRESS GROUPS, each with its own syntactical stress:

>Mr. and Mrs. °Brown | live in a big °house.
>Herr and Frau °Braun | wohnen in einem großen °Haus.

Even our original short sentence, however, can be spoken with two stress groups. We would probably say it that way if we were speaking very slowly:

>°John | lives °here.
>°Hans | wohnt °hier.

In theory, at least, each word in a sentence can bear its own syntactical stress. To a very poor stenographer we might dictate the sentence <u>John lives here</u> as °John | °lives | °here, making a separate stress group out of each word. In ordinary speech, however, there are certain types of phrases which are rarely split into smaller stress groups. The following sentence can be split into four stress groups, but hardly more than that:

>The Browns have bought the house on the °corner.
>The °Browns | have bought the house on the °corner.
>The °Browns | have °bought | the house on the °corner.
>The °Browns | have °bought | the °house | on the °corner.

10.3 WORD STRESS

The syntactical stress which we have just examined is normally the strongest stress in any stress group. As we have seen, it is part of the structure of syntactical expressions—phrases, clauses, and sentences. In addition to syntactical stress, both English and German have three further, weaker degrees of stress. Since they are part of the structure of words, we shall call them different degrees of WORD STRESS.

1. PRIMARY STRESS. This is the degree of stress which falls on the first syllable of English /'dɪskəs/ <u>discus</u>, German /'augʊst/ <u>August</u> (man's name); or on the second syllable of English /dɪ'skʌs/ <u>discuss</u>, German /au'gʊst/ <u>August</u> (the month). Following the practice recommended by the International Phonetics Association and used in the Kenyon and Knott <u>Pronouncing Dictionary</u> and in the <u>Siebs</u>, we shall mark primary stress by means of a raised tick in front of the stressed syllable, as in the above examples. Another common way of marking primary stress is by means of an acute accent over the stressed vowel: /dɪ́skəs/, /dɪskʌ́s/; /áugʊst/, /augʊ́st/. Most American dictionaries use a heavy acute accent following the stressed syllable: <u>dis´cus</u>, <u>discuss´</u>. The Duden <u>Rechtschreibung</u> leaves primary stress unmarked in native words which are stressed on the first syllable: <u>fallen</u>, or on the first syllable following one of the common unstressed prefixes: <u>befallen</u>, <u>entfallen</u>, <u>gefallen</u>, etc. Otherwise it marks primary stress by placing a line under long vowels and diphthongs: <u>August</u> (man's name), but a dot under short vowels: August (the month).

2. SECONDARY STRESS. This is the degree of stress which falls on the first syllable of English /ˌovɜ'flo/ <u>(to) overflow</u>, German /ˌʊntər'rɪçtən/ <u>unterrichten</u>; or on the

third syllable of English /'ovɜ,flo/ (the) overflow, German /'untər,riçt/ Unterricht. The use of a lowered tick to mark secondary stress is again the practice recommended by the International Phonetics Association and used in Kenyon and Knott. The Siebs, unfortunately, usually omits it. Secondary stress can also be indicated by means of a grave accent over the stressed vowel, but then a /+/ is needed to mark the syllable break: /òvɜ+flô/, /óvɜ+flò/; /ùntər+rîçtən/, /úntər+rìçt/. Most American dictionaries use a light acute accent following the syllable with secondary stress: (to) o´ver·flow´, (the) o´ver·flow´. The Duden does not usually mark secondary stress.

   3. WEAK STRESS. This is the degree of stress which falls on the first syllable of /dį'skʌs/ discuss, /au'gųst/ August (the month), and on the second syllable of /'dįskəs/ discus, /'augųst/ August (man's name). Syllables bearing weak stress are customarily (though inaccurately) said to be UNSTRESSED, in contrast to syllables with primary or secondary stress which are said to be STRESSED. Weak stress is customarily left unmarked. Where we wish to indicate stress patterns, we shall mark it with a hyphen. Thus discus has the stress pattern /'-/; discuss has the stress pattern /-'/; Unterricht has the stress pattern /'-,/; and unterrichten has the stress pattern /,-'-/.

10.4 SYNTACTICAL STRESS VS. PRIMARY STRESS

   Thus far we have spoken of stress largely in impressionistic phonetic terms, without bothering to ask whether the four degrees we have assumed are meaningfully distinctive and hence phonemic. We now need to perform this latter task.

   It is easy to show that the placement of syntactical stress is meaningfully distinctive. In effect, we have already done so, since such sentences as °John lives here vs. John °lives here, or either of these vs. John lives °here, constitute minimal pairs. It may be objected that the contrast in meaning in such a pair is very different from that in such a pair as pill vs. bill. This is quite true; but this merely reflects the difference between vowels and consonants on the one hand, and syntactical stress on the other. Vowel and consonant phonemes are used to distinguish words: pill vs. bill, bill vs. bell, etc. Syntactical stress is used to distinguish stress groups: °John lives here vs. John °lives here, etc. That these two stress groups mean quite different things is clear from the fact that only the former, never the latter, could be said in answer to the question: Who lives here?

   Can we establish a contrast between syntactical stress and primary stress? From a very strict point of view this is impossible. That is to say, we cannot give one utterance containing only syntactical stress, and then contrast with it another utterance containing only primary stress. This is because every normal utterance must consist of at least one stress group; and each stress group, by definition, contains one syntactical stress. Such words as "John," "live," and "here," as words, have only primary stress: /'ǰan/, /'lįv/, /'hir/; but, as utterances, they must also have syntactical stress:

Who lives here?	—	John.	/°'ǰan/
What does John do here?	—	Live.	/°'lįv/
Where does John live?	—	Here.	/°'hir/

This means that a word with primary stress, like /'jan/, is unpronounceable as such. As soon as we pronounce it, all by itself, it becomes a stress group; and every stress group has a syntactical stress: /°'ǰan/.

By definition, then, we cannot contrast one utterance containing only syntactical stress with another containing only primary stress, since utterances of the latter type do not occur. The best we can do is to contrast parts of utterances, e.g. the primary stress of /'ǰan/ in John lives °here vs. the syntactical stress of /°'ǰan/ in °John lives here.

10.5 PRIMARY STRESS VS. SECONDARY STRESS

We can show that the contrast between primary and secondary stress is distinctive by citing such a pair as the following:

/'nu/ in (1) /'nu 'ǰ3zi °'kau/
vs. /ˌnu/ in (2) /ˌnu 'ǰ3zi °'kau/

Americans generally agree immediately that utterance (1) refers to a Jersey cow that is new (a "new Jersey cow"), whereas (2) refers to a cow from New Jersey (a "New Jersey cow"). Since (1) has /'nu/ with primary stress and (2) has /ˌnu/ with secondary stress, this shows that the difference between primary and secondary stress is meaningfully distinctive and hence phonemic. We need to note one other phonetic difference between these two utterances. In (1) the transition from /'nu/ to /'ǰ3zi/ is relatively slow, but in (2) the transition from /ˌnu/ to /'ǰ3zi/ is relatively fast. This difference in speed of transition seems to be automatically conditioned by the difference in stress: slow transition from primary to primary: /'nu 'ǰ3zi/ new Jersey, but fast transition from secondary to primary: /ˌnu 'ǰ3zi/ New Jersey.

As a German example of the same general type, we may cite the following:

/'bre:/ in (1) /ịm 'bre:mər 'ha:fən °'ạrbaitən/
vs. /ˌbre:/ in (2) /ịn ˌbre:mər'ha:fən °'ạrbaitən/

Here the difference in stress signals the difference between (1) the phrase Bremer Hafen ("im Bremer Hafen arbeiten") vs. (2) the place name Bremerhaven ("in Bremerhaven arbeiten"). Other German examples are: /'tsvai 'brǖkən/ in the phrase zwei Brücken vs. /ˌtsvai'brǖkən/ in the place name Zweibrücken; or /'ja:r 'hụndərt/ in the phrase (im) Jahr Hundert vs. /ˌja:r'hụndərt/ in the compound noun (im) Jahrhundert.

10.6 SECONDARY STRESS VS. WEAK STRESS

To show that the contrast between secondary and weak stress is meaningfully distinctive, and hence phonemic, we may cite such pairs as the following:

/ˌǰi/ in /'rẹfjəˌǰi/ refugee
vs. /ǰi/ in /'ẹfəǰi/ effigy

/ˌsi/ in /'færəˌsi/ Pharisee
vs. /si/ in /'fæləsi/ fallacy

Comparable German examples:

/ˌtĭš/ in /ˈ ẹk,tĭš/ Ecktisch

vs. /tĭš/ in /ˈhẹktĭš/ hektisch

/ˌfĭš/ in /ˈhai,fĭš/ Haifisch

vs. /fĭš/ in /ˈhöːfĭš/ höfisch

Note how the use of secondary stress in hektisch and höfisch would change the meaning. /ˈhẹk,tĭš/, with secondary stress on /ˌtĭš/, would mean something like 'stern table' ("Hecktisch"), in contrast to a hypothetical 'bow table' ("Bugtisch"). Similarly, /ˈhöːˌfĭš/, with secondary stress on /ˌfĭš/, would be a new name for some sort of fish, spellable perhaps as Höhfisch.

10.7 CONFLICTS IN THE USE OF SYNTACTICAL STRESS

The sentences John lives here, German Hans wohnt hier, have shown us the way in which syntactical stress functions in both languages. It serves as a method of putting one particular word in a stress group at the center of attention: °John lives here, John °lives here, etc. But, we might ask, how is syntactical stress handled when there is no one word which the speaker wants to single out as the center of attention? The answer seems to be that, by and large, both languages then put syntactical stress on the last word in the stress group. Compare the following sentences, all spoken "neutrally," that is, without singling out any one word for special attention:

John °works.   Hans °arbeitet.

John works in a °factory.   Hans arbeitet in einer Fa°brik.

John works in a factory in   Hans arbeitet in einer Fabrik in
    °Hamburg.   °Hamburg.

Since both languages handle syntactical stress in such neutral sentences in the same way, there are generally no conflicts in structure between them.

Conflicts of a minor sort arise when the word order of corresponding sentences is different in the two languages. Then, either (1) syntactical stress falls at corresponding places within the stress group but not on corresponding words; or (2) syntactical stress falls on corresponding words but not at corresponding places within the stress group.

An example of the first type of conflict is the following:

We're going to the movies at   Wir gehen um sieben Uhr ins
    seven o°'clock.   °Kino.

Here syntactical stress falls at corresponding places in both languages, namely on the last word of the stress group. The word order of the two sentences, however, is different: place expression before time expression in English, but time expression before place expression in German. Therefore the syntactical stress falls on the time expression in English but on the place expression in German.

Two examples of the second type of conflict are the following:

I'm going °home tomorrow.   Ich fahre morgen nach °Hause.

I have to go °home.   Ich muß nach °Hause fahren.

Here syntactical stress falls on corresponding words (<u>home</u> in English, <u>Hause</u> in German), but not at corresponding places in the stress group. In the first pair of sentences it falls on the next to last word in English, but on the last word in German; in the second pair of sentences it falls on the last word in English, but on the next to last word in German.

Conflicts like these seldom cause serious teaching problems, but the teacher will need to be on guard against occasional errors caused by them. For example, it is common for beginning students to say <u>Wo °kommen Sie her?</u>, putting syntactical stress on <u>kommen</u> because it falls on <u>come</u> in English <u>Where do you °come from?</u> In German the syntactical stress normally falls on the word <u>her</u>: <u>Wo kommen Sie °her?</u>

10.8 SIMILARITIES IN THE USE OF WORD STRESS

In the common words of everyday speech, the stress patterns of English and German are remarkably similar. Both languages have large numbers of one-syllable stems which, as independent words, bear primary stress:

Type /'/	house	hand	mouth	bed	door
	Haus	Hand	Mund	Bett	Tür

Beside these there are many two-syllable stems with primary stress on the first syllable, weak stress on the second:

Type /'-/	hammer	wander	open	bottom	apple
	Hammer	wandern	offen	Boden	Apfel

Stems of both types can also occur with various unstressed inflectional and derivational suffixes, giving stress patterns of the following types:

Type /'-/	houses	waited	running	holy	friendly
	Häuser	wartet	laufend	heilig	freundlich

Type /'--/	wandering	hopefully	bettering	bitterest
	Wanderung	hoffentlich	Besserung	bitterste

In addition, such stems can be preceded by unstressed prefixes or other unstressed syllables:

Type /-'/	begin	forbid	along	alone
	Beginn	Verbot	entlang	allein

Type /-'-/	betraying	forgetting	allowing	together
	betrügen	vergessen	erlauben	zusammen

Because of the nature of its inflectional system, German words often have one more unstressed syllable than their English counterparts:

/'/	hands	/'-/	Hände
/'-/	waited	/'--/	wartete
/'--/	wanderings	/'---/	Wanderungen

Since the basic patterns are the same, however, differences of this type seldom cause teaching problems.

English and German also agree in having comparable classes of words which typically bear secondary or weak stress rather than primary stress. A few examples:

Pronouns:	he, as in he comes	/ˌhi°ˈkʌmz/
	or if he comes	/ˌɪf i °ˈkʌmz/
	er, as in er kommt	/ˌẹr °ˈkọmt/
	or wenn er kommt	/ˌvẹn ẹr °ˈkọmt/
Conjunctions:	if and wenn in the above examples	
Prepositions:	on, as in on the street	/ˌan ðə °ˈstrit/
	auf, as in auf der Straße	/ˌauf dẹr °ˈštra:sə/
Articles:	the and der in the above examples	

In both languages a few words of this type show unstressed forms with a full vowel reduced to /ə/ or even lost. Though the words may not correspond from language to language, the principle is the same in both languages and such forms do not cause any serious teaching problems. Examples:

and:	you and I	/ˈju ən °ˈai/
ein:	hat ein Kind	/ˌhạt ən °ˈkịnt/
is:	it's here	/ˌɪt s °ˈhir/
es:	hat's gesehen	/ˌhạt s gə°ˈzẹ:ən/
them:	give 'em time	/ˈgịv əm °ˈtaim/
dem:	auf 'm Dach	/ˌauf əm °ˈdạx/

Especially common in German are such reduced forms of the definite article (and, often, of the preposition also) as: im (in dem), ins (in das), zum (zu dem), zur (zu der), etc.

10.9 THE STRESS PATTERNS OF COMPOUND WORDS

The typical stress pattern for compound words in both English and German is: primary stress on the first part, secondary stress on the second part. A few examples:

Type /ˈ ˌ/			
	redcap	railroad	doorknob
	Rotwein	Bleistift	Lehnstuhl
	tablespoon	pigeon-toed	applesauce
	Eisenbahn	Bücherschrank	Apfelmus
	housekeeper	typewriter	belt buckle
	Schulmeister	Bettdecke	Dampfkessel
	window dressing	babysitter	undercoating
	Speisekarte	Magenschmerzen	Badewanne

This same stress pattern is also used in many words which, from a grammatical point of view, are not compounds because the second part is a suffix rather than an independent word: ˈfriendˌship, ˈFreundˌschaft; ˈchildˌhood, ˈKindˌheit; etc. Cf. also such further German suffixes as -sal (ˈSchickˌsal), -tum (ˈReichˌtum), -keit (ˈEitelˌkeit), -igkeit

(Ge'schwindig,keit), -haft ('leb,haft), -sam ('lang,sam), -bar ('trag,bar), etc. Since both languages make extensive use of the pattern /' ,/, it does not usually constitute a teaching problem. There is of course a conflict in spelling. Where German almost invariably writes such compounds together, without a space or a hyphen, English sometimes writes a space: belt buckle, sometimes a hyphen: pigeon-toed, and sometimes neither: tablespoon.

A second stress pattern, considerably less common in both languages, has the structure: secondary stress on the first part, primary stress on the second part. Examples:

Type /, '/			
New York	northwest	untie	
Heilbronn	Nordwest	umfaßt	
overwhelm	understand	nevermore	
Paderborn	allerdings	überhaupt	
New Jersey	however	northwestern	
Saarbrücken	barmherzig	nordwestlich	
undertaken	overbearing	everlasting	
Bremerhaven	Apfelsine	unterdessen	

A third type of compound, the least common in both languages, has the structure: primary stress on the first part, primary stress on the second part; and, if the word bears syntactical stress, it usually falls on the second part. Some examples:

Type /' '/	ice cold	snow-white	blood red	open-eyed	tightfisted
	eiskalt	schneeweiß	blutrot	haarscharf	nagelneu

For German, contrast 'blut'arm 'very poor' vs. 'blut,arm 'anemic'; 'stein'reich 'very rich' vs. 'stein,reich 'containing much stone.' Cf. also such forms as 'Pik'as 'ace of spades,' 'Karo'könig 'king of diamonds,' 'Mords'spaß 'tremendous fun,' 'riesen'groß 'terrifically big'; and such country names as 'Sachsen-'An,halt, 'Öster,reich-'Un,garn. It is questionable whether the English forms cited above should be considered to be compounds. They may simply be sequences of two words, like 'front 'door, 'kitchen 'table, 'atom 'bomb. (Note the contrast between the pattern /' '/ in these English phrases and the pattern /' ,/ in the corresponding German compounds 'Haus,tür, 'Küchen,tisch, A'tom,bombe.) Somewhat less questionable as compounds are forms like 'over'due (different from both the 'over,flow and to ,over'flow), or 'under'rate (different from both the 'under,cut and to ,under'cut).

10.10 CONFLICTS IN LONG COMPOUNDS

The compounds discussed in the previous section consist of only two parts each. When we examine sequences of three or more parts, we find that stress is no longer used consistently to mark them as compounds. In English, for example, the three-part sequence life insurance policy may be stressed /' , ,/: 'life in,surance ,policy; but it may just as well be /' , '/: 'life in,surance 'policy (assuming, in both cases, that the syntactical stress falls on some other word, e.g. ,my 'life in,surance ,policy °'lapsed, or ,my 'life in,surance 'policy °'lapsed). In the latter case it is no longer marked in any way as a compound and could be analyzed as a phrase consisting of two words: life insurance plus policy. Similarly, German Lebensversicherungspolice may be stressed /' , ,/: 'Lebensver-,sicherungspo,lice, but also /' , '/: 'Lebensver,sicherungspo'lice. In the latter case it is marked as a compound not by the stress pattern, but by the fact that Lebensversicherung appears in its special compounding form with final /s/: Lebensversicherungs-.

A conflict in stress pattern arises in sequences of four or more parts. For example, English constructions like railroad workshop seem always to be treated as phrases: 'rail,road 'work,shop, with /' ,/ on each of the two words. German can use the same stress pattern in a compound like Rathauseingang: 'Rat,haus'ein,gang, with /' , ' ,/. Unlike English, however, it can also use the stress pattern /' , , ,/: 'Rat,haus,ein,gang, and it is this fact which marks such forms as compounds rather than as phrases. Since the stress pattern /' , , ,/ does not seem to be used in English, it may present a minor teaching problem.

Further complications in forms of this type can be illustrated by the following example:

Normal:	'jet 'bomber °'air,plane	°'Düsen,kampf,flug,zeug
Contrastive:	'jet °'bomber 'air,plane	'Düsen°'kampf,flug,zeug

Two different types of conflict are involved here. First, in expressions of this type English typically uses phrases with the stress pattern /' ' ' . . ./, whereas German typically uses compounds with the stress pattern /' , , , . . ./. Second, English normally puts syntactical stress on the last word in such a phrase; it puts it elsewhere only for reasons of contrast, e.g. contrasting a jet °bomber airplane with a jet °fighter airplane. This is precisely the opposite of German, which normally puts syntactical stress on the first part of such a compound and puts it elsewhere only for reasons of contrast, e.g. contrasting a Düsen-°kampfflugzeug with a Düsen°jagdflugzeug.

Because such long German compounds may contain a series of secondary stresses, and because they normally have syntactical stress at the very beginning, they often constitute a teaching problem. Reasoning from his English stress habits, the student is likely to read contrastive meaning into the initial syntactical stress of °'Düsen,kampf-,flug,zeug. He will need to be told that this is the normal stress pattern and that placing it elsewhere would give contrastive meaning.

10.11 THE STRESS PATTERNS OF VERBS

Both English and German show extensive traces of an old Germanic stress distinction between nouns and verbs. Many two-part nouns show the pattern "primary + secondary"; many two-part verbs show the pattern "secondary + primary," or "weak + primary." Compare German 'Unter,richt vs. ,unter'richten, 'Über,fall vs. ,über'fallen, 'Ur,teil vs. er'teilen, 'Ur,laub vs. er'lauben; and English the 'under,cut vs. to ,under'cut, the 'over,hang vs. to ,over'hang, the 'fore,sight vs. to fore'see. English also uses this pattern extensively in words borrowed from Latin: the 'con,trast vs. to con'trast, the 'in,sert vs. to in'sert, the 'subject vs. to sub'ject. (It should be emphasized that these stress patterns do not by any means apply to all nouns and verbs. The English verb 'side,step has the same stress pattern as the noun 'side,step; the German verb 'ant,worten has the same stress pattern as the noun 'Ant,wort; the German noun ,Unter'haltung has the same stress pattern as the verb ,unter'halten, etc.)

In both English and German, compound verbs of this type are clearly distinguished from phrases made up of the same elements. Compare the following:

Compound verb	Verb phrase
(I) overstep (it)	(I) step over
(I) undergo (it)	(I) go under
(ich) übertrete (es)	(ich) trete über
(ich) unterhalte (es)	(ich) halte (es) unter

In these examples there are two features which distinguish the compound verbs from the verb phrases. The most obvious difference is in the order of the elements: the compound verbs consist of adverb + verb, whereas the verb phrases consist of verb + adverb. But there is also a difference in stress. The compound verbs have the pattern /, '/: ,over'step, ,under'go, ,über'trete, ,unter'halte; whereas the phrases have the pattern /' '/: 'step 'over, 'go 'under, 'trete 'über, 'halte 'unter.

In English, these two types of construction are always distinguished from one another in these two different ways: both by order and by stress. In German, however, when the verbs are used in dependent clauses or as infinitives, the order of the elements in the two constructions becomes identical, and they are then distinguished only by stress:

Compound verb		Verb phrase	
(wenn ich es)	,über'trete	(wenn ich)	'über,trete
(wenn ich es)	,unter'halte	(wenn ich es)	'unter,halte
(ich muß es)	,über'treten	(ich muß)	'über,treten
(ich muß es)	,unter'halten	(ich muß es)	'unter,halten

In the compounds, the adverb keeps its secondary stress and the verb its primary stress: ,über'treten, ,unter'halten. In the phrases, the adverb keeps its primary stress, but the verb usually reduces its primary stress to secondary stress: 'über,treten, 'unter,halten (rather than 'über'treten, 'unter'halten). To this extent, therefore, these "phrases" become "compounds," since they show the stress pattern /' ,/ which is so typical of other types of compound words. It is probably for this reason that most German speakers think of forms like 'über,treten and 'unter,halten as single words (despite the fact that they are obviously two words in such constructions as ich trete . . . über, ich halte es . . . unter), and that the spelling system writes them without a hyphen or a space: übertreten rather than über-treten or über treten.

Though the stress alternation between /' '/ in 'trete 'über vs. /' ,/ in 'über,treten seems to have arisen in a limited number of forms of this type, it is now quite widespread in other types of forms as well. Compare the following:

Same Stress	⎰ er 'hält die 'Rede °'frei	'speaks without notes'
	⎱ er 'hält ,seine 'Freunde °'frei	'treats his friends'
Different Stress	⎰ er 'wird die 'Rede °'frei 'halten	'speak without notes'
	⎱ er 'wird ,seine 'Freunde °'frei,halten	'treat his friends'
Same Stress	⎰ er 'bleibt °'sitzen	'remains seated'
	⎱ er 'bleibt °'sitzen	'repeats the grade'
Different Stress	⎰ er 'muß °'sitzen 'bleiben	'remain seated'
	⎱ er 'muß °'sitzen,bleiben	'repeat the grade'

The spelling reflects this difference in stress by writing frei halten 'speak without notes' vs. freihalten 'treat'; sitzen bleiben 'remain seated' vs. sitzenbleiben 'repeat the grade.' We may recall that, along with this difference in stress, there is also a difference in transition: slower transition with /' '/, faster transition with /' ,/.

The stress contrast between sitzen bleiben with /' '/ vs. sitzenbleiben with /' ,/ is a rather minor teaching problem; many—perhaps most—German speakers do not maintain the distinction consistently. The stress contrast between ich trete über with /' '/ vs. ich übertrete with /, '/ is not a teaching problem at all, since it is so exactly matched by English I step over with /' '/ vs. I overstep with /, '/. The contrast between (wenn ich) übertrete, (ich muß) übertreten with /' ,/ vs. (wenn ich es) übertrete, (ich muß es) übertreten with /, '/ causes a real teaching problem, but it probably results more from English-German differences in word order than from any conflict in stress patterns. The stress patterns /' ,/ and /, '/ are familiar to the student from many types of English words. On the other hand, the word order alternation between ich trete . . . über and ich muß . . . übertreten (or wenn ich . . . übertrete) is quite unfamiliar to students, since English phrases of this type, such as step over, always maintain the order "verb + adverb" and never shift to the order "adverb + verb."

A teaching device which may prove useful is to place parallel forms of the German compound verb and phrase verb side by side, to show the consistent differences between them:

	ich	,über'trete	ich	'trete . . .	'über
wenn ich	. . .	,über'trete	wenn ich	. . .	'über,trete
	ich	,über'trat	ich	'trat . . .	'über
als ich	. . .	,über'trat	als ich	. . .	'über,trat
ich habe	. . .	,über'treten	ich bin	. . .	'überge,treten
weil ich	. . .	,über'treten habe	weil ich	. . .	'überge,treten bin
ich muß	. . .	,über'treten	ich muß	. . .	'über,treten
um	. . .	zu ,über'treten	um	. . .	'überzu,treten

One can then go on to point out that, if only it had the same rules of word order as German, English would probably show exactly the same types of forms.

I ,over'step	I 'step . . . 'over
if I . . . ,over'step	*if I . . . 'over,step
I ,over'stepped	I 'stepped . . . 'over
when I . . . ,over'stepped	*when I . . . 'over,stepped
etc.	etc.

The starred forms do not, of course, occur in English—because the rules of English word order are different from those of German.

10.12 CONFLICTS IN THE STRESS PATTERNS OF LOANWORDS

The stress patterns which we have examined thus far are those which occur in "native" words, that is, in words built up of stems which have long been in use in each language. As we have seen, despite many differences in detail, both languages use basically the same sets of stress patterns. When we turn now to an examination of the great masses of words which have been borrowed from other languages, principally Latin and Greek, we discover a very fundamental difference between English and German. By and large, English continues to use much the same stress patterns as in native words (or combinations of such patterns), whereas German uses many stress patterns which never occur in native words. Consider the following English words:

democrat	stress pattern /' - ,/ like overcoat
democratic	stress pattern /, - ' -/ like understanding
democracy	stress pattern /- ' - -/ like belatedly

Contrast with these familiar stress patterns the unusual ones in the corresponding German words:

Demokrat	stress pattern /- - '/
demokratisch	stress pattern /- - ' -/
Demokratie	stress pattern /- - - '/

In §9.12 we stated that words of this type are given a special status within the German vocabulary, that of Fremdwörter, because of the fact that they show full vowels in unstressed syllables. A second feature which sets them apart from ordinary words is the fact that they show these unusual stress patterns. And just as the use of full vowels in unstressed syllables creates a teaching problem, so also does the use of these unfamiliar stress patterns. In §9.12 we contrasted the unstressed vowels of the following pairs of words; we need to note here the contrasts in stress patterns, particularly the long series of unstressed syllables which may occur in German as opposed to the up's and down's of stressed and unstressed syllables in English:

English		German	
/,-'-/	philosophic	/--'-/	philosophisch
	affidavit		Affidavit

English		German	
/ˌ--'--/	anthropological	/----'-/	anthropologisch
	entomological		entomologisch
/ˌ-ˌ-'-/	immatriculation	/----'-/	immatrikulieren
	excommunication		exkommunizieren
/-ˌ---'-/	Americanization	/-----'-/	Amerikanisierung

In examples like these the student must learn to use weak stress where he has been accustomed to using secondary stress. If he fails to do so, his German will sound a bit peculiar, though it will not be seriously distorted. This is, therefore, a relatively minor conflict. A far more serious conflict arises in the many words where primary stress falls on different syllables in English and German. The following examples are only a tiny sample of such words; hundreds of others could be given:

English		German	
/'-/	atom, altar	/-'/	Atom, Altar
/'--/	energy, president	/--'/	Energie, Präsident
/'-ˌ/	dialogue, dynamite	/--'/	Dialog, Dynamit
/'-ˌ-/	apoplexy, architecture	/---'/	Apoplexie, Architektur
/-'--/	academy, diagonal	/---'/	Akademie, diagonal
/-'-ˌ/	acetylene, aristocrat	/---'/	Azetylen, Aristokrat
/ˌ-'-/	opposition, anesthesia	/---'/	Opposition, Anästhesie
/ˌ-'--/	bibliography, archeology	/----'/	Bibliographie, Archäologie
/-ˌ'--/	elasticity, electricity	/----'/	Elastizität, Elektrizität
/-ˌ-'-/	assimilation, emancipation	/----'/	Assimilation, Emanzipation
/ˌ--'--/	sentimentality, meteorology	/-----'/	Sentimentalität, Meteorologie
/-ˌ-'--/	eventuality, superiority	/-----'/	Eventualität, Superiorität
/ˌ-ˌ-'-/	immatriculation, excommunication	/-----'/	Immatrikulation, Exkommunikation

10.13 STRESS SHIFT

English has a large number of words in which primary stress shifts toward the end when a suffix is added. We may call this phenomenon "stress shift." A few examples:

'atom	—	a'tomic	'auto,mat	—	,auto'matic
'subject	—	sub'jective	'abdi,cate	—	,abdi'cation
'courage	—	cou'rageous	'influence	—	,influ'ential
'brutal	—	bru'tality	'secre,tary	—	,secre'tariat

This phenomenon is by no means unknown in German. There are a good many cases in which the derived word may or may not have stress shift:

'All,macht — 'all,mächtig or ,all'mächtig
'Ur,sprung — 'ur,sprünglich or ,ur'sprünglich
'aus,führen — 'aus,führlich or ,aus'führlich
'offen — 'offen,bar or ,offen'bar

There are also a few words in which stress shift is compulsory:

'Leben — le'bendig   'wahr,haft — ,wahr'haftig

In particular, German has a fairly large class of nouns (of Latin or Greek origin) which regularly show stress shift in the plural:

'Autor	—	Au'toren	'Atlas	—	At'lanten
'Doktor	—	Dok'toren	Cha'rakter	—	Charak'tere
'Pastor	—	Pas'toren	'Dämon	—	Dä'monen

A conflict in the use of stress shift arises from the fact that, though it unquestionably occurs in both languages, it is by no means so widespread in German as in English. Its great frequency in English often leads students to use it in such inflected forms as the following, in which the underlying words show full vowels in unstressed syllables:

Underlying word	Erroneous stress shift	Should be
'Monat	Mo'nate	'Monate
'Arbeit	Ar'beiten	'Arbeiten
'arbeiten	ar'beitete	'arbeitete
'Obacht	beo'bachten	be'obachten
be'obachten	beo'bachtete	be'obachtete

Except for the class of plurals like 'Doktor, Dok'toren, German never shows stress shift in inflected forms.

Because stress shift is so widespread in English, there are relatively few long words with primary stress at or near the beginning. As a result, students often have trouble in using primary stress at or near the beginning of long words in German. Examples of the kinds of words which cause trouble are the following, all of which have primary stress on the first syllable:

Mißverständnis	Ungewißheit	Arbeitslosigkeit
eigentümlich	Einheitlichkeit	Eigenwilligkeit
Ehrerbietung	Nachlässigkeit	Götterdämmerung

10.14 CONFLICTS BETWEEN STRESS CONTRASTS AND LEXICAL CONTRASTS

Consider the following English-German equivalents:

1a. 'Show ,me the °'hat.   1b. 'Zeigen ,Sie ,mir den °'Hut.
2a. 'Show ,me 'that °'hat.   2b. 'Zeigen ,Sie ,mir 'den °'Hut.

3a. 'Give ‚me a °'pound.	3b. 'Geben ‚Sie ‚mir ein °'Pfund.
4a. 'Give ‚me 'one °'pound.	4b. 'Geben ‚Sie ‚mir 'ein °'Pfund.

In both English and German, the articles the, der and a, ein belong to the class of words (see §10.8) which usually bear only secondary or weak stress; cf. sentences 1a and 1b, 3a and 3b. In English, the and a bear primary stress when they are specifically contrasted with each other or with some other word: "the (a) hat, not my hat"; otherwise the bears primary stress only in the special meaning 'the ideal, the best': "he's the man for the job," and a does not bear primary stress at all. In German, on the other hand, der and ein frequently bear primary stress. Der then serves as a demonstrative, as in sentence 2b; and ein serves as a numeral, as in sentence 4b. In these uses, therefore, stressed der corresponds to English that (sentence 2a) and stressed ein corresponds to English one (sentence 4a); that is to say, much the same contrast in meaning is signaled in German by the use of different degrees of stress (a stress contrast), but in English by the use of different words (a lexical contrast).

The absence in German of a pair of words corresponding to English a and one often frustrates beginning students. Having learned to equate ein with a, they find it hard to believe that they must also learn to equate it with one. In their search for a better equivalent, they often try to find it in German eins, and then produce such things as "Geben Sie mir eins Pfund" to match English "Give me one pound." The interlanguage conflict which bothers them here is perhaps best presented in the form of a diagram. The term article is used in its customary sense (a 'pound; ein 'Pfund); the term modifying numeral refers to usage as a stressed noun modifier ('one 'pound; 'ein 'Pfund); and the term independent numeral refers to usage in counting (one, two, three; eins, zwei, drei), but not as a noun modifier.

	Article	Modifying numeral	Independent numeral
English	a, an	one	
German	ein		eins

As this diagram shows, German ein corresponds as an article (with secondary or weak stress) to English a, an, but as a modifying numeral (with primary stress) to English one; and English one corresponds as a modifying numeral to German ein (with primary stress), but as an independent numeral to German eins. A diagram of this type may perhaps help students to understand this conflict intellectually; they will overcome it linguistically only through frequent practice.

Many beginning students are equally frustrated when they fail to find in German a pair of noun modifiers corresponding to English the and that. Having learned to equate der (in its various forms) with the, they find it hard to believe that they must also learn to equate it with that. This time, in their search for a better equivalent, they may hit upon either one of two wrong solutions. The correspondence between English What's that? and German Was ist das? may lead them to say "Zeigen Sie mir das Hut!" as the

equivalent of "Show me that hat"; and the dictionary entry "that = jener" may lead them
to say "Zeigen Sie mir jenen Hut." Both of these solutions are impossible, one for reasons
of grammar, the other for reasons of style. Das cannot be used to modify a masculine
noun like Hut; and jener cannot be used in such an everyday situation as that implied in
this sentence but is restricted to use in very formal speech or, more particularly, in writing. The interlanguage conflict in this more complicated case can be diagrammed as follows:

	Article	Modifying demonstrative	Independent demonstrative	Formal demonstrative
English	the	that		
German	der		das	jener

Here German der corresponds as an article (secondary or weak stress) to English the,
but as a modifying demonstrative (primary stress) to English that; and English that corresponds as a modifying demonstrative to German der (primary stress), but as an independent demonstrative to German das. German makes a distinction between the normal modifying demonstrative der (primary stress) and the very formal modifying demonstrative jener;
English has no such distinction, but uses that in all styles of speech and writing.

 The German contrast between stressed and unstressed der is paralleled by the
use of stressed and unstressed da(r)-. Compare the following:

1a. ‚I °'write 'with it.
2a. ‚I 'write ‚with °'that.

3a. ‚I °'sit 'on it.
4a. ‚I 'sit ‚on °'that.

1b. ‚Ich °'schreibe da'mit.
2b. ‚Ich 'schreibe °'da‚mit.

3b. ‚Ich °sitze da'rauf (or 'drauf).
4b. ‚Ich 'sitze °'da‚rauf.

Here again a lexical contrast in English: with it vs. with that corresponds to a stress contrast in German: da'mit vs. 'da‚mit.

INTONATION

11.1 INTRODUCTORY

As we have seen in the preceding chapter, the term "stress" refers to the relative prominence of syllables in the flow of speech, to what we might call the dimension "strong—weak." In contrast to this, the term "intonation" refers to patterns of voice pitch in speech, to what we might call the dimension "up—down." Intonation is the factor which allows us to distinguish a question such as "No?" (with rising intonation) from a statement such as "No." (with falling intonation). Like the stress dimension "strong—weak," the pitch dimension "up—down" is a continuum. We shall therefore be interested not in absolute levels of pitch along the musical scale but only in relative levels.

Not a great deal is known as yet about the intonation of English and German, and our remarks must be even more tentative than they were in the case of stress. From the little we do know, it appears that English and German have identical intonational systems and that they both use them in much the same way. They are certainly far more similar to one another than either of them is to French, for example. Unlike stress, intonation does not function in either English or German as part of the structure of words. This fact distinguishes them from the so-called "tone languages" (such as Chinese), where the same sequence of vowel and consonant phonemes may have totally different meanings depending on the intonation that is used with it. In both English and German, the domain of intonation is the stress group, and it is here that we may begin our investigations.

11.2 TERMINALS

Every stress group in English and German seems to end in one of only three different intonations. Since these intonations signal the end of a stress group, they are often called TERMINALS. We can illustrate them in the following examples:

1. Fade /↓/

°Yes.	°Ja.
Mr. °Meyer.	Herr °Meyer.
It's °raining.	Es °regnet.

2. Rise /↑/

°Yes?	°Ja?
Mr. °Meyer?	Herr °Meyer?
It's °raining?	Es °regnet?

3. Sustain /|/

°Well . . .	°Nun . . .
Mr. °Meyer . . .	Herr °Meyer . . .
If it's °raining . . .	Wenn es °regnet . . .

1. **Fade** /↓/. The three utterances in the first group are to be spoken as normal, matter-of-fact statements: "Are you ready?"—"°Yes"; "Who's in charge?"—"Mr. °Meyer"; "What's the weather like?"—"It's °raining." In each of them, the pitch of the voice is highest at the onset of syntactical stress; from this point on it trails downward and then fades out at the very end. We shall call this terminal a FADE and symbolize it with an arrow pointing downward: /↓/. Its typical meaning is something like "completed utterance."

2. **Rise** /↑/. These three utterances are to be spoken with the intonation which we use in the meaning, "Is that what you said?" In each of them the pitch of the voice is relatively high at the onset of syntactical stress; it then stays at this level but rises slightly just at the end. The level stretch is short in the case of °Yes?, because only this one syllable follows the /°/; it is longer in the case of °Meyer? and °raining?, because two syllables follow the /°/; it would be still longer in such an utterance as The °life insurance policy?, where seven syllables follow the /°/. In each of these examples, a slight rise occurs on the last syllable. We shall call this terminal a RISE and symbolize it with an arrow pointing upward: /↑/. Its typical meaning might be given as "interrogation."

3. **Sustain** /|/. These three utterances are to be pronounced as if the speaker were going to continue speaking but had paused briefly at this point to collect his thoughts. In each of them, the pitch of the voice is highest at the onset of syntactical stress; but then, instead of rising, or falling and fading, it is sustained at the same level until phonation ceases—or until the speaker goes on to complete his utterance. We shall call this terminal SUSTAIN and symbolize it with a vertical line: /|/. Its typical meaning is something like "incomplete utterance."

11.3 PITCH LEVELS

Let us take a typical three-syllable statement like it's raining, German es regnet, and examine the pitch levels which occur in it. In (a) below, we give it with an indication of word stresses, syntactical stress, and terminal; in (b), (c), and (d) we repeat it with the pitch levels symbolized in three different ways. To avoid confusion between an apostrophe and the symbol /'/ for primary stress, we write English it's as it-s.

(a)   ˌit-s °'raining↓   ˌes °'regnet↓

(b)   ˌit-s °'rai_ni_ng↓   ˌes °'re_gn_et↓

```
        °_                    °_
   -          -↓       -           -↓
(c)   ,it-s 'raining       ,es 'regnet

   2   °3   1↓          2   °3   1↓
(d)   ,it-s 'raining       ,es 'regnet
```

In both languages the lowest pitch level occurs at the end of the stress group, just before the fade; we shall call this pitch level /1/. Somewhat higher than this is the pitch on the first word; we shall call it pitch level /2/. Still higher is the pitch level which coincides with the syntactical stress; this is pitch level /3/. The whole sentence then has the following intonation: it begins on the first syllable at level /2/; at the onset of syntactical stress it shifts to level /3/; from here on it glides down to level /1/; it ends in a fade; we can symbolize all of this by writing /2 °3 1 ↓/. In (b) we have attempted to indicate these three pitch levels by writing the letters at corresponding heights. In (c) we have written all the letters on a straight line but have placed dashes at appropriate levels above them. In (d) we have written number symbols for the three pitch levels. Because this third type of symbolization is by far the easiest to manipulate, we shall use it from now on. Note that we write above the line not only the symbols for pitch levels but also the other symbols which refer to syntactical structure: the /°/ symbolizing syntactical stress, and the symbol /↓/ for the terminal.

It will be useful to have terms for the three parts of the intonation /2 °3 1/. In his helpful book, Grundzüge der hochdeutschen Satzintonation (Ratingen/Düsseldorf: A. Henn Verlag, 1956), Otto von Essen speaks of the Vorlauf, the Schwerpunkt, and the Nachlauf. We shall call the Schwerpunkt the "stress point"; it is of course the point at which syntactical stress falls. What precedes the stress point we shall call the "pre-stress segment" and what follows it the "post-stress segment."

11.4 THE INTONATION /(2) °3 1/

The example it's raining, German es regnet, contains only three syllables—one each for the pre-stress segment, for the stress point, and for the post-stress segment. We need to experiment a little to find out what happens when the number of syllables in the pre- and post-stress segments is increased or decreased. First, consider the post-stress segments in the following examples:

```
   2    °3              1↓      2   °3                1↓
(a)   ,it-s 'raining ,this 'evening    ,es 'regnet 'heute 'abend

   2  °3          1↓            2  °3             1↓
(b)   ,it 'snows ,too 'much       ,es 'schneit ,zu 'viel

   2   °3   1↓                  2   °3   1↓
(c)   ,it 'snows                ,es 'schneit
```

Examples (a) and (b) illustrate post-stress segments containing two to five syllables. The pitch contour is now somewhat different, but only because the post-stress segment is longer; the basic intonation is still the same. Example (c) illustrates what happens when the stress point falls on the last syllable of the group: this single syllable then functions simultaneously both as stress point and as post-stress segment. The pitch contour is again somewhat different, but only because the fall from /3/ to /1/ occurs within a single syllable; the basic intonation is still the same, namely /2 °3 1/.

Next, consider the pre-stress segments of the following examples:

	2	°3 1↓	2	°3 1↓
(a)	,he 'gave ,me the 'book		,er 'gab ,mir das 'Buch	

	2 °3	1↓	2 °3	1↓
(b)	,my 'brother 'gave ,me the 'book		,mein 'Bruder 'gab ,mir das 'Buch	

	°3	1↓	°3	1↓
(c)	'John 'gave ,me the 'book		'Hans 'gab ,mir das 'Buch	

In (a) the pre-stress segment contains four syllables. Though it begins at pitch level /2/, it does not necessarily remain precisely at this level, but may wander considerably, especially downward. In (b) the pre-stress segment consists of only one syllable; the intonation is still the same, namely /2 °3 1/. Example (c) illustrates what happens when the stress point falls on the first syllable in the group: here there is no longer any pre-stress segment, and the intonation is now /°3 1/. However, since /°3 1/ and /2 °3 1/ are in complementary distribution with one another, they can be taken as examples of one and the same basic intonation, which we can symbolize as /(2) °3 1/.

The following examples illustrate this same intonation in stress groups consisting of only one syllable:

°3 1↓	°3 1↓
'come	'komm

°31↓	°3 1↓
'no	'nein

Since the stress point falls on the first syllable in the group, there is no pre-stress segment; and since this syllable is at the same time the last syllable in the group, it is also the post-stress segment. The intonation is still the same: /°3 1/, an automatic variant of /(2) °3 1/.

In all the above examples, /(2) °3 1/ is used with the fading terminal /↓/, and the meaning is that of statement. If it is used with the rising terminal /↑/, the meaning becomes one of surprised interrogation: "Really? I never would have thought so." Examples:

2 °3 1↑	2 °3 1↑
,it-s 'raining?!	,es 'regnet?!

If /(2) °3 1/ is used with the sustaining terminal /|/, the meaning is one of incompleteness:

2 °3 1|	2 °3 1↓
,it-s 'raining	I 'have to ,go 'home

2 °3 1|	2 °3 1↓
,es 'regnet	,ich 'muß ,nach 'Hause

English spelling usually indicates this /|/ by writing a comma: "It's raining, I have to go home," or a semicolon: "It's raining; I have to go home"; German spelling uses a comma: "Es regnet, ich muß nach Hause." If the first stress group had the fading terminal /↓/, the spelling would usually show a period: "It's raining. I have to go home"; "Es regnet. Ich muß nach Hause."

11.5 THE INTONATION /(2) 3 °1 1/

A second intonation often used in statements, but less common than /(2) °3 1/, is the following:

2	3	°1	1↓	2	3	°1	1↓

,it ,was a 'lovely 'warm 'evening   ,es ,war ein 'schöner 'warmer 'Abend

3	°1	1↓	3	°1	1↓

'evenings ,it-s 'very 'warm   'abends ,ist es 'sehr 'warm

The first occurrence of primary stress has pitch level /3/; any preceding syllables with secondary or weak stress have pitch level /2/. From /3/ the pitch falls in a gradual glide to level /1/ at the stress point; this level is then maintained until the fade. Note the difference between the first example of /(2) 3 °1 1/ and the following example of /(2) °3 1/:

2	°3	1↓	2	°3	1↓

,it ,was a 'lovely 'warm 'evening   ,es ,war ein 'schöner 'warmer Abend

In this latter example, pitch level /3/ is at the stress point; the fall to /1/ is then much more abrupt.

11.6 THE INTONATION /(2) °3 3/

This is the intonation which is typically used with the rising terminal /↑/ in questions which call for a yes-or-no answer:

2	°3	3↑	2	°3	3↑

,is ,your 'brother 'here?   ,ist ,Ihr 'Bruder 'hier?

°3	3↑	°3	3↑

'John ,is 'here?   'Hans ,ist 'hier?

°3 3↑	°33↑

'yes?   'ja?

The stress point has pitch level /3/; any preceding syllables have pitch level /2/. After the stress point, pitch level /3/ is maintained, with a final rise at the end representing /↑/.

An interesting use of /(2) °3 3/ plus /|/ plus /3 °1 1/ occurs in what may be called "alternative questions":

2	°3 3	3	°1	1↓	2	°3 3	3	°1	1↓

,is ,it 'red ,or ,is ,it 'blue?   ,ist ,es 'rot ,oder ,ist ,es 'blau?

| 2 | °3 | 3⎸3 °1 1↓ | 2 | °3 | 3⎸3 °1 1↓ |

‚is ‚his 'name 'Brown ‚or 'Meyer?   'heißt ‚er 'Braun ‚oder 'Meyer?

11.7 THE INTONATION /(3) °2 3/

An intonation perhaps less commonly used for questions in American English is the following:

| 3 | °2 | 3↑ | | 3 | °2 | 3↑ |

‚is ‚your 'brother 'here?   ‚ist ‚Ihr 'Bruder 'hier?

| 3 °2 | 3↑ | | 3 °2 | 3↑ |

'how 'old ‚are ‚you?   'wie 'alt ‚sind ‚Sie?

| °2 3↑ | | °2 3↑ |

'well?   'nun?

The stress point has pitch level /2/; any preceding syllables have pitch level /3/. After the stress spoint, the pitch level rises gradually to /3/.

11.8 THE INTONATIONS /(1) °1 1/, /(3) °3 3/

The intonations discussed thus far can all be used with complete sentences, provided they are followed by /↑/ or /↓/. Intonations not used for complete sentences are the following; they very often occur in clauses which identify the speaker of what precedes:

(a)
2   °3   1⎸1   °1   1↓
‚it-s 'raining ‚said the 'old 'woman

(b)
2   °3   1⎸1   °1   1↑
‚it-s 'raining ‚she ex'claimed 'unbe'lievingly

(c)
2   °3   3⎸3   °3   3↑
‚is ‚it 'raining 'asked the 'old 'woman

(d)
3   °2   3⎸3   °3   3↑
'how 'old ‚are ‚you 'asked the 'old 'woman

It is characteristic of these intonations that they continue the final pitch level of the preceding stress group and that they end in the terminal which the preceding stress group would have if it stood alone. In (a), the final /1/ of the first group is continued throughout the second; and the /↓/ which would otherwise have terminated the first group is postponed until the end of the second. So also in (b), (c), and (d); and similar examples could easily be given for German. These intonations are therefore very useful for testing the final pitch level and the terminal of a stress group, if we are uncertain about them. The test consists of saying the stress group and immediately adding to it some such phrase as "said the old woman," or "sagte die alte Großmutter." The pitch level and the terminal of the second group are those which the first group has when said alone.

11.9 INTONATIONS, TERMINALS, AND OTHER GRAMMATICAL STRUCTURES

It is characteristic of intonations and terminals, in both English and German, that they are quite independent of other grammatical structures. In theory, at least, any intonation and any terminal can occur with any type of stress group. Intonations, terminals, and stress groups are dependent upon one another only to the extent that no one of them can occur without the other two—that is to say, in normal speech we never say a stress group without giving it some kind of intonation and ending it in one of the three terminals.

Despite their independence of one another, it is also true that certain intonations typically occur with certain types of clauses. In the preceding sections we have tried to describe some of the commonest intonations (there are certainly many more—just how many, no one as yet knows); here we shall try to describe some of the clause types with which they typically occur.

1. Statements. We define a statement, in German, as a clause which has the finite verb in second position, and which does not contain a question word. Examples: er kommt morgen; morgen kommt er; mich friert. German statements, and their English counterparts, typically have /(2) °3 1/, or /(2) 3 °1 1/, with /↓/. Examples:

```
   2              °3   1↓          2              °3   1↓
   ,he-s 'reading the 'paper       ,er 'liest die 'Zeitung

   2    3         °1   1↓          2    3         °1   1↓
   ,he-s 'reading the 'paper       ,er 'liest die 'Zeitung
```

When used with /↓/, these intonations have the meaning of simple declaration. If /|/ is used instead of /↓/, the meaning is one of incompleteness, usually with more to follow: "He's reading the paper, but he should be doing his homework." If /↑/ is used instead of /↓/, the meaning is one of surprised disbelief: "He's reading the paper . . .? Is that really true?"

An intonation often used to soften the effect of statements, and to make them sound more polite, is /3 °2 3/ with /↑/. Note how the same sentence sounds somewhat sharp with /2 °3 1/ plus /↓/, but more friendly with /3 °2 3/ plus /↑/:

```
   2    °3                1↓        2    °3                1↓
   ,you 'mustn-t 'do 'that          'das 'darfst ,du ,doch 'nicht

   3    °2                3↑        3    °2                3↑
   ,you 'mustn-t 'do 'that          'das 'darfst ,du ,doch 'nicht
```

2. Word questions. We define a word question, in German, as a clause which contains a question word (usually in first position) and has the finite verb in second position. Examples: wann kommt er?, warum friert dich?, wer kommt? German word questions, and their English counterparts, often have the same declarative intonations and terminal as statements, namely /(2) °3 1↓/ and /(2) 3 °1 1↓/. Examples:

2	°3	1↓		2	°3	1↓
'where-s the 'paper				'wo ,ist ,die 'Zeitung		

3	°1	1↓		3	°1	1↓
'where-s the 'paper				'wo ,ist ,die 'Zeitung		

The use of /2 °3 1↓/ is very widespread in American English, and it is also very common in Northern Germany. In the south of the German-speaking area, however, /2 °3 1↓/ tends to sound slightly rude and officious; it often carries overtones of Beamtentum and Prussian efficiency. In both English and German, the use of /3 °1 1↓/ makes the question sound brusque ("Come on, no more of this nonsense, give me the paper!"), or even threatening ("Give me that paper or else . . . !").

A politer intonation in German (von Essen calls it the "Höflichkeitsmelodie") is /3 °2 3/ with /↑/:

3	°2	3↑		3	°2	3↑
'where-s the 'paper				'wo ,ist ,die 'Zeitung		

3	°2	3↑		3	°2	3↑
'what-s ,your 'name				'wie 'heißen ,Sie		

This is in more general use in the south of the German-speaking area and is said to be coming into wider use in the north as well. Though widespread in American English, its repeated use in a series of questions carries overtones of childish inquisitiveness: "What's your name? Where do you live? What does your father do?" The same series of questions with /2 °3 1/ plus /↑/ in English sounds somewhat less polite, but also more adult and matter-of-fact. In German, however, it begins to sound like an inquisition.

In both English and German, the use of /(2) °3 3/ plus /↑/ with word questions has the special meaning of request for corroboration: "Is that what you said?"

3. Order questions. We define an order question, in German, as an independent clause which has the finite verb in first position. Examples: kommt er?, kommt er morgen?, friert dich? Such questions are of course always a request for corroboration, and they often have the intonation /(2) °3 3/ with /↑/:

2	°3	3↑		2	°3	3↑
,has the 'news,paper 'come				,ist die 'Zeitung ,schon 'da		

2	°3	3↑		2	°3	3↑
,do ,you 'live ,in 'Ham,burg				'wohnen ,Sie ,in 'Ham,burg		

An intonation which is more polite than this—in English it may even be deferential or patronizing—is /(3) °2 3/ with /↑/:

3	°2	3↑		3	°2	3↑
,has the 'news,paper 'come				,ist die 'Zeitung ,schon 'da		

Still another intonation is /(2) °3 1/ with /↑/:

2	°3	1↑		2	°3	1↑
,has the 'news,paper 'come				,ist die 'Zeitung ,schon 'da		

If /(2) °3 1/ is used with /↓/ in order questions, they may carry an air of brusqueness, or the implication may be: "I didn't get very far with that last question; now let's try this one." An example:

2	°3	1↓	2	°3	1↓
ˌhas the ˈnewsˌpaper ˈcome			ˌist die ˈZeitung ˌschon ˈda		

4. Commands. We define a command, in German, as a clause containing an imperative verb form: <u>bleib hier!</u>, or as the polite transform of this: <u>bleiben Sie hier!</u> Commands spoken with /(2) °3 1/ plus /↓/ tend to sound rather brusque:

2	°3	1↓	2	°3	1↓
ˈgive ˌme the ˈnewsˌpaper			ˈgib ˌmir die ˈZeitung		

The use of /3 °1 1/ plus /↓/ sounds rather matter-of-fact:

3	°1	1↓	3	°1	1↓
ˈgive ˌme the ˈnewsˌpaper			ˈgib ˌmir die ˈZeitung		

More polite—almost wheedling in English—is the use of /3 °2 3/ plus /↑/:

3	°2	3↑	3	°2	3↑
ˈgive ˌme the ˈnewsˌpaper			ˈgib ˌmir die ˈZeitung		

11.10 ENGLISH-GERMAN CONFLICTS IN THE USE OF INTONATION

Until far more is known than at present about the intonations of English and German, it will not be possible to make a contrastive analysis of the two systems and to reveal the points of conflict between them. Teachers of German can make important contributions by noting their students' errors in intonation and revealing the English-German conflicts which lie behind them. Much interesting work can also be done within German itself. What are the features in the intonation of a southerner (e.g., from Bavaria or Austria) which make him sound <u>schlampig</u> to a northerner (e.g., from Berlin)? What are the features in the intonation of a northerner which make him sound aggressive and "Prussian" to a southerner? We know almost nothing about such matters.

The following are a few random remarks about conflicts in the intonations used in greetings in English and German.

A friendly way of greeting another person in American English is to divide the greeting into two stress groups, the first containing the actual greeting and the second the name of the person spoken to. The first stress group has the intonation /(2) °3 1/ plus /|/; the second has /(1) °1 1/ plus /↑/. Examples:

2	°3	1|	1	°1	1↑
ˌgood ˈmorning ˌMrs. ˈMeyer					

°3	1|	°1	1↑
ˈmorning ˈJohn			

As far as the writer knows, this combination of intonations and terminals is never used in German greetings. Instead, the commonest type of greeting consists of the single intonation /(2) °3 1/ with /↓/:

    2   °3   1↓
,guten 'Morgen ,Frau 'Meyer

    °3   1↓
'Morgen 'Hans

When used with a greeting in English, this intonation sounds like a reproof. It is the kind of intonation an office manager might use to an employee who comes to work late:

    2   °3   1↓
,good 'morning ,Miss 'Brown

with the implication:

    2   °3   1↓
,it-s a'bout 'time 'you 'showed 'up

A more intimate and friendly type of greeting in German has an intonation which we have not yet described, namely /1 °2 2/, plus /|/:

    1   °2   2|
,guten 'Morgen ,Frau 'Meyer

To an American, this intonation carries the implication that the speaker is suffering from acute boredom or that he considers the person spoken to rather moronic. It is the intonation an American would use in such a clause as:

    1   °2   2|
,well if 'that-s 'all ,you 'know

A third type of German greeting is often used when a speaker wants to single out the one person in a group to whom he has not yet said good morning. He then says:

    2   °3 1↓
,guten 'Morgen 'Hans

This is of course the familiar /2 °3 1/ plus /↓/ which is so common in statements. An American, however, would use /2 °3 1 | °1 1↓/ in such a greeting; and he is likely to interpret /2 °3 1↓/ as meaning something like his American:

    2   °3 1↓
'what-s the 'matter ,with 'you

These are a few examples of the many kinds of misunderstandings which can arise because of the different ways in which German and English handle intonation. Though our knowledge of such things is rudimentary, perhaps these few examples are enough to show the kinds of conflicts which exist and the real need we have for a better understanding of them.

JUNCTURE $\boxed{12}$

12.1 PHONOLOGICAL CLUES TO GRAMMATICAL STRUCTURE

In order to introduce the topic of juncture, we need to consider some of the ways in which the sounds of English and German give clues to the grammatical structure of utterances. Let us suppose that a speaker, A, has uttered the phrase that sphericity, using a word completely unknown to his hearer, B. What B has heard phonemically is /ˈðætsfəˈrɪ̩səti/. If he were familiar with the word sphericity, he could immediately break the utterance grammatically into the units /ˈðæt/ and /sfəˈrɪ̩səti/. Not knowing the word, however, he does not know whether to break the utterance into these two grammatical units, or into three: /ˈðæt/, /s/, /fəˈrɪ̩səti/, i.e., a non-existent but quite possible that's phericity. In this situation, what can A do to make clear the grammatical structure of what he has said? He can of course say: "Sphericity, not phericity." But English also allows him to use another device. He can repeat what he has said, putting a clear syllable break or even a slight pause between the two grammatical units he wants to indicate. If we symbolize this clear syllable break or slight pause as /+/, what he then says is: /ˈðæt+sfəˈrɪ̩səti/. The grammatical structure is now clear to B: it is /ˈðæt+sfəˈrɪ̩səti/ that sphericity, and not /ˈðæts+fəˈrɪ̩səti/ that's phericity.

Speakers of German can use exactly the same device. If A has said /ˈdi̩:zəsfɛ:rǫˈi̩:də/ diese Sphäroide, and B does not know whether to break this into /ˈdi̩:zə/ plus /sfɛ:rǫˈi̩:də/ or /ˈdi̩:zəs/ plus /fɛ:rǫˈi̩:də/, A can repeat the utterance, using a clear syllable break or a slight pause: /ˈdi̩:zə+sfɛ:rǫˈi̩:də/. B then realizes that is is diese Sphäroide rather than a non-existent but quite possible /ˈdi̩:zəs+fɛ:rǫˈi̩:də/ dieses Phäroide.

12.2 OPEN AND CLOSE JUNCTURE

The above examples show us two different ways in which /s/ can be followed by /f/—or, to use the technical term, they show us two different kinds of JUNCTURE. In English /ˈðæt+sfəˈrɪ̩səti/ that sphericity, German /ˈdi̩:zə+sfɛ:rǫˈi̩:də/ diese Sphäroide, /s/ and /f/ are in CLOSE JUNCTURE; in the hypothetical /ˈðæts+fəˈrɪ̩səti/ that's phericity, /ˈdi̩:zəs+fɛ:rǫˈi̩:də/ dieses Phäroide, they are in OPEN JUNCTURE.

Two characteristics of open juncture, in both English and German, need to be emphasized. First, open juncture very frequently marks the grammatical boundary between two words, between the constituents of compound words, or between a word stem and a prefix or suffix. However, there are types of grammatical boundaries which are never marked by open juncture; and there are occurrences of open juncture (particularly in words of foreign origin) at points where no grammatical boundary occurs. Second, the occurrence of open juncture is often determined partly by style, partly by the need which the speaker feels for using it. For example, in a formal public address on linguistics, the speaker might use a platform style of speech in which the phrase that's phonemic (or German man dieses Phonem) would regularly show open juncture between the /s/ and the /f/: /'ðæts+fə'nimɨk/ (German /'di:zəs+fo̜:'ne̜:m/). He might also use open juncture in informal talk with people who were not familiar with this term. But in shoptalk with fellow linguists, where there is no need to emphasize the grammatical boundary between the two words, he would be more likely to use close juncture: /'ðætsfə'nimɨk/ (German /'di̜:zəsfo̜:'ne̜:m/). What is generally called "precise" or "carefully articulated" speech is characterized (in both English and German) by extensive use of open juncture; "slurred" or "sloppy" speech, on the other hand, where "words are run together," is characterized by a relatively infrequent use of open juncture.

12.3 JUNCTURE AND TERMINALS

Open juncture probably always occurs at the terminals which mark the boundaries between stress groups. Consider the following examples:

```
2          °3   3|2            °3   1↓
'old ,Mr. 'Kraus  for'got ,his 'ticket

2                °3   3|2            °3      1↓
,der 'alte ,Herr 'Kraus  ver'gaß ,seine 'Fahr,karte
```

Because the terminal /|/ falls between them, the final /s/ of Kraus and the initial /f/ of forgot (German vergaß) clearly stand in open juncture with one another. This is definitely /'kraus+fɜ'gat/, German /'kraus+fɛr'ga:s/, and not—even if such forms existed— /'krau+sfɜ'gat/, German /'krau+sfɛr'ga:s/.

12.4 JUNCTURE AND ONSET OF STRESS

Open juncture occurs next most consistently before onset of strong stress. If we leave stress unmarked for the moment, the English phoneme sequence /maisfir/ is usually quite clearly either /mai+sfir/ my sphere, with open juncture between the /ai/ and the /s/, and with onset of primary stress falling on the /s/; or else it is clearly /mais+fir/ mice fear, with open juncture between the /s/ and the /f/, and with onset of primary stress falling on the /f/. In the symbolization of stress which we have been using, the likelihood of open juncture at these points is indicated by the position of the stress marks: /'mai'sfir/ vs. /'mais'fir/. A German example of this type is the phoneme sequence /kauflaks/. This is usually quite clearly either /kau+flaks/ kau Flachs!, or /kauf+laks/ kauf Lachs! In the notation we have been using, these utterances are /'kau'flaks/ vs. /'kauf'laks/.

Open juncture occurs less consistently, especially in English, before onset of secondary stress. English stratosphere and atmosphere both end in syllables bearing secondary stress, but it is not always clear whether this secondary stress begins with the /s/

or with the /f/, and hence whether the point of onset of secondary stress is the same or different in the two words. Kenyon and Knott write /'strætə₁sfir/ vs. /'ætməs₁fir/, implying a consistent difference between the two words: open juncture before /s/ in stratosphere, but before /f/ in atmosphere. It might, however, be preferable to use a system of stress notation which did not force the issue in this way: /strætəsfîr/, /ǽtməsfîr/. Open juncture could then be written when it clearly occurs: /strætə+sfîr/, /ǽtməs+fîr/. In German, onset of secondary stress is more consistently accompanied by open juncture. A word such as Bundesfähre is quite clearly /'bundəs+₁fɛːrə/ and not /'bundə+₁sfɛːrə/. (Bundessphäre is of course still different: /'bundəs+₁sfɛːrə/.)

Onset of weak stress is very often accompanied by close rather than open juncture; or, to put the same matter in a different way, English and German often give no clear indication as to just where onset of weak stress occurs. Our examples in §12.1 illustrate this point. A speaker may use open juncture in English /'ðæts+fə'nimik/, German /'diːzəs+foː'neːm/, so that weak stress clearly sets in with the /f/; but he may also use close juncture and say /'ðætsfə'nimik/, /'diːzəsfoː'neːm/, in which case it is no longer clear just where the weak stress sets in.

12.5 JUNCTURE AND CONSONANT CLUSTERS

In both English and German, open juncture is often a corollary of the limitations placed on the sequences of consonants which may occur in close juncture. Perhaps the most striking limitation is the fact that no consonant may follow itself in close juncture. In such forms as /'pen₁naif/ penknife, /'an₁naːmə/ Annahme, there is always a clear break between the two /n/'s, so that these forms are clearly /'pen+₁naif/, /'an+₁naːmə/. If the juncture is closed up, the double consonant is automatically shortened to a single one. For example, if the open juncture in English /'kæn+'nat/ can not is closed up, the result is /'kænat/ or /kæ'nat/ cannot, with a single /n/. A somewhat different example of this same type of shortening is such a form as German (du) sitzt. Archaically, this is (du) sitzest /'zitsəst/; but if, as in normal present-day speech, the /ə/ drops out, the result is automatically /'zitst/ and not /'zitsst/.

In both English and German, an /n/ may stand in close juncture with a following stop only if the stop is dental (or, in English, palatal). That is to say, we can have /nt/, /nd/ (and in English /nč/, /nǰ/), but only /n+b/, /n+g/, etc. This means that such German forms as unbedacht, angenehm have /n/ only if open juncture follows: /'un+bə₁daxt/, /'an+gə₁neːm/. If the juncture is closed up, the nasal is automatically labial or velar, respectively: /'umbə₁daxt/, /'angə₁neːm/. In all such forms the Siebs prescribes open juncture, i.e., the more careful, precise style of speech.

In German, obstruents (= stops, fricatives, sibilants) may stand in close juncture with one another only if all of them are voiceless. (Cf. §5.14, and the one exception noted there.) This means that a form like sagbar will have /b/, and a form like biegsam will have /z/, only if they are preceded by open juncture: /'zaːk+₁baːr/, /'biːk+₁zaːm/. If the juncture is closed up, the consonants automatically become voiceless: /'zaːk₁paːr/, /'biːk₁saːm/. Again, in all such cases the Siebs prescribes open juncture.

The limitations on clusters of obstruents and on the occurrence of double consonants are both illustrated in the colloquial pronunciation of such phrases as <u>wo bist du</u>. If the last two words are spoken in open juncture, this phrase is /'voː+°'bɪst+ˌduː/. But if the last two words are spoken in close juncture, it is /'voː+°'bɪstuː/. The cluster /td/ is not permitted in close juncture. Unvoicing would give /tt/, but double consonants are also not permitted in close juncture. Hence the result is single /t/.

12.6 JUNCTURE AND ASPIRATION

A characteristic of both English and German is the fact that /p t k/ are strongly aspirated when they stand in open juncture with a preceding phoneme, or when they stand at the beginning of an utterance. Note such contrasts as the following, in which open juncture and aspiration are written in the transcription:

Aspirated		Unaspirated	
/'gris+ˌpʰat/	grease pot	/'fli+ˌspat/	flea spot
/'mai+'tʰren/	my train	/'mait+'ren/	might rain
/'ðɪs+'kʰɪd/	this kid	/ðə+'skɪd/	the skid
/'tʰauš+ˌpʰrais/	Tauschpreis	/'tʰau+ˌšplais/	Tauspleiß
/'an+ˌtʰraːt/	antrat	/'lant+ˌraːt/	Landrat
/das+'kʰɪtsəln/	das Kitzeln	/diː+'skɪtsə/	die Skizze

The voiceless stops are weakly aspirated in other positions, especially in German (cf. §5.10); but strong aspiration occurs only after open juncture.

12.7 JUNCTURE AND THE GLOTTAL STOP

A characteristic of German, and to a far lesser extent of English, is the allophonic use of a glottal stop before vowels which stand in open juncture with a preceding phoneme, or which stand at the beginning of an utterance. Though these glottalized allophones of vowels are not common in American English, all speakers apparently use them when they feel some particular need to separate words clearly. One such instance is when they are told to correct "sloppy" pronunciations, and not to "run their words together." For example, many Americans normally pronounce <u>not at all</u> as ['natə+'tʰɔˑl]; when told to correct this, they often do so by saying ['nat+ˌʔæt+' ʔɔˑl], using a glottal stop to separate the words clearly from one another. Or they may be reproved for pronouncing <u>an old auto</u> as [ə'noˑl'dɔto], and then correct this to [ˌʔæn+' ʔoˑld+' ʔɔto].

Glottalized allophones of vowels after open juncture are far more common in German than in English, though the <u>Siebs</u> no longer insists on them as it did up to 1933. The <u>Siebs</u> now prescribes open juncture before vowels in the following words: "Alle Vokale im Anlaut eines Wortes oder einer Silbe (<u>Alt</u>, <u>ohne</u>, <u>ein</u>; <u>Verein</u>, <u>überall</u>) werden neu eingesetzt" (p. 36). In the north of the German speaking area, this <u>Neueinsatz</u> of a vowel is almost universally accomplished through the use of an allophone with preceding glottal stop; in the south the glottal stop is far less common. The Siebs warns specifically against close juncture in such forms as the following:

	Close juncture condemned	Open juncture prescribed
der Affe	/deː'rafə/	/deːr+'afə/
erübrigen	/e'rüːbrɪgən/	/er+'üːbrɪgən/
veralten	/fe'raltən/	/fer+'altən/
Himmelsau	/'hɪməl‚zau/	/'hɪməls+‚au/

12.8 SYLLABIFICATION AND TRANSCRIPTION

In all the instances of open juncture discussed in the preceding sections, the one common feature has been the fact that, when two phonemes are in open juncture with one another, there is a clear syllable break between them. If this is the case, one might ask whether we cannot eliminate juncture altogether by analyzing English and German in terms of their syllable structures. Unfortunately this simple solution cannot be used, because of the cases in which the syllable structure is not clear. As we have seen, the syllable structure of the segment /sf/ is clear neither in English /'ðætsfə'nimɪk/ that's phonemic nor in German /'diːzəsfoː'neːm/ dieses Phonem when these words are spoken in close juncture.

One might also ask: If open juncture is an essential part of both English and German, why should it not be made a regular part of our transcription? The answer to this question is of a different sort. In transcribing any given utterance, as it is spoken, we can easily write a /+/ at every open juncture. But in devising a transcription for the language as a whole, we need to allow for the fact that open juncture may or may not occur at a given point. Except in this chapter, we have indicated such points by either or both of two different devices: either by writing a space, as in /'diːzəs foː'neːm/ dieses Phonem; or by the position of a stress mark, as in /fer'altən/ veralten; or by both, as in /deːr 'afə/ der Affe. Only where these two devices fail is it necessary to use the special symbol /+/. An example is such a form as /'landəs+poː:liː‚tsai/ Landespolizei, where the /+/ is needed to indicate that the /p/ is generally strongly aspirated.

12.9 ENGLISH-GERMAN CONFLICTS IN JUNCTURE

The preceding sections have shown us that, by and large, English and German handle juncture in much the same way. In terms of general tendencies, we may say that open juncture is less frequent in English than in German. We can try to correct for this by telling our students that German should be spoken more precisely than English and that words should not be run together as much as in English. Their English habit of using open juncture more frequently in precise speech will then help them to use open juncture properly in German.

The one case where a serious conflict arises is in the use of open juncture before vowels. We have seen, in §12.7, that Americans very commonly use close juncture before word-initial vowels, and that, when reproved for this, their way of achieving open juncture is by inserting a glottal stop before the vowel. We have also seen that there are many types of forms where standard German pronunciation requires open juncture before a vowel, and that, though it is not prescribed, the glottal stop is used in such instances by speakers in Northern Germany. The simplest device for achieving open juncture in the speech of our students is therefore to have them use this northern pronunciation, since it agrees with articulatory habits which they already possess.

Though the Siebs implies that open juncture—with an optional glottal stop—is used before all words beginning phonemically with a vowel, this is not the case in normal conversational speech. Very commonly, a word-initial vowel is pronounced in close juncture with a preceding phoneme, provided the vowel is unstressed and both phonemes belong to the same stress group. For example, in Kann ich °gehen?, close juncture is normally used between the first two words: /ˈkɑ̩nɪç °ˈgeːən/. This is exactly like English Can I °go? /ˈkænai °ˈgo/. But open juncture is consistently used in German if the word-initial vowel is stressed, e.g. Kann °ich gehen? is /ˈkɑ̩n °ˈ[ʔ]ɪç ˈgeːən/. This in sharp contrast to English, where Can °I go? is commonly /ˌkæ°ˈnai ˈgo/.

In constructing drills on the use of open juncture before vowels, it is perhaps helpful to begin with precisely the types of forms just discussed. The following examples are given in a symbolization which might be used with students. An underline indicates syntactical stress; a tie-line indicates close juncture; and an asterisk indicates open juncture and, in the speech of many Germans, a glottal stop.

Kann ich gehen?	—	Kann *ich gehen?
Will er kommen?	—	Will *er kommen?
Was ist das?	—	Was *ist das?
Wer ist da?	—	Wer *ist da?

In this last example it should be noted that, though wer and ist may be in close juncture, the syllable division remains unchanged: it is always /ˈveːr ɪ̩st/ = [ˈveːʌ̩ɪst], and not /veː rɪst/ = [ˈveːʀɪ̩st]. If the first word in such a construction ends in an unstressed vowel, it is in open juncture with a following unstressed vowel: Heute ist Montag, with /ˈhoitə+ɪst/ and not /ˈhoitəɪst/.

The above drill purposely introduces the student to the glottal stop in an environment where he occasionally uses it in his English, e.g. in strongly stressed /ˌkæn °ˈ[ʔ]ai ˈgo/ Can °I go? Further drills will need to include environments where the glottal stop is uncommon in English. Examples:

die *Oper	der *Anfang
die *Uhr	das *Ende
sie *arbeiten	wir *essen
sie *antworten	er *eilt
*Ur*enkel	*ein*atmen
*über*all	*um*armen

der *Empfang	der Fernseh*empfang
der *Entwurf	der Gesetz*entwurf

It may also be helpful to drill forms which contrast close and open juncture in comparable environments:

bereinigen	—	ver*einigen
bereisen	—	ver*eisen
Schuhlatz	—	Schul*amt
Beiname	—	Bein*ader
Weihnachten	—	Wein *achten